Wild Curiosity

Wild Curiosity

How to Unleash Creativity and Encourage Lifelong Wondering

Erik Shonstrom

ROWMAN & LITTLEFIELD
Lanham • Boulder • New York • London

Published by Rowman & Littlefield
A wholly owned subsidiary of The Rowman & Littlefield Publishing Group, Inc.
4501 Forbes Boulevard, Suite 200, Lanham, Maryland 20706
www.rowman.com

Unit A, Whitacre Mews, 26-34 Stannary Street, London SE11 4AB

British Library Cataloguing in Publication Information Available

Library of Congress Cataloging-in-Publication Data Available

ISBN 978-1-4758-1528-3 (cloth : alk. paper)
ISBN 978-1-4758-1530-6 (electronic)

♾ ™ The paper used in this publication meets the minimum requirements of American National Standard for Information Sciences Permanence of Paper for Printed Library Materials, ANSI/NISO Z39.48-1992.

Printed in the United States of America

This book is dedicated to Cindy; my true love, partner in crime, and best friend.

Contents

Author's Note

Parts of this book draw on interviews and published research. I have tried to appropriately credit those who have written about curiosity and related subjects as well as the people I interviewed—any misinterpretation or omissions are purely my own fault. Some names and minor details have been changed out of respect for privacy. If something sparks your curiosity, a complete list of sources can be found in the back of the book.

Introduction

Song of the Sirens

ON THE TIP OF A MOUNTAIN IN THE MIDDLE OF NOWHERE

The wind sheared through the ice-encrusted crevices on the summit of Telescope Peak. Frigid air blasted the bare rocks and dwarf, mutant bristlecone pine that for some ungodly reason had purchased a roothold and survived in this Martian landscape. I struggled with the cord attached to the tarp, trying to get it tied down to something. It was dark. The nearest tree was fifty yards away. There was nothing to tie it to.

Twelve middle school students lay like stacked cordwood, shivering and crying, eyes wide in the darkness. They were scared, and with good reason. The temperature was dropping, and it was already well below freezing. With the screaming winds, the wind chill was obscene. We were at 11,331 feet. Our gear was spread out over a mile of trail below; I'd told them to ditch their packs and hustle to the top as night fell and the temperature went from mildly uncomfortable to face shattering. It was December in Death Valley, California, and the whole stupid thing had been my idea.

The concept had been to get the kids to hike up a peak in the winter and sleep overnight on the summit without tents. Just bivouac under some tarps, teach them how to be tough. Get them in touch with the natural world. But my hands were frozen lobster claws, and I couldn't tie the tarp down. Kids were screaming and crying—and maybe I was too.

I had, in my optimism, brought a giant-sized bag of Peanut M&M's with me. This was before the peanut allergy craze and subsequent quarantine seized schools in its grip. I imagined us celebrating on the peak in the early evening, munching candy and admiring the view. One of the shy, more reticent students would come sit next to me as the sunset burned vermillion over the Panamint Range and say quietly, "I never knew how beautiful the world was until you took us here, Erik. I've decided to dedicate my life to helping orphaned pandas because of your selfless example." Or something like that—but it wasn't turning out that way.

I had to do something to salvage their fragile emotions, to delicately let them know that I was calm, in control, and that their lives were not, despite convincing evidence to the contrary, in danger. I lurched to my pack, deftly shaving layers of skin from my shins with razor-sharp slabs of rock as I flailed in the blackness. I pulled the big yellow bag of candy from my pack and hunched over against the wind, crab-walked back to where the kids were freaking out.

"Here!" I yelled. "Peanut M&M's!"

It was the desperate move of a desperate man. I tossed the bag to them. One girl, named Erin, looked up at me with woeful eyes.

"But I don't like peanuts!" she said.

I lost it. I had dragged these kids up here. Now we were freezing to death, and I was going to be responsible for killing them all. I was out of my comfort zone. I snapped.

I tore the bag of M&M's from the girl's hands and hurled it into the void that yawned below us, on the tip of a mountain in the middle of nowhere.

THE TEACHINGS OF *CYPRINODON SALINUS SALINUS*

I was a mediocre student. It wasn't because I lacked curiosity, however. Like many kids, I was curious about a great many things, and that curiosity was often the motivating force behind discovery, exploration, adventure, and learning. What occurs to me now, looking back on my experiences in school, is that my curiosity didn't fit within the expectations of traditional education.

It's ironic, then, that despite my lackluster performance as a student, I'm an educator. Teaching has been my primary profession for almost twenty years. The word "curiosity" has popped up regularly during that time, in curriculum descriptions, marketing literature, mission statements, competencies, and conversations with colleagues.

Brown University admissions states that they're looking for applicants with "intellectual curiosity," Harvard's Medical School claims their scholars are "curiosity seekers," and the Association of American Colleges and Universities states that "fostering student's curiosity about the world" is an essential aim of education.

It's not just higher education; it's hard to find a description of a Montessori school without curiosity being listed front and center as a central focus of the program. The National Science Teacher's Association lists nurturing "scientific curiosity" in the early elementary grades as part of a six point strategic plan. Curiosity—or invocations of it, at least—runs through every level of education, from kindergarten through medical school.

Culturally, we've embraced curiosity as a kind of synonym for daring, exciting adventure. NASA named its Mars rover "Curiosity." Film director and deep-sea explorer James Cameron has a TED talk in which curiosity is noted as the most essential tool humans have in their quest for knowledge. In the PBS series *First Peoples*, which documents the spread of humans around the globe in prehistory, curiosity is often called upon as an explanation for human migration out of Africa and through Asia, the Americas, and beyond.

After hearing the word so often and for so long, I got—pun intended—curious about curiosity. What is it, and how does it relate to learning? I often found myself with other teachers, bemoaning student's lack of curiosity. They were unengaged in class, unwilling or unable to read deeply and think critically about coursework. Discussions dragged, and there seemed to be this collective inertia in the classroom.

Yet, when I looked around the campuses of the schools where I worked, I'd see students deeply absorbed in their phones, swiping and scrolling their way through some digital universe. Or they'd be in packs, jostling and laughing and arguing and oblivious of the adults who hovered around the periphery. Their conversations about music, movies, video games, and *each other* bespoke of a highly engaged, roving curiosity.

But wait, I said to myself—these were the same students I'd just been lamenting for their lack of curiosity. It dawned on me that it wasn't that they weren't curious. They were deeply curious about many things—if I just let go of my expectations of what was worthy of curiosity.

I'm also a parent. My children have given me a window into how curiosity forms us from the get-go. For instance, I've watched my stepdaughter transition from high school to college, and now she stands poised to enter graduate school. Watching Vivien as she went from the kid she was to the adult she's become afforded me a firsthand account of how curiosity informs not just what we are interested in, but the experiences we have, what and how we learn, and ultimately the direction our lives take.

Vivien is a gifted writer, an artist of exacting skill, a talented photographer, and a deep reader. I watched as she went through a traditional four-year liberal arts curriculum at a small college, and noted how her curiosity picked up various threads for a time and dropped them, trying to find a path that best suited her.

As she settled into a study of anthropology, I began to realize two distinct phenomena that related to her curiosity. The first was that her curiosity literally propelled her into the world; she's done research in Kenya, Tanzania, New Mexico, and Georgia. By letting go and allowing Vivien to choose her path based on her curiosity and passions, she found a trajectory that was fulfilling. She discovered subjects that she was invested in and that made her happy.

The second understanding that developed was that this curiosity of hers could be traced all the way back to when she was a child in elementary school. Her mother—my wife—had completed college while Vivien was still a child, and *she* had studied anthropology back then. Vivien had grown up going to the Los Angeles Zoo, staring at the chimps, gorillas, and other primates. Books by Jane Goodall, Frans de Waal, and other primatologists surrounded her as a child.

One of Vivien's greatest gifts has always been observation—her skill was in her quiet, steady noticing of the natural world. She was always listening and exploring the world that her mother and I chatted about. The curious pursuits of children—their daydreams, games, and fantasies—are not just play. They can be the very deep roots of lifelong passions—and the first evidence of living a curious life.

Curiosity was the connective tissue running through three distinct spheres in my life. I was a learner, a teacher, and a parent. Curiosity defined my success and struggles in all three areas.

It began to occur to me, however, that there was a chance that curiosity was not being given its due. We speak of "idle curiosity" as though it is a minor player in the field of emotions and behaviors. I began to suspect that the group of traits and motivations that are herded under the umbrella term "curiosity" might be far more fundamental to learning than I previously thought.

Why did my passions rage as a child, my obsessions pinball from topic to topic, and yet my performance as a student was relatively lackluster? Am I nurturing my children's appreciation of the world, igniting their own curiosity, or trying to impose my own? And why do my students seem so hyperfocused and engaged sometimes, and yet at other moments seem so intensely apathetic and disinterested?

Up on the top of Telescope Peak, I had an epiphany—or a realization in a long line of realizations—about learning and experience. After that disastrous trip, the students were energized and excited. They retold the stories of our adventure again and again. I began to realize that the experience was directly tied to how we learn. In fact, learning couldn't really happen *without* direct experience.

It was something I'd known in some form or another by the time I chucked the bag of M&M's off the mountainside. (I had to sheepishly clamber down the sheer rocks to find it the next day, after my students sharply abused me for littering.) I'd already been an instructor with Outward Bound, worked in schools, and had noted that the learning that mattered to students was always tied to experience and lack of structure—it was when the lesson was over or the plan failed or the route was unclear that all the cool stuff began to take shape.

I began to think about the way structure—and by that I mean *institutionalized* structures like required curriculums, state standards, and their ilk—was so antithetical to what I thought learning should be: an adventure. Not only that, but I began to question my own approach to learning. My students were so deeply and intensely curious about so many things—skateboarding, movies, food, nature, each other—that I began to understand why they were at times so uninterested in what I was teaching them.

On that frigid, rocky slab of Telescope Peak, a single domino got tipped in my brain that has led me to this inquiry, to this book. What the hell was I doing up there? How did I end up on that exposed, shrieking mountain in the first place?

The answer, of course, is curiosity.

I'd heard about Death Valley. Initially, it was the name that got me curious. *Death Valley?* Why is it called that? Who named it with such terrifying directness, and why? These events predated the Internet and the instant gratification of Google, so my curiosity was left to ferment, to become bolder and more potent with time. It bubbled and grew, and I began to subconsciously—and actively—glean information about Death Valley wherever I went.

I would forage for tidbits of information that just drove my curiosity to a higher and higher pitch: Death Valley is the largest wilderness area outside of Alaska, one of the hottest places on earth, and one of the lowest places on earth (over 200 feet below sea level). I was fired up, salivating. I haunted bookstores and libraries, reading travel guides and old pioneer accounts. I learned about *Cyprinodon salinus salinus*, the Death Valley pupfish, a hardy little guy who scrapes out an existence in the highly salty, pee-warm puddles that collect at the base of the valley.

I cast my net far and wide, and began to associate Death Valley with other ideas, places, and things. I learned that a scene from *Star Wars* was filmed there. The adventures on Tatooine were shot in part at Zabriskie Point in Death Valley. Just learning the name of the location made me glad.

I began to collect names of places and features in and around the park, and they sounded like poetry: *Panamint Range, Eureka Dunes, the White Mountains.* Death Valley became Mordor in my imagination, and I could imagine battle-hardened orcs in rank and file, chugging across the blazing landscape. I found an article about a woman in her 70s named Marta Beckett who performed solo Broadway-esque shows at the Amargosa Opera House in Death Valley Junction, like something straight out of a David Lynch film. I found out about Ubehebe Crater, a huge pit that sits in the middle of the flaming landscape.

And then, the coup de grace: a parent of a student told me about Telescope Peak, which rises to over 11,000 feet above the flaming flats of Death Valley. The rise from the salt pan of the basin to the peak is similar in scope to the rise from the Tibetan Plateau to the tip of Everest, he said.

That's it, I thought. I'm going.

And so curiosity bred experience, and my own learning began.

THE CURIOSITY CONNECTION

While this book is about curiosity—what it is, how to nurture it, and what can impede it—I won't be sticking to any hard and fast rules about how curiosity works, or even offer a singular explanation of what it is. I'm hesitant to even make a stab at a standardized definition. This isn't out of cowardice or some mincing, academic anxiety. Curiosity, like many of our human idiosyncrasies, is complex. This book is intended to suss out its many forms and become intimately familiar with its many haunts.

Perhaps a better way to say it is that I won't be providing a stand-alone definition of curiosity; I'll be providing multiple meanings. Like anything worth looking at, curiosity is an incredibly complicated idea and sits nested within all kinds of behaviors, traits, interpretations, and cultural notions.

Was Einstein's quest to understand space-time curiosity, but my need to click on the latest Internet story about Kim Kardashian's drama with Kanye West simply vulgar voyeurism? Well, yes and no. They're both curiosity, or are both spurred by curiosity. But they're different kinds, have different aspects. We'll explore both.

Curiosity is not necessarily a deep, important, intellectual trait. Curiosity can compel us to ponder our own existence, but it's also the insistent itch we feel when our phone dings and we wonder who just texted us.

THE GLEAM

One of the incongruities in curiosity is that some of the ways it manifests itself could be seen as a negative behavior, particularly the way in which curiosity is often impulsive and intense. However, despite often being an impulsive, it's included in Christopher Peterson and Martin Seligman's handbook of *Character Strengths and Virtues*.

Seligman and Peterson sought to define mental states not in a negative light, where the pathology of behavior is the focus, but rather through the lens of positive psychology. And wouldn't you know it—curiosity is right up there toward the top of the list as a positive attribute and shared as a universal strength across time and culture. Essential parts of curiosity, according to Seligman and Peterson, include interest, novelty seeking, and openness to experience, all of which we'll investigate.

An acknowledgment here: I'm a white, middle-class, college educated, heterosexual American male. As such, I have more privilege than most people on the globe. This book would be different if I were a recent Southeast Asian immigrant, or an African American woman from Alabama, or a Central American migrant laborer on a vast industrial tomato farm in the San Joaquin valley. But, as Seligman and Peterson note, curiosity cuts across cultures, genders, and nationalities.

While I belong to one of the more privileged demographics in history, I can try to pursue the truths of curiosity in a way that celebrates its universality and commonality as a human characteristic. I don't think my interest in how my children learn or my concern for their schooling, or ruminations about my own crooked path toward knowledge is mine alone; I share all these with people across the world and through time.

In fact, we've been aware of curiosity as a central part of what it means to be human since we began telling each other stories. Perhaps the greatest story of curiosity in literature appears in Book 12 of Homer's *Odyssey*. It's in this passage of the epic that Odysseus and his crew must sail past the sirens—monstrous bird-women who sing a song so sweet that sailors are driven mad and steer their ships straight onto the rocks, killing themselves and their crew. "Around them is a great heap of the bones of rotting men," the enchantress Kirke tells Odysseus.

The story goes that Odysseus plugs his men's ears with wax and has them tie him to the mast so that he alone can hear the song of the sirens. The question, of course, is why? Why risk madness and insanity, not to mention your life and that of your crew, when you've been warned of the death of all those who hear the siren's song? Why does Odysseus not plug his own ears with wax while they sailed past? What compels Odysseus to hear the song of the sirens?

Some scholars—and some translations—seem to suggest that Kirke demands that he listen to the sirens. In the 2014 translation of Homer's poem by Barry Powell, Odysseus tells his sailors: "She [Kirke] advised me alone to hear their voice." However, earlier in Book 12, what Kirke *actually* says is: "If you yourself want to hear, let them bind your hands and feet in the swift ship, upright in the hole for the mast, and let the ropes be fixed to the mast itself so that you might take delight in hearing the voice of the two sirens."

Odysseus wants to hear the sirens—he's curious. Sly, ambitious fox that he is, he wants to be the first man to survive the siren's song, to hear their sweet entreaties but live to tell the tale. Odysseus as a character demonstrates why we get the phrase "curiosity killed the cat." After all, without his premeditated effort to have himself bound and his men's ears plugged against the siren's entreaties, the Greeks would've been drawn to the rocks and the *Odyssey* would've been a whole lot shorter. And rather depressing.

Literature is full of curious characters who push limits in order to explore, discover, and learn. "O young Mariner, / Down to the haven, / Call your companions / Launch your vessel, / And crowd your canvas, / And, ere it vanishes / Over the margin / After it, follow it / Follow The

Gleam," exclaims the narrator of Tennyson's famous poem "Merlin and the Gleam."

Robert Burns curiously imagines the life and familiar travails of a field mouse in his poem "To a Mouse, On Turning Her Up In Her Nest With the Plow": "Wee, sleekit, cow'rin, tim'rous beastie / O, what a panic's in thy breastie!"

Huck Finn explores the river, investigates the humanity of Jim, and resists being "civilised" by society, suggesting that his curiosity about the world is puckish and represents the wildness of the uncontained curious mind.

One of the consistent mechanisms in stories about curiosity is the way in which the hero—usually a child—is left to his or her own devices, enters a state of boredom, and sets off on an adventure.

In the Hayao Miyazaki animated film *My Neighbor Totoro* there are two sisters, Mei and Satsuki. One day, while Satsuki is at school and her father busy with work, Mei wanders the fields near their rural home. A mixture of boredom, freedom, and the outdoors compels Mei to explore, and soon enough she discovers a magical land populated by fantastical creatures and the adventure begins. This plot device can be seen again and again, and in it we can see the way curiosity gives rise to experience.

The entire genre of science fiction could be said to be derived from the initial question "What else could be out there?" and then suddenly William Shatner is dressed in a polyester V-neck and boldly going "where no man has gone before." Peppy Laura Ingalls Wilder, brave Jo from Louisa May Alcott's *Little Women*, John Muir's fascination with the towering pines of the Sierra and wrinkled glaciers of Alaska, and Dorothy Parker famously writing "The cure for boredom is curiosity. There is no cure for curiosity." All of these examples have a rich vein of curiosity running through the substrate.

In fact, many of our favorite literary heroes exhibit a certain impish curiosity about the world and those around them. It seems that many protagonists who figure in iconic literature are curious. Their curiosity about the human condition and the world is what moves the plot forward. Their internal ruminations about what makes other people tick is what drives their actions and activates experience (something us boring pedants call *plot*). Had Lizzie not had such a high degree of curiosity, she would've dismissed Darcy as an uptight prig, and we wouldn't have one of the greatest love stories of all time in *Pride and Prejudice*.

Curiosity doesn't just drive the characters of novels, but drives the reader reflexively in a very "meta" sort of way. Ishmael's curiosity about Queequeg drives our own curiosity, which fuels our reading. It could be argued that the act of reading literature itself is one of sustained, curious exploration of the text.

Reading is a helpful example to demonstrate how curiosity works. We can read feverishly at times—late in book two of the *Hunger Games*, we speed through pages to find out what happens next to our heroine Katniss Everdeen. But we often read more passively, even with a certain amount of boredom. In the latter case, we can't predict when curiosity will appear; it is by nature difficult to predict.

Much of what we find curious through reading is based on personal interpretation. What I find curiously absorbing about a given text will not resonate with you and vice versa. Personal mythologies play a huge role in how we read, interpret, and ultimately assign meaning to the books we read. But there are times when we're reading when for some reason a particular passage or word catches our attention, and curiosity compels us forward in the text.

THE WELLSPRING OF GENIUS AND DISSENT

One of the earlier psychological descriptions of curiosity comes from a textbook from 1854 by Leopold George called *Lehrbuch der Psychologie*, which described curiosity thus: "[It] searches neither truth nor exact knowledge; it is satisfied with the most superficial and most confused apprehension of things and is content to accept their existence when only parts of them are perceived."

Curiosity is a multifaceted phenomena, and George's early description is a good case in point. However, even in this nineteenth-century description, we can hear some of the consistent themes begin to emerge — curiosity can be capricious and fickle, and have less to do with defining facts and more to do with the process of exploration.

To begin with, we can rely on some basic descriptions to help get us started in a conversation about curiosity that come from the field of animal behavior and psychology, a sort of shorthand that will keep us from being hamstrung by a profusion of meanings all dependent on context and discipline. The most basic definition that we can rely on may as well come from Hans-Georg Voss and Heidi Keller from their book *Curiosity and Exploration*: "It is clear that exploratory behaviors share common elements. These are visual, linguistic, haptic, motoric, or intellectual activities that make new information available to the individual." Directly — curiosity is how we find stuff out.

But Voss and Keller fall short, I think, when they write that these intellectual activities "[a]re used to reduce uncertainty, and to solve a problem or contradiction." Yes, they do, but they also have other forms that we'll investigate; they can also seek out and maintain states of ambiguity. It's also entirely possible that the way these behaviors express themselves are the very things that differentiate us from other species.

If there's one thing we can be sure of, it's that curiosity will take us to weird and unexplored places. "Gaining specialized knowledge requires seeking the uncommon," wrote Daniel W. Gade in a book called *Curios-*

ity, Inquiry, and the Geographical Imagination. Curiosity is not just about exploring the vast landscapes of the world—physical and intellectual frontiers—but also the nooks and crannies of our own psyche. "Learning cannot be isolated from motivation and that one wants to begin to understand his or her own life," Gade tells us.

The aim of this book is to see how curiosity works under certain conditions: in school, at work, and during our own development as thinking, feeling beings. We'll explore its depths and see what a single deep dive can teach us about what makes us learners so maybe we can become better teachers, parents, and citizens. After all, if there's one thing this book will hopefully show, it's that curiosity research is well-trodden ground.

My own efforts were undertaken with a huge boost from a large pool of men and women who have explored this quirky tendency of ours for centuries. In fact, even the very word "curiosity" has a book focused on its origins and the etymology of the term. While the idea of an entire book dedicated to the meaning of a single word may sound a bit excessive, it's actually not. The book is a surprisingly delightful read. When scholar Neil Kenny penned a tome called *Curiosity in Early Modern Europe Word Histories,* even he had to stand in awe of the word and its implications within Western culture:

> Although "curiosity" became, especially between mid-seventeenth and the mid-eighteenth century, a key "concept" serving to construct a seductive symmetry between desire for knowledge and objects of knowledge, it remains surprisingly impossible to sum up neatly its meanings. Those meanings varied endlessly according to the infinite contexts out of which they emerged. "Curiosity" differed from decade to decade, from language to language, from dictionary to dictionary, and from dictionaries to other discursive contexts; it differed depending on exactly how it was collocated with neighboring terms in a particular text, depending on those terms to which it was being made equivalent and on those to which it was being presented as opposite; it differed depending on whether it was taken to mean what it explicitly denoted or else also what it implicitly connoted; and it differed depending on whether it was read as constative or performative.

But Kenny not only parses the various meanings of curiosity from a linguistic standpoint; he theorizes on its many uses and misuses: "If people endlessly defined and redefined 'curiosity,' this was not, on the whole, because they were interested in semantics per se, but because the semantics of 'curiosity' were an important verbal tool for a wide range of goals, such as legitimizing or discouraging certain activities (whether travel, divination, collecting, or delving into court or state secrets), producing hostile attitudes to certain groups (such as women), earning money by making certain objects valuable, and so on."

So on indeed. Within the nineteenth century, particularly in Britain, learned gentry often had a "curio cabinet" to display artifacts from around the world: fossils, gemstones, art from "exotic" peoples around the world. Through this lens, curiosity took on an almost taboo air, as if by association it was related to controversial ideas like evolution, or the complex and compelling cultures of non-Western European peoples.

Curiosity has, of late, been neutered and reduced to something institutionalized and codified by schools. It was not always that way, as Kenny points out, and in fact has historically been seen as a negative attribute and something to be discouraged, giving us the phrase "curiosity killed the cat."

That is, in a way, a good introduction to the shadow agenda for this book. While I am sincere and committed to the goal of unearthing the particularities of curiosity to help us understand teaching, learning, parenting, and creativity better, I have other plans as well.

I want to imbue curiosity with a sense of danger, to reinvigorate the term and introduce you to its subversive power. For example, while curiosity drives the gears of innovation and commerce in the tech world through the likes of Apple's Steve Jobs; Pinterest engineer Tracy Chou; inventor of the personal computer, Steve Wozniak; Apple special projects developer Divya Nag; and Facebook's Mark Zuckerberg, it also sublimates market paradigms and social inequities through its refusal to be commoditized and corralled.

Curiosity is the wellspring of both genius and dissent.

But beyond that, it is curiosity that connects us. It is how we find people who matter. It is the ignitable stuff that makes us "click" with certain individuals. It can be how we find love. When we meet someone, we begin to wonder and be curious, and that spurs us to action, to declarations of love and commitment.

Curiosity is many things, but hopefully, we can discover that curiosity can serve the most humble—and yet most noble—purpose of all. Curiosity can be the source of empathy and compassion.

ONE

Resurrecting the Cat

ALL I NEED

When I was a kid I played a game. I imagined I was stranded—on an island in the middle of the ocean, in a forested wilderness, in the desert, or on an iceberg—and that I had to survive with whatever was at hand. Riding in the car, I'd examine the contents of the glove box: registration, vinyl-cover car manual, food wrappers—and then, look!—an old Phillips head screwdriver, languishing forgotten. And more: a book of matches, half used, from a convenience store. That would be all I'd need. Matches and the screwdriver: matches for fire, the screwdriver sharpened to a point—a weapon, a tool.

Sitting at school, I'd look through my backpack. The oval rings of my binder could be fishhooks, the pencil sharpener taken apart and the tiny blade used to slice through scales and gut fish. The thrill I remember in thinking about how I could survive with only what was at hand, with the world pared down not just to essentials, but random objects whose true utility was hidden, was real and visceral.

Like most kids, I was pretty curious. My curiosity was feverish at times, insistent and provoking. It was also a selfish kind of curiosity—my imaginary games rooting through the glove box didn't get me any awards in schools or praise from my parents. My behaviors were of a particular kind of curiosity, something researchers call *epistemic curiosity*.

EPISTEMIC VERSUS INTELLECTUAL CURIOSITY

Epistemic curiosity is motivated by intellectual uncertainty and spurs behaviors to acquire further knowledge such as asking questions. However, the key difference here is that epistemic curiosity is not necessarily

1

conducive to traditional education. A person who is epistemically curious may be interested in only information and learning that satisfies their personal interests—the conscientious piece may be missing.

This type of curiosity, where people who are curious are seeking answers to questions they've posed themselves, is slightly different from *intellectual curiosity*. The two terms can be used interchangeably, but in terms of our investigation into how curiosity helps us learn, there's an important distinction.

Intellectual curiosity is what we most commonly think of when we discuss curiosity. Good students often rate high in intellectual curiosity. They solve puzzles and understand systems like geometry and democracy well. They look up key terms in the index of a book. In short, they rate high in what we'd consider typical intelligence.

They have a tendency to be conscientious listeners and well adapted to traditional education. Tell them that sharks have a cartilaginous skeleton, and they'll be asking, "What is that? Why do they have that kind of skeleton? Do other fish have the same kind?" and so on. Epistemic curiosity is concerned with answering questions to reduce uncertainty or gain knowledge, whether or not there is some extrinsic reward.

Ivan Illich, a twentieth-century political theorist and philosopher who popularized anti-institutional sentiment through books like *Deschooling Society*, believed that institutional education negated the possibility of the "autodidact." Self-taught individuals are examples of folks who could very well rate high in epistemic curiosity. While deeply curious, they may choose to pursue interests outside of traditionally rewarded pathways—differentiating them from an intellectually curious person who responds to traditional learning environments like school.

Whether or not they are two truly different types of curiosity is up for debate—clearly, circumstance and motivation matter. But to understand this form of curiosity, whether we label it epistemic or intellectual, first we need to go back to the mid-twentieth century, and then all the way back to the dawn of humankind.

THE BLACK OBELISK

One of the founding fathers of curiosity research was Daniel Berlyne. Berlyne, a native of the United Kingdom, developed the idea that not knowing stuff created uncertainty and was uncomfortable; therefore, we developed curiosity as a way to find out information and reduce this unpleasant feeling.

He also theorized about different types of curiosity, particularly the different qualities of epistemic versus perceptual curiosity. Berlyne's research career was at its height in the mid-twentieth century. Berlyne's idea is often referred to as "curiosity-drive" theory. The idea inherent in

Berlyne's work is that humans don't like cognitive gaps or uncertainty. In other words, we don't like not knowing what's behind door number three.

The first act of Stanley Kubrick's *2001: A Space Odyssey* takes place at the dawn of human evolution, when humans were all hairy and apelike. In the film, a mysterious black, upright extraterrestrial monolith of unknown origin suddenly appears in the prehistoric landscape. The troop of protohumans approaches the weird new thing in their environment, shrieking and jumping, hooting and hollering. They're upset, because this new thing disrupts what is previously understood about the landscape where they live.

Curious, they finally get up the gumption to scurry closer and closer and finally touch the obelisk. Curiosity satisfied, pretty soon they go back to scratching themselves and hanging out.

This scene could've been acted out to demonstrate Berlyne's theory. The hominids are uncertain about the new object in their midst. A towering 20-foot-high sleek, black monolith is perhaps the classic definition of "unusual stimuli" used by Berlyne. But once they've satisfied their curiosity, they ignore it and go about their business of being primates.

It should be noted that Berlyne was aware of other potential types of curiosity, such as perceptual curiosity. He developed a more nuanced approach to understanding curiosity as his research progressed. In his book, *Conflict, Arousal, and Curiosity* (which sounds like either a great or terrible recipe for an amorous relationship, depending on the order), he began to investigate how curiosity could work not just in terms of reducing unpleasantness, but increasing pleasure. He wrote:

> The reward value of acquiring knowledge would then be ascribed to the mechanism of secondary reward or that of fear reduction. On other occasions, stimuli, especially symbolic stimuli, may be sought purely for their secondary reward value, derived from their association with concrete satisfactions, regardless of any practical value that they might have. But the kind of free-association fantasy that forms daydreams is capable of serving this purpose without the element of belief that is one of the hallmarks of knowledge. Often the reward value of knowledge depends on some social usefulness like gaining prestige or passing an examination.

This idea, that curiosity could exist as a something other than a fear-reduction impulse, would eventually be fleshed out by contemporary researchers like Jordan Litman, whom we'll meet in a bit. But science being science, it didn't take long after Berlyne put forth his ideas that someone soon came up with an alternate hypothesis to explain the origins of curiosity.

Eventually, even Berlyne came around to the idea of optimal arousal. The idea came about from researchers like Donald O. Hebb, who in the mid-twentieth century wrote a book that's become a classic in psychology called *The Organization of Behavior*. Hebb agreed with researchers such as James Leuba and believed that curiosity was a mechanism used to create optimal levels of arousal—a level of interest that doesn't tilt toward boredom or overstimulation.

According to the theory, if things get too intense—think a high-decibel rave with black lights and hordes of sweaty dancers crowding around—avoidance behavior is motivated. We get the heck out of there. Conversely, if things get dull—think about that lecture you went to last week where you started staring at the earlobes of the person in front of you and wondering about earlobes, and then idly considered doing a series of weird black-and-white photos of only earlobes—humans will explore their environment to find new stimuli to raise their level of stimulation to an arousal level that is pleasurable.

For those of you teachers out there, picture your students surreptitiously scrolling their phones under their desks while you drone on about concepts of community in Puritan England. (Unfortunately, that example is from my own experience.)

Hebb and his crew basically saw curiosity as a means to achieve a pleasurable state of mind and being. This idea is based on a central tenet of learning known as the Yerkes-Dodson Law, developed by Robert Yerkes and John Dodson in the early-twentieth century, which states that psychological performance increases with mental arousal, but only up to a point.

Things get too nutty and intense, and we freak out and can't concentrate. This is why our current emphasis on testing students with relentless regularity may be out of step with how learning actually works, as the heightened importance of student scores more and more reflects teacher salaries, school funding, and student success. Stakes that are that high—and have little or nothing to do with a student's intellectual development—skew the balance and performance suffers.

These two theories duked it out well into the twenty-first century. In the 1990s, researcher George Loewenstein of Carnegie Mellon University reframed the conversation. While not dismissing the idea that curiosity was an attempt to reduce uncertainty, Loewenstein thought that curiosity was an attempt to solve "deprivation," meaning that when we are deprived of understanding we seek information to bridge that knowledge gap.

THE BATMAN AND JOKER SCALE OF AMBIGUITY TOLERANCE

Currently our understanding of curiosity is evolving. In 2005, researcher Jordan Litman published a paper in the journal *Cognition and Emotion* titled "Curiosity and the pleasures of learning: Wanting and liking new information." This paper rejects both linear models in which curiosity is a means of reducing knowledge gaps and thus reducing the pain of unknowing, and the rewards-based system of searching out stimuli that get our dopamine centers going. Rather, Litman has postulated that curiosity exists upon a spectrum, dependent on a number of factors. His work suggests that there are different kinds of curiosity, each performing a different function.

Before, with Loewenstein, Berlyne, and others, curiosity was seen as either one of two responses to stimuli or lack thereof. It was either a situation of optimal arousal or curiosity drive. But Litman argues that recent research and neurological evidence suggest that the two modes of curiosity discussed above are no longer accurate.

But let's back up here and try to understand a little more clearly what Loewenstein and others are actually trying to say. A key part of curiosity theory lies with the concept of feeling of knowing, or FOK—an unfortunate but serviceable acronym.

Basically, a FOK is a state where you think you know something, but can't quite grasp it, tip of the tongue type stuff. The idea here is that when you feel like you're close to figuring something out, the feeling of curiosity intensifies, as the motivation to discover the desired information becomes a bit clearer. Lowenstein called this relationship between wanting to know and how close we are to knowing as the "knowledge gap/approach gradient."

All of which is fine and dandy, according to Litman, but it leaves out two very crucial elements: types of information desired and environmental factors. Litman proposes a more nuanced view of curiosity. He places the expression of curiosity within the same framework as other appetites such as food or sex. Similar to those drives, curiosity corresponds to scales of wanting, which regulate dopamine production, and liking, which stimulates opioid activity in the brain. Taking this more complex view helps to explain curiosity's various forms and its fluctuation in intensity, relationship with learning, and role in self-regulation.

Litman's work is a far cry from the initial work of researchers like Loewenstein and Berlyne, who argued for a basic "drive state" wherein a knowledge gap resulted in uncomfortable uncertainty. It also builds on the work of twentieth-century psychologists like Harry Fowler, who suggested that boredom created low levels of arousal that stimulate exploratory behavior to create optimum arousal levels. In both cases, curiosity is seen as a basic novelty-seeking motive.

In his research, Litman defines two distinct types of curiosity. There is "curiosity as feeling of deprivation" and "curiosity as feeling of interest," D-type and I-type, respectively. The concept behind these two types of curiosity is that in some conditions, that knowledge gap described by Loewenstein is acutely felt as a deficit.

With D-type, there is an intensity and transactional nature to the information, as in, "Boy, am I curious about the answer to the question on my history quiz!" That curiosity is driven by a feeling that you're lacking vital information that *matters*. The stakes could be low, like on the history quiz, or quite serious, like figuring out a cure for cancer. One of the defining characteristics of D-type is that the problem you're trying to solve is important; it matters.

It's different with I-type. On this end of the spectrum, we don't feel any particular need to discover new information. No black-robed, ruler-wielding nun stands before us ready to bloody our knuckles should we forget the correct recitation of *Pater noster*. Instead, we're just kind of interested in knowing about something. For whatever reason, some bit of information or a particular experience has made us prick up our ears and wonder.

The difference is that I-type is related to pleasure. We happily anticipate finding out the new information. I-type represents a stress-free scenario, where we don't necessarily need to know the information—we *want* to. Litman offers general examples of the types of categories this desired knowledge falls into: "information of a more casual, unessential, entertaining, or aesthetically pleasing nature, such as juicy gossip, an amusing anecdote, or an entertaining story."

Litman offers an example of potato chips to help understand this dynamic—again, reinforcing the concept that curiosity is similar to other appetites, like hunger. An analogous hunger state to D-type curiosity is when we are sodium deprived and we eat potato chips; we chow them down and experience a deep satiation. An I-type metaphor of this kind would have us eating potato chips and enjoying them not because we need the salt, but simply for their deliciousness. This is something Litman refers to as "hedonic value."

It comes down to a basic contextual scenario. With D-type, you need to know the information or else. With I-type, there's no external pressure to be curious, but you're attuned to the pleasure that results from discovering things anew.

As you can imagine, certain personalities are more likely to experience D-type. People who are task-oriented go-getters often fit into this category. Litman says that those who experience D-type are motivated by "tension, dissatisfaction, or anger." Sounds fun.

Conversely, those who fall on the I-type side of the spectrum are more likely to seek emotions that feel good such as humor, appreciating aesthetically pleasing scenes, and exciting situations.

So here's our scale:

Curiosity as feeling of deprivation ↔ Curiosity as feeling of interest

We can see these two types play themselves out in cultural icons. They often take the form of stereotypes. The is D-type bad cop. The I-type is good cop. Batman, especially the Batman of Christopher Nolan's recent

Dark Knight Trilogy, is starkly D-type, whereas his antagonists are often playfully I-type.

In the second film of the series, as Batman interrogates the Joker, we see this duality played out. "Then why do you want to kill me?" demands a violently angry Batman as he hurls the Joker around the room. "I don't want to kill you. What would I do without you?" replies the Joker. Batman is driven to paroxysms of madness trying to find the location of Harvey Dent, whom the Joker has kidnapped. The Joker is content with—coaxes, even—the unresolved situation, the ambiguity of who is on the right side of morality.

One of the Joker's arguments in the film is that people adopt morality when it suits them, something the D-type Batman struggles with. For the Caped Crusader, the world's greatest detective, ambiguity is unwanted. What the Dark Knight wants is answers. Now.

Our personalities play a role in terms of whether or not we develop one type of curiosity versus another, as do environmental factors. Most of us faced with a test or some thorny, complicated problem at work would be under the strain of D-type.

Imagine this scenario: you're working at the bank and keeping the books. Suddenly, there's a thousand dollars missing from the bank. Your boss will most definitely fire you if you can't figure out where the money went. So as you search for the information you need, the explanation and reason for the missing money, the curiosity you feel amid scouring spreadsheets and bank statements will be one based in deprivation, as in *where the hell is the cash?*

EXPLORING *MIDDLEMARCH*

Now, think of the classroom. How do we set up our students, to experience D-type or I-type curiosity, deprivation or interest? While I was a grade school teacher, I found motivation much easier through inspiring a sense of need and capitalizing on D-type—work equals grades sort of transaction. And while I tried, on some level, to incite their interest level and I-type grade curiosity, it was not as prevalent in my demeanor, lesson plans, or overall approach.

My own struggles as a teacher may have come from a misunderstanding of the relationship between learning, curiosity, and inquiry. The expectation is that our students practice inquiry; they engage in sustained investigation of a subject or problem with some eventual goal in sight.

Inquiry methods are skills that must be taught and learned over time. The catch is that we don't capitalize on our students' curiosity as an essential first step in developing learning skills. While curiosity may in fact be intense, sporadic, and transient, it is also personal to the learner and a powerful motivating force. But by identifying what the student is curious about and fostering that exploration, we can establish a framework through which to begin building higher-level skills of inquiry and sustained study.

But there are some more nuanced neurological underpinnings here. Two psychologists, Kent Berridge and Terry Robinson of the University of Michigan, have been digging into the mechanisms behind *wanting* and *liking* as neurologically based systems. Their research describes wanting as a means by which dopamine is produced, whereas liking involves opioid production.

As noted earlier, Litman uses their work to delineate the different types of curiosity. He writes, "Wanting is influenced by a variation in deprivation states, the presence of learned incentives for rewards, and the anticipated potential for a given stimulus to satisfy one's desire based on past experience."

This is basically how school and employment work. We are incentivized not to sneak out of the office at 10:30 in the morning to go for a swim in the lake because we know that working through the day will reward us with income. Our students struggle mightily through our lectures and lessons in the anticipation of getting home, opening a package of Oreos, putting in their earbuds, and surfing the Internet in glorious oblivion.

But *liking*, according to the research presented in various papers by Berridge and Robinson, is a bit trickier. There are different strengths and different types. For instance, desire can be strong or weak. Stimuli such as sweetness factor in how much we desire a certain food. Carrots have a sweetness to them, but I don't desire them with the same intensity as a pint of Ben & Jerry's New York Super Fudge Chunk.

Liking is even more complicated—and has more to do with how we learn—when we integrate how much we are able to interpret the thing we are curious about, and therefore like. The degree of our ability to interpret something cognitively bears directly on how much we like it.

Researchers such as Paul Reber from Northwestern University call this "processing ease" or "fluency." It works like this: the more skill we have in interpreting and understanding novel stimuli, or better yet, the more competency we have in digesting certain categories of novel stimuli (thus categorizing elements in our environment in a way that increases our ability to identify and use information), the more we like the stimuli. Back to Litman, who writes, "With repeated exposure, stimuli become progressively more interpretable, more easily understood, and therefore better liked."

This is how learning works. As we become progressively more "fluent" in interpreting new and stimulating information, we come to like it more—"it" being both the state of unknowing and the search for information that satisfies it. The liking comes from the anticipatory feeling of looking forward to the pleasure of discovery.

This is a precarious situation, and one that only develops with time. It actually falls into a category Berridge calls "subrational." That's because it's a state of high liking but low wanting, which doesn't seem to make much sense. How can we *like* something but not *want* it too?

Stimuli that are enjoyed but not really all that sought after fall into this category. An example of this would be reading Victorian novels. While not something I seek actively all the time, when I do find myself doing it, I enjoy it and like it. But compared with a wide array of other activities—trekking in the mountains with my family, kayaking Lake Champlain, having a barbecue with friends and drinking Vermont microbrews—it rates low on the wanting scale.

Take *Middlemarch*. I was looking around for something to read, and in clicking idly around the Internet one day I came across a review of Rebecca Mead's *My Life in Middlemarch*, a quirky but absorbing memoir of the author's relationship with George Eliot's masterpiece. A book about a book—super nerdy, I know, and having since read it can say that Mead's book is a compelling read.

Anyway, I got curious about *Middlemarch* for two reasons. Partly it was because of a general affinity I have for nineteenth-century English novels like *Far from the Madding Crowd* or *Jane Eyre*. While I don't actively dig them up, or study the books with any kind of scholarly acumen (indeed, I'm a pretty lazy reader as far as that goes), I like them. So low wanting, high liking.

My other reason was based in curiosity. I began to wonder why so many men (Joyce, David Foster Wallace, Pynchon) write these behemoth novels, rambling on for hundreds, sometimes thousands of pages. It seemed so phallic, sort of, a bunch of dudes trying to see who is biggest. But then there's George Eliot—or Mary Ann Evans, as she was named at birth—a woman who wrote a gargantuan novel way before all the guys.

Weird, I thought. What's up with that? I barely knew what *Middlemarch* was about, and was vaguely aware that George Eliot was actually the pen name for a female author. So I had all these Loewensteinian *gaps* in my understanding. There was information deprivation, but it didn't bother me all that much. The thing is though, that because I had read long novels before and found the experience—while not the most exciting thing in the world—to be pleasurable, I had developed "processing ease," and thought I might like *Middlemarch*. Turns out I did.

In fact, Eliot's monster of a book is perhaps one of my favorite novels for a few reasons. While there are books with writing I like more from a style perspective and novels that have more compelling content (as much as I like reading, plowing through chapter after chapter of the minutiae of a nineteenth-century industrial town was never what I would call fun), I have grown to love *Middlemarch* because of its pure scope.

It actually functions within the "processing ease" situation as a major tool; I feel I can understand so much more because of it. Other novels and complicated scenarios are more easily interpreted because of the way *Middlemarch* nudges one to understand complexity. But more importantly, I feel I understand myself better, somehow, because of *Middlemarch*.

Not only that, I'm in awe of Eliot's book. The appreciation of a book of that scope, or anything that inspires awe, is actually on a larger continuum that contains curiosity. In a footnote to his paper (footnotes are proof of curiosity—I usually read them only when the thing I'm reading is good enough to spur curiosity), Litman wrote, "Related to aesthetic appreciation is the study of awe, which involves intense emotional responses to stimuli that are perceived as vast in size or scope and that are difficult to comprehend fully."

Litman is basing this on research done by Dacher Keltner of the University of California, Berkeley, and Jonathan Haidt of New York University. He goes on to write, "The nature of the complex relationships between awe, aesthetic experience, and curiosity are not well understood and will be an interesting topic for future study."

Perhaps part of the reason I so thoroughly enjoyed George Eliot's *Middlemarch* is because I didn't particularly want to read it, but ended up doing so under no pressure from anyone other than myself.

But one of Loewenstein's main precepts was that curiosity was impulsive, that it was an urge, a scratch. Now, the scratch could be strong—a *need* to know—or less strong—a *want* to know. But curiosity doesn't sit well. Eventually, it drives us to do things, to make things happen.

Remember Telescope Peak, where this book started? That was an experience in impulsivity, the way curiosity makes us do things without a lot of thought. It's why when my son wants to know if Storm (aka Ororo Munroe) from the X-Men can create tornadoes, and I respond with an "I don't know," he gets agitated.

THE SPUR OF THE MOMENT

Impulsivity, transience, and intensity are frequently prevalent aspects of curiosity. These three traits offer us some helpful clues in discussing curiosity and how it plays a role in learning and schools. By *impulsive* what is meant is that it comes on suddenly and at times unexpectedly—this can be a lovely surprise or not, depending on the circumstance. Curiosity is often *transient* in that just as it comes on suddenly, it goes away after a certain amount of time.

While we may remain passionate about art our whole lives, when standing in front of a given Jackson Pollock painting, we experience curiosity about the work and artist briefly, and then it dies down as we drift into the Renaissance art wing of the museum. And more often than not, curiosity is *intense*. We experience it as a heightened state. It's not necessarily some low-level hum of mild interest; it can be a powerful motivating force.

In addition, curiosity can arise due to states of uncertainty, such as ambiguity. It can also take root in boredom. This doesn't mean that it can't also be an intrinsic drive, but the research suggests that environmental conditions like ambiguity and boredom can give rise to curiosity.

One would think that learning through curiosity is a relatively simple approach. However, when we take into account Litman's scale of I-type and D-type, and our own messy lives and prickly tastes when it comes to how and what we learn, difficulties begin to emerge. While school and traditional learning do stimulate some students, and usually do so through D-type situations, there are other types of learning where curiosity plays a role.

CHAOS THEORY AND VIRGINIA WOOLF

Learning is viewed as a form of reception (in other words, the student receives the learning in packaged form from a program or teacher or book in a linear fashion). It is generally held to be purpose driven. There's a reason for that, and we experience it thus in schools. And if we are teachers, we construct our lesson plans and curricula in such as way as to build idea upon idea.

Skill sets that are foundational provide support for more convoluted and complex forms of knowledge. This is as it should be. It makes sense. You learn a few letters of the alphabet, then the whole twenty-six letters, then the sounds they make, then the little two- and three-letter words like *at* and *hot*, and suddenly BOOM! The next thing you know, you're furtively reading *Fifty Shades of Grey* on the bus to work.

I've depended on this progression of skill sets and knowledge as a teacher and used it to inform my practice. It's similar to how managers teach their employees and parents teach their children. But as a person, as a chaotic and messy and not-terribly-organized human, I can't say that what I see as the *trajectory* of my learning resembles the ruler-straight, FAA-approved contrail of a jet across the sky as it dependably reaches higher and higher altitudes of understanding.

My learning—the learning that makes me who I am, not the learning that adds up to what I know—has been more like the fully inflated balloon you let go and watch as it rockets about the room going haywire, fart noises providing the soundtrack.

I think there are two types of learning—more possibly, but in terms of curiosity and learning, two that are important in our quotidian, daily lives. The first we recognize as learning with a capital "L." This is institutional learning, where we depend on governmental departments, educational organizations, and businesses to provide us with the raw building blocks of understanding: school, publishers, media, professional teachers, uniform assessment, hierarchical schema, literary canons, educational policy—you get the idea.

I've supported myself more or less consistently for almost twenty years as a purveyor of just these types of goods. But there is a shadow learning process that exists in parallel to learning with a capital "L." To my mind, it's a deeper, more personal learning. It's less easily codified, but defines us and determines who we are, like intellectual dark matter.

Virginia Woolf was the master of this shadow land where wandering and rumination took center stage, and where the journey was the point rather than the destination. Arriving at meaning is key—both in terms of learning and understanding ourselves as active beings with agency in our own lives. Woolf was somehow able to demonstrate in her writing exactly this kind of subtle unspooling of thought, a willingness to engage in happenstance and let the world teach her. But what it teaches, and whatever learning occurs at the end, is up to fate. Or for the more mathematically minded, chaos theory.

What I don't know about chaos theory could fill books—actually, it does. But as a metaphor it may be helpful. Basically, chaos theory suggests that systems of determination that have minor deviances at the onset end up with unpredictable results. The "butterfly effect" it's sometimes called.

The idea is that a small experience in the initial phases of a system that plays out over time causes unanticipated and incalculable results. It's a fun idea to think about. Some tiny little event early in our lives, let's say, led us to some great change that no one saw coming later on because of the domino effect of random causality.

In much of Woolf's writing—*To the Lighthouse* comes to mind—travel plays a key role, even if the journey is no more exotic than a walk through her neighborhood in London.

In *A Room of One's Own*, Woolf describes the kind of thinking that is intimately tied to the kind of learning we're talking about. In doing so she opens a door to a vast and variegated internal terrain and personal mythology that exists within anyone willing to stop and plunge the depths of their own experience. In the novella-length essay, we find Woolf sitting by the side of a river, watching the light as it reflects the bushes and trees on the water.

> Thought—to call it by a prouder name than it deserved—let its line down into the stream. It swayed, minute after minute, hither and thither among the reflections and the weeds, letting the water lift it and sink it, until—you know the little tug—the sudden conglomeration of an idea at the end of one's line: and then the cautious hauling of it in, and the careful laying of it out? Alas, laid on the grass how small, how insignificant this thought of mine looked; the sort of fish that a good

fisherman puts back into the water so that it may grow fatter and be one day worth cooking and eating.

This kind of thinking—though I agree with Woolf that it's not really like thinking, more like a subconscious percolating of stuff that may bubble up from time to time given the right conditions—is the very action of the type of learning that interests me. It requires two things, however, both of which are in short supply in America in the twenty-first century: time and a well-wrought and decently calibrated dowsing rod of the Self.

In Sven Birkerts's book *The Gutenberg Elegies*, Birkerts discusses this very passage of Woolf's. He writes, "She reveals how incidental experience can encounter a receptive sensibility and activate the mainspring of creativity." Learning is ultimately experiential. We have to be doing things, going places, in order to inoculate ourselves with this type of knowledge. It depends on two crucial factors: the active, participatory self and what Birkerts calls the "receptive sensibility," that dowsing rod I just mentioned.

In our breakneck, fast-paced lives and within the hectic multitude of digital selves and all their demands that now exist, how are we to access this kind of space, this reverie? It sounds quaint even to me, an acolyte of unmitigated, noninstitutionalized idle; I cringe and think of parasols, shoes that button, and words like *waistcoat* and *phaeton*.

We miss out on a special kind of learning when we don't actively create moments of exactly this kind of reverie and idleness, or do the work of having experiences and reading books to get that dowsing rod buffed to a high shine. If my college students are any example, if they let their lives float downstream they'd be snagged by professional pressure, smartphones, family demands, six classes, work study, and the ceaseless and addictive demand to participate in the digital dialogue that consumes our lives.

I wish, actually, that I was some hoary, old man, complaining about youngsters and their gadgetry and ruefully shaking my shaggy head at their attention-shattering distraction and self-absorption. I'm not, though (at least not entirely). I'm talking about myself.

Take this morning. As I write this, I'm in a study carrel in the basement of the library on campus, which isn't even called a library but rather an information commons, whatever that is. I'm writing longhand on white legal pads with a cheap pen. Birkerts's book is here, as is Woolf's. I don't bring a laptop down here—I can't resist its siren's song. It's currently 9:25 a.m. on a Wednesday.

It sounds like discipline, but it's fear and addiction that force me to run, not walk but run, down to this windowless, airless closet of a study room. Because in my daily life, I am a man beset by the plague of digital information—which I love and hate in equal measure.

I clumped up the stairs to my office this morning around 8:00 a.m. On the way I saw a friend and colleague to whom I'd sent an interesting article from Gawker the day before. We chatted, and he followed my lead and opened a window on his computer to show me a related piece from Deadspin.

I bustled off to my desk, and with the push of a button brought my computer to life and opened the door to the universe—literally. Anything I wanted to learn or do—learn Finnish, watch a video that describes how they built the Mars Curiosity rover, research the early life of Malcolm X, peruse fund-raising sites and give money to causes I believe in—or anything I wanted to discover or even anyone I wanted to talk to was there. I could've tweeted Hassan Rouhani if I so desired.

I did none of those things. Instead, I allowed myself to be distracted and pitched about by the heaving seas of the Internet for awhile instead of work. But in this milieu, I am susceptible to the same influences as my students. And while I love the ease and accessibility of the Web, and millions of things I can do with it, I know that for me it represents the anathema of what real learning feels like. Because at the end of the day, no matter how interesting or captivating or global or prescient the information is that I absorb through the screen, when I am engaging with it I am not doing anything. I am not having experiences. I'm sitting on my butt in a chair, slack jawed and finger twitchy. As Montaigne said in his *Essais*, "My thoughts fall asleep if I make them sit down. My mind will not budge unless my legs move it."

Birkerts calls Woolf's writing a kind of "exploratory digressiveness," and offers the idea that thinking doesn't necessarily have to be "utilitarian." Thinking is not only the critical, problem-solving tool of schools and teachers and institutions—a mechanical rendering of useful fact and LEGO-like ideas snapped together to create some sort of by-the-numbers stronghold. He suggests that thinking can also be "a kind of narrative travel that allows for picnics along the way."

If I haven't lost you yet—sent you harrumphing off at my artsy-fartsy notions of how learning of this kind can work—let me try one last arrow from my quiver.

FINDING FATTER FISH

I've worked in the business world and now teach at a career-oriented college. Two of the buzzwords at the moment, though they're never really out of style, are *innovation* and *creativity*. In the chaotic and rapidly mutating job market, employers are clamoring for innovators, creative types. Outside-the-box thinkers. I don't necessarily mean the next Warhol or Pollock, though that's a part of it, but also workers who can make software do interesting things, market products in ways that are successful, reimagine companies to make them more profitable. The CEOs and bosses of America are saying that they want these types of inventive employees.

Virginia Woolf wouldn't have been a good regional manager for Boring & Cos widgets and gizmos, but she knew a thing or two about creativity. Remember Birkerts talking about how the "receptive sensibility" gets the creative juices flowing? He follows up by pinpointing what it is, exactly, about this kind of free-associative and deschooled learning that gives rise to imagination of the sort that Woolf embodies so keenly.

Birkerts looks at the way Woolf ordered her thoughts on the page to arrive at a deep understanding of this type of thinking: "This is her triumph: the trust in serendipity, which proves, when unmasked, to be an absolute faith in the transformative powers of the creative intellect."

Can this type of learning and thinking be nurtured—where we give students and ourselves time to compost their own thoughts, digress and transform, until the random memories and experience provide fertile soil for creation—for a "fatter" fish good for "cooking and eating?" Yes and no.

It's possible, of course, to structure the lives of our students and ourselves to give time, space, and unmediated experience. It's unlikely though. Not something parents anxious about the employment prospects of their progeny want to hear. Not something eager undergrads want to invest tens of thousands of dollars of loan money in. And not something we, ourselves, feel particularly comfortable with. Certainly not something purveyors of institutionalized education like the Educational Testing Service, the U.S. Department of Education, educational software program developers, ed tech companies, and professional associations want to hear.

Hard to put a dollar sign next to daydreams; hard to enter the valuation of idle reverie into a spreadsheet. Is it possible that we could transform education—and our own lives—in such a way as to foster this amorphous experience of careful yet unfocused listening to the world and ourselves? Yes. Give the students—and ourselves—time to read, to think. Give in to our curiosity.

TWO

Hardwired for Adventure

TUBERS AND MILEY CYRUS

The question is whether we can even help ourselves from checking Facebook or resist the impulse to click whatever Internet fodder pixelates before our eyeballs. Is it just our own inability to control ourselves, or is there something deeper at work—are we biologically programmed to be impulsively curious? Is our "exploratory digressiveness" nothing more than a twenty-first-century form of foraging, but instead of looking for tubers and carcasses to scavenge, we're hunting for the latest news on Miley Cyrus?

Whether or not curiosity is an innate, biological drive has fascinated researchers from biologists to neuroscientists for ages. Much of the research has attempted to discover the source of motivation in a given scenario.

For instance, is an animal that explores its environment driven by hunger looking for a new food source, or is it in search of novel stimuli? And does this behavior result from an inner urge to explore, or is it simply a result of the environment? If a rat within a maze takes the time and energy to explore the whole maze, how can we be sure it's not just driven by hunger? How can we assign the exploratory behavior as curious?

Curiosity is, like many behaviors and traits, a difficult aspect of behavior to define. One of the reasons for this is its inherent complexity. As we'll see, there are several types of curiosity with different strengths, and they are often dependent on a variety of environments and stimuli.

Curiosity may be one of the only attributes that distinctly sets us apart from other animals—or not. The research on what curiosity exactly is—and if it's similar to the way animals will explore new stimuli or a new environment in the hopes of finding food—is a dense and many layered field that includes research from education, neuroscience, psychology, philosophy, and biology.

If the way we express curiosity is one of the things that makes humans human, then it behooves the question whether the trait is genetic and thus biologically rooted or just a facet of culture, something inherited socially rather than genetically.

This is an important question to consider. Whether or not curiosity in humans is an inherent, genetic set of behaviors or something we learn culturally affects the way we think about teaching, learning, and creativity itself. If curiosity is genetically inherited, then we can begin to confront questions about creativity, schools, and how we perceive our children's behaviors.

However, we then must grapple with the fact that if curiosity exists on the genetic level, we are in league with animals and curiosity isn't the thing that makes us different from animals. We'd have to accept the fact that we're in league with mole rats and wallabies.

CURIOUS BIRDS

While animals engage in all kinds of exploratory behavior, it's safe to say they don't fuss about the origin of the universe in the same way we do or wonder about how life might have begun at volcanic fumaroles under the sea. Our particularly human expression of curiosity, be it intellectual or epistemic, is not observable, at least at this point, within the cognition of animals. But that doesn't mean that animals can't be curious or that curiosity is purely a human trait.

Back in 2007 researchers at the Max Planck Institute identified a gene that may have a link to curiosity. The gene is labeled as the DRD4 gene, and its function is to build receptors in the brain for the neurotransmitter dopamine. However, this gene was not identified in humans, but in the great tit, a smallish songbird native to Europe and Asia.

Discovery of this gene was significant for two reasons. One, it identified a potential biological root of curiosity. Two, it suggested that curiosity was an adaptive trait—otherwise it wouldn't show up in genes.

Further studies have shown that your Indiana Jones–type folks (explorers and adventurers) who carry more of the curiosity gene and one of its variants known as DRD4-7R are more likely to explore new foods, places, and cultures. They explore and adventure, and are often what psychologists would describe as *perceptually curious*.

People who rate highly in perceptual curiosity have an intense interest in novel sights, sounds, or environmental cues. For them, it motivates visual exploration; they look around to identify the stimuli. Or they listen closely. The best way to think of perceptual curiosity is of someone who enters a new place, let's say a crowded street bazaar, and is enveloped in the sights and sounds, eager to investigate and explore.

That suggests that folks with this gene—about 20 percent of the population according to a 2013 article in *National Geographic* that reviews the research—are the explorers, adventurers, and risk takers among us. Fill up a hypodermic with the stuff, and you're Richard Branson, trying to float a balloon around the world, or you're Felix Baumgartner, the Red Bull–sponsored nut who parachuted from 128,000 feet. Right?

Not quite.

Humans are unbelievably complex. Our behaviors and traits are dependent on so many factors that narrowing down causality to this one gene variant, while seductive, is ultimately too simple to do any real good. In his fascinating book *Sapiens*, author Yuval Noah Harari writes that to understand complicated human development, "it is not enough to comprehend the interaction of genes, hormones and organisms. It is necessary to take into account the interaction of ideas, images and fantasies as well."

But what the research seems to suggest is that there is a correlation on some level between curiosity and impulsivity. Whether or not they're connected in terms of cause and effect is unclear, but they seem to coincide enough to warrant investigation.

In the *National Geographic* article, Yale University evolutionary and population geneticist Kenneth Kidd states it this way: "You can't reduce something as complex as human exploration to a single gene." Other factors are equally as important.

For instance, a stable childhood where an individual is able to explore and learn and play for an extended period into adolescence would contribute to exploratory, inquisitive behavior. So although there is a biological link to curiosity behavior within our genetic makeup, it is not the only—or even necessarily the most important—piece of the puzzle of curiosity.

Looking at curiosity from the perspective of how impulsivity informs our behavior helps to color in the picture a bit more clearly and gives us a more nuanced view of how curiosity operates.

IMPULSIVITY RESEARCH IS VERY IMPORT.... HEY! LOOK AT THAT SQUIRREL!

Impulsivity has been given a bad rap. It's the very thing that inhibits learning, or at least that's the conventional understanding. Students go pinballing around the classroom, asking nonsensical questions, straying off topic, leading the discussion off on tangents. In fact, if we look at techniques for classroom management as a whole, they almost seem designed to inhibit impulsivity: we keep students engaged in such a way that non sequitur thoughts, flashes of emotion, and curious asides are kept to a minimum.

This is for the most part a good thing. To tackle any large, ambitious learning project, the opposite forces of impulsivity come into play: perseverance, stick-to-itiveness, directedness, focus, delayed gratification, the project management-esque deliberate consciousness of and adherence to an axis of time and deliverables—all these are tried-and-true ways to get stuff done. These elements are necessary for any big project, but that's not the whole story.

(VERVET) MONKEY BUSINESS

On an evolutionary scale, it's always been a gamble to be impulsive. However, as with all gambles, you win some, you lose some. But with impulsivity in human primates it seems we've won enough to have the trait passed down as an adaptation. The question is, why and under what circumstances is impulsivity successful?

Impulsivity as a drive and fundamental expression within human behavior hasn't always been a bad thing, nor is it a bad thing under all circumstances. For most of us, it is an unfortunate behavioral tick: all of a sudden you get the urge to ditch work; you decide to party the night away despite the fact you have to be up early the next day; you display vulgar, symbolic hand gestures to other drivers during your morning commute. None of this bodes well for increasing your standing in society.

But change the environment to more natural settings, and the outcomes of impulsivity can shift under certain circumstances. Impulsivity can be great, dependent on one factor: you need to be a vervet monkey.

Lynn Fairbanks is a professor emeritus of primatology at UCLA. Though officially retired, Fairbanks keeps an office on campus and retains her charming, enthusiastic lecture style in conversation. You can tell from talking to her that she's a good teacher and digs primates in a big way and that she finds why and when they engage in certain behaviors helpful in figuring out why their evolutionary cousins—us humans—are so damnably quirky.

Fairbanks studies vervet monkeys. Vervets are interesting primates for a variety of reasons. They exploit multiple environments—savannah and fractured forest, urban land and agricultural areas—and can be found from South Africa all the way up to the horn of East Africa. Their adaptability to various environments is one token of their success. But there are other ways in which vervets are often studied to help understand various qualities of *Homo sapiens*:

- They have hypertension just like us, and can be spiteful just like us.
- The little buggers also have specialized communication.

- They vocalize specific warnings depending on the threat (in other words, they have different alarm calls for different predators. Their "holy moly, an eagle!" call is different from their "run away, it's a leopard!" screech.)
- In addition to being uncanny in their communication, male vervets also capitalize on impulsivity.

Fairbanks studied both captive vervets and monkeys in the wild, and her research has shown a direct correlation between impulsivity and success. In a 2004 paper published in the *American Journal of Primatology* with the spoiler of a title, "Adolescent Impulsivity Predicts Adult Male Dominance Attainment in Male Vervet Monkeys," Fairbanks and her coauthors discovered that the more impulsive adolescent male vervets were, the more likely they were to attain the rank of alpha within the troop. And in the world of vervets, there is no greater measure of success than being head honcho and having access to the ladies. Continuing genes is the name of the game after all in evolution.

In analyzing the research she and her colleagues completed on vervets, Fairbanks wrote, "These results support the idea that there are benefits of a high-risk, high-gain strategy [and that it] is beneficial for adolescent and young male vervets."

It seems counterintuitive at first. Risk takers would appear to be at a disadvantage in the natural world—the curious and exploratory wildebeest who decides to go swimming just for the hell of it on a hot day quickly becomes croc bait. According to natural selection, which favors adaptations and behaviors that increase the likelihood of passing genes from one generation to the next, impulsivity as a drive should've disappeared in vervets, our primate ancestors, and ourselves.

It doesn't pay to go sticking your nose where it doesn't belong in the natural world, we assume; it might get bitten off. But when I asked Fairbanks about this, she responded, "[Impulsivity] wouldn't exist on such a large scale in evolution if it wasn't an adaptation." Touché, madam professor.

But the literature on impulsivity points strongly toward detrimental behaviors in human primates associated with a propensity for risk taking: binge drinking, crime, promiscuity, and so on. Fairbanks responded, "You have to take the value system out of it."

She went on to describe what she saw the vervets do. When confronted with a new male vervet in their midst—stranger danger!—Fairbanks noted that some adolescent males in the troop would "rush over to the adult male stranger."

This is not good behavior for vervets or humans; acting rashly like that toward a strange male is likely to get the young vervet walloped or bit by the interloping adult male (which is exactly what will happen to us if we try a similar approach to strange males we encounter at night in downtown Los Angeles).

However, Fairbanks and her colleagues noted that those youngsters became alphas, or at least more dominant males within the troop's hierarchy, over time. And here's the kicker: "The males that became alpha were significantly higher in impulsivity as adolescents, but then declined to the same mean level of impulsivity as the lower-ranking males after they had achieved alpha status as adults." These impulsive monkeys turned out to be good leaders.

So the next time you see a bunch of skateboarders careening wildly about, trying to ollie a 10 stair and grinding the curb in front of your office, just remember: you could be working for that kid some day.

When Fairbanks explained this to me, I found what I thought was a chink in the armor. Stress in primates, vervets, baboons, or humans produces cortisol. Cortisol is a glucocorticoid, a hormone that triggers all kinds of reactions within our bodies during times of intense stress.

It's an excellent thing to have if all of a sudden a hockey-mask-wearing serial killer jumps out of the bushes and starts chasing you with a machete. Cortisol and other glucocorticoids like it help us get the hell out of there; they fire up the fight-or-flight system in our bodies. But under constant, chronic stress, when we repeatedly fire up our adrenal glands to produce cortisol, it's not so great.

For instance, if your response to your boss is similar to the response you'd have to said hockey-masked killer and you have to face the boss man every day, it will have negative physical and psychological consequences. Our bodies begin to exhibit physical symptoms of chronic stress, and it breaks us down—think ulcers, hair loss, lack of sleep, acid reflux, and loss of sex drive. It's all from stress.

But what Fairbanks and her cohort discovered was that those risk-taking adolescents and other more adventurous adult females have *lower* than normal levels of cortisol. These crazy teenage monkeys (or risk-taking individuals) should be under a constant barrage of cortisol and exhibit all the telltale signs of stress. But that's not what the researchers found. They weren't stressed out. "They were the chill ones," said Fairbanks.

Fairbanks called this a "blunted reaction," and it's unclear whether the cortisol response of the adventuresome vervets is "intentionally deregulated" or they've just worn down the system over time with repeated exposure to stressful stimuli.

But impulsivity payoff is clear in evolutionary terms. Natural selection has, according to Fairbanks and her crew, favored impulsivity. Otherwise, impulsivity wouldn't exist.

Impulsivity can still have its drawbacks, to be sure. As Fairbanks noted, when you're an individual who acts impulsively, "you're more likely to lose your job, get in a fight, or be arrested." But by the same token, being a risk taker—a devil-may-care adventurer, a job quitter, an innovator, a rule breaker, or a rebel—may have rewards that are rarer but more spectacular. As Fairbanks pointed out, "You can't be an entrepreneur without overestimating your chance of success."

Heeding the siren's song of impulsivity—for ourselves or our students—produces experience. Something happens. Risk takers come into contact with the world under all kinds of conditions. There's a downside to be sure. But if learning is best activated through direct experience, then venturing away from our desks, out of the classroom, and into the unknown is a good thing. So is occasionally allowing impulse and capricious whim to guide our thinking and exploration.

We can learn traditionally, in school, with the teacher lecturing, but there are other forums for personal development. As Fairbanks said to me at the end of our conversation, "It's more interesting to be out there."

What she meant by "out there" was impulsively engaged in the environment and with those around you. Consider the more standard definition of "out there": being outside. The connection between impulsivity and adventure seems clearer. Potentially, both exploration and a willingness to launch into the fray, to confront the unknown, have a biological root. It also seems that perceptual curiosity—interest in visual stimuli that provoke an investigative response—must be only part of the story.

If perceptual curiosity is the response to novel stimuli to gain knowledge, what about curiosity that seeks to create sensations such as excitement, fear, or a bit of a thrill? Turns out, there's just such a set of behaviors and traits within the spectrum of curiosity.

THREE

Inside Bad, Outside Good

SAN JACINTO PEAK

I turned back briefly to look at my stepdaughter. We were almost 10,000 feet above sea level near the summit of San Jacinto Peak, and I was walking away, leaving Vivien on a 24-hour solo camping trip in the middle of the wilderness. She was ten years old.

Her mother and I jokingly called her "Victorian Vivien." She has always been quiet, introverted, and smart as a whip; she's also fond of her creature comforts. The joke has grown ironic: she is anything but the stereotypical delicate Victorian lady now.

In the past half-dozen years she's traversed the globe, researching wildlife populations in Africa, scrabbling around on her hands and knees in the Sevilleta National Wildlife Refuge in New Mexico researching whiptail lizards, partying down in a small village in Spain when they won the World Cup in 2010. But there was a time when she was a child when adventure of the thrill-inducing kind didn't seem to be a fit for her.

Even today, that moment on San Jacinto stands out to me as the singular moment when I felt the overwhelming feeling of pride mixed with love—and a decent dash of fear. What was it in Vivien that made her seek out that experience?

When I went back to get her 24 hours later, she told me she'd made herself pancakes for breakfast. She'd slept in the open, without a tent. A coyote had trotted through her camp. Not many adults I know would have the courage to do what Vivien did. The other kids were so excited by the feat she'd achieved, and she did it all in her quiet, assured way.

Sensory curiosity is the essence of what compelled her to take on this adventure.

EVOLVING CURIOSITY

School is a relatively recent phenomenon, especially school as we know it. The history of formal schooling goes at least all the way back to ancient Mesopotamia, roughly 4,000 years ago, and included the instruction of scribes who had to learn to record how many goats farmer Etel-pisha sold to Sin-ishmeni and so forth.

You can almost imagine disheartened schoolboys in the mud-walled city of Ur slouching home, hand-knotted bags full of clay tablets to complete for homework for strict, rod-bearing and loinclothed schoolmasters. But as far as the whole human endeavor goes—our history as a distinct and identifiable species—formal schooling is just a flash in the pan. It could stand to be the one hit wonder of human history, an institutional Milli Vanilli.

We've been anatomically human for about 200,000 years, meaning you could dress up a *Homo sapiens* from 200 centuries ago in a uniform, and you wouldn't recognize her as she collected tolls for the Washington Bridge. That means that for roughly 98 percent of our evolutionary history, we haven't had formal schools.

We didn't have to head off to some horrible Soviet-looking brick building, endure trigonometry or earth science, eat something euphemistically called "Chef's special shepard's pie" in the cafeteria. There was (blessedly) no homework. No curricula, no formal expectations, no Common Core.

Most of our experience as humans was completely devoid of anything resembling what we now call education. And yet whatever we did for those eons leading up to civilization led us to create those very civilizations: their cities, languages, laws, and tools like the Garden Weasel and Flowbee.

The question of what, exactly, was going on for approximately 196,000 years before three-ring binders and notebook checks is a fair one, as whatever mode of learning we employed during that time not only lasted for the majority of our time as anatomically modern humans, but also encouraged and supported the human species' greatest accomplishment: we migrated and adapted and colonized every corner of the globe.

Just within this past century, we've added Antarctica and the Earth's orbit to the list. No small feat, and our radical settling of every possible environment in the world may stand the test of time as the most fundamentally human event in the history of our kind on this planet: a global exploration fueled by curiosity.

So how did we do it? How did we spread across the globe, develop language, cooperation, culture? What were we doing to build the necessary skills, pass on knowledge, and make sure our little groups had the information needed—the creativity demanded—to survive? What conditions fostered the explosion of exploration that occurred as we spread from east Africa all over the entire world? And more to the purposes of this book, how did curiosity play a role in our progression from a skinny, naked, upright primate stealing carcasses from hyenas on the savannah to the species that would eventually give rise to Grand Theft Auto?

As we've seen, curiosity functions in a number of ways. But in its most basic forms, it exists as a group of behaviors and traits that ping-pongs between the urge to probe the unknown out of intrinsic, epistemic desire and the need to close gaps of understanding that cause us discomfort.

Curiosity in its most elemental form lives between these two poles. Think again of our ancestors depicted in Kubrick's *2001: A Space Odyssey*. It was curiosity that spurred the primates to explore the new monolith that suddenly appeared in their midst. This is external motivation. Many studies in curiosity and exploratory behavior have noted that when novel stimuli are introduced, like a giant obsidian-like block of flawless alien stone, we investigate them until they are no longer novel.

What then of our desire to cross the Bering Land Bridge between Siberia and Alaska some 15,000 to 35,000 years ago and spread down all the way to Patagonia in just a few thousand years? Competition for resources among our Paleolithic forebears, overcrowding, the search for a more delicious mastodon burger all probably played a part, but there's something else there as well—the intrinsic need to explore, to go farther, to see what's over the next rise.

Anyone who's ever been the passenger of a car driven by someone stubbornly trying to find their destination as they drive aimlessly down streets, bent over the wheel while offering hollow assurances that it's "definitely just around the next corner," will recognize this scenario.

It could be that the compulsion to explore the unknown is a form of sensory curiosity. Individuals high in sensory curiosity seek stimuli in order to provoke a sensory response often associated with risk or thrill seeking. Clearly, exploring a continent with a rock-tipped spear qualifies as thrilling.

In looking at this vital stretch of our history, two things become clear:

- Learning was communal and autonomous, unforced and inclusive. Learning was relational. Whether learning to make a Clovis point spear or the story of the creation of the world through myth and song, we learned from people we knew and who knew us.
- We learned outside, in the natural world.

These two factors—the time and freedom to learn and explore whatever we want and the endlessly fascinating classroom offered by the wild, natural world—are the perfect ingredients to foster curiosity. It was through these two elements that we experienced the most radical and rapid advance in human evolution: exploration, creativity, and innovation on a global scale.

DECONSTRUCTING PLAY STRUCTURES

In his 2013 book, *Free to Learn*, Peter Gray focuses on exactly this relationship. Gray is a psychologist who studied learning and education through the lens of biological evolution and human development. Realizing that the way we do school now is an anomaly rather than some tried-and-true approach to learning, Gray reviewed research and undertook his own experiments to figure out how we approached the cultural transmission of knowledge—learning—during the hunter-gatherer phase of human evolution, which as noted earlier, comprises 98 percent of our time as humans.

What he found was that a lack of structure—time to play and explore, and the negation of responsibility for children—was consistent across multiple hunter-gatherer societies, if not all of them. But his work also points out that these groups, including the Ju/'hoansi of South Africa, Hazda of the Tanzanian rain forest, and Inuit of the far north, had sharing, egalitarianism, and a sense of openness and community as central tenets.

In his research, Gray notes that within these open, unstructured and noncoercive environments, children find the perfect circumstances for learning, primed, as they are, by their own curiosity:

> Children come into the world burning to learn and genetically programmed with extraordinary capacities for learning. They are little learning machines. Within their first four years or so they absorb an unfathomable amount of information and skills without any instruction. They learn to walk, run, jump, and climb. They learn to understand and speak the language of the culture into which they are born, and with that they learn to assert their will, argue, amuse, annoy, befriend, and ask questions. They acquire an incredible amount of knowledge about the physical and social world around them. All of this is driven by their inborn instincts and drives their innate playfulness and curiosity.

Not only are the children of these tribes actively ready to learn; they are supported by adults who realize that sometimes the best thing to do is get out of the way. Gray writes, "The general belief among hunter-gatherer adults, borne out by centuries of experiences, is that children educate themselves through their self-directed play and exploration."

Gray's findings stand in stark contrast to contemporary schools. Education is instructed, delivered, packaged, and programmed. We, as a culture, intervene in every aspect of our children's lives, going so far as to introduce the idea of "play dates" instead of play and changing the name of the "monkey bars" to "play structures."

Gray is right. Curiosity is ignited under unencumbered free time. But add to that experience the natural world—the woods, fields, mountains, deserts, and seashores—and curiosity bursts into flame.

Richard Louv's well-known treatise on children's rapidly eroding contact with the natural world, *Last Child in the Woods*, echoes many of Gray's sentiments, but also narrows the argument. Louv, founder of a global movement to introduce kids to more time outdoors, suggests that it is exposure to the outdoors in an unstructured way that is the wellspring of curiosity and creativity, even spiritual health. Louv's work is a perfect parallel for Gray's.

Through *Last Child in the Woods*, Louv makes a compelling argument for the importance of getting kids outside and playing in the woods. Curiosity, it would seem, responds to the natural world. Only within the universe that exists in the scrubby patches of trees that dot our landscape can children fully explore their own imaginations.

OUTSIDE THE BOX

There's a solid body of research that strongly supports the idea that being outside improves our thinking. University of Michigan researchers found that memory retention could improve simply when we spend time outside or in green spaces, as reported in *Psychological Science* in 2008.

Multiple studies have shown that children respond positively to being in nature and that a natural environment can reduce stress and anxiety, and even mitigate learning challenges such as ADHD. But you don't need the research to know this—we all experience it. You're at work, you're stressed, and you're freaking out. You feel the urge to walk somewhere, to bolt from your cubicle and get out in the fresh air. Once outside, the dominance of the work-bot mentality of your job seems a bit less deadly. You feel better. You look at trees, listen to the birds. You may even smile.

All good things. But the link between large amounts of unstructured time outdoors and curiosity is of an even deeper, more profound sort.

We spent most of our evolutionary journey in nature. It is there that our brains developed, where we learned how to think, where instincts grew that encouraged exploration and innovation. What is it about being outside—without much of anything to do—that helps us foster curiosity?

To answer the question, we return to the research of Jordan Litman. Remember the scale of curiosity in regard to intensity and context? There are two sides of the spectrum: curiosity as a feeling of deprivation (D-type) and curiosity as a feeling of interest (I-type). I-type is usually accompanied by positive feelings. It's neat to learn new stuff and it makes us happy. Some negative associations can accompany D-type curiosity: a knowledge gap created by a lack of information, sort of like an itch we can't quite scratch. Litman categorizes I-type as a "take it or leave it" approach to new information and novel stimuli.

I-type—the state of being interested in a musing sort of way—is best engendered through long stretches of time in the woods without any set agenda. This is, after all, how we've spent the majority of our evolutionary history.

Multiple studies have shown that hunter-gatherer cultures worked a lot less than we do now—a couple of hours a day—leaving plenty of time for lying about and kicking back, skipping stones, watching the leaves blow in the wind. What is going on in that time spent outdoors, though it may not appear to be all that substantial, is in reality a vital experience for human development.

PLAYING IN THE WOODS, PLAYING WITH IDEAS

Picture a little kid, somewhere between two and five years old, alone in the woods.

You don't talk to her; you just watch what she does and follow her movements. She may get fussy and complain, but you don't try to entertain her. You don't alleviate her boredom. You let her wander.

She totters about in that adorable, simian bow-legged walk of toddlers, gesturing and asking questions. Or maybe she ignores you completely, intent in her little world. Given enough time, she'll begin to explore on her own. Not explore in the iconic sense, but exploring nonetheless, touching leaves, picking up rocks, balancing on logs, and listening to the scurrying in the undergrowth and the birds overhead.

Every movement, sound, texture, and bit of light is collected through her senses—sometimes cognitively, sometimes by default. What she is experiencing is *sensory curiosity*, a whole-body exploration of the physical world.

As scientists, psychologists, educators, and parents look more closely at the experience of kids in the outdoors, we're beginning to see (or rediscover) the importance of what's going on as children interact with the natural environment. Richard Louv's two books on the subject, the aforementioned *Last Child in the Woods*, and his follow-up, *The Nature Principle*, provide an insightful analysis of what exposure to the wild world outside does for children developmentally and how it's essential for growth.

The growing evidence strongly supports the concept that getting kids outside to play—once the default activity of children everywhere, now an organized, regimented, parentally monitored experience in the West— may be instrumental in nurturing kids who grow up to be healthy adults.

The research has become more and more compelling as reports keep rolling in of our bodies' and minds' integral connection with the wild world. It seems clear that being outdoors in natural environments is good for us. Various researchers have discovered that bacteria found in the soil are vital to keeping us healthy, boosting serotonin levels, and making us happier.

Researchers Stephen and Rachel Kaplan have reported multiple studies that strongly suggest that exposing yourself to green spaces makes you more contemplative, better rested, and ready to think. Our vestibular system (balance) is kept honed sharpest by scrambling around the woods barefoot, making our bodies connect with our minds in an intimate dance. Getting outside makes our bodies healthy. It makes us whole.

But let's not forget about our little tyke wandering out in the field! What she seems to be doing is a whole lot of nothing. Squatting down to flip over a rock. Grabbing some grass in her plump, grimy hands. Hopefully, she's barefoot and smooshing around the mud and sand and forest detritus with her toes.

There's a part of us that bridles—just a bit—at the thought of this. Shouldn't she be at a Little Tikes Taekwondo lesson? Learning to count with primary colored plastic things? Listening to Baby Bach? Doing yoga? Eating more omega-3s? Isn't a kid bumbling around the woods with neglectful supervision kind of wasting her time?

We know exploration is the thing she's supposed to be doing, but still, we don't really see the value in it. But as I'm sure you've guessed—and if you've made it this far, you may even agree a bit—the best thing to do is to leave her alone for as long as possible. She's fostering curiosity, without our big, fumbling, overzealous, adult interference.

SEEKING SENSATION

Sensory curiosity is a cluster of traits within the broader construct of curiosity in general that hasn't received quite the same level of research attention as epistemic or perceptual curiosity. The first real peer-reviewed presentation of sensory curiosity comes by way of our good buddy Jordan Litman and his crew, Robert Collins and Charles Spielberger, and their work, which exhibits sensory curiosity as a funky set of behaviors and responses that differ slightly, but importantly, from other forms of curiosity.

Curiosity motivates exploratory behavior, and as we've seen, we continually discover various ways in which curiosity defines behavior and vice versa over the past half century. We've moved from a mitigation of uncertainty to optimal arousal and have now come to see curiosity as a multifaceted phenomenon not easily corralled.

For instance, there are a whole bunch of experiences—seeking novelty and adventure, for instance—that seem to correlate very closely to the spectrum of curiosity traits and behaviors. One of these traits is called "sensation seeking" and was first defined by a psychological researcher named Marvin Zuckerman.

Sensation seeking is best described in the context of adrenaline junkies, looking to get that rush from skydiving or driving fast or wrestling alligators. Generally, sensation seeking is a group of exploratory behaviors that try to find experiences that are "novel, complex, and intense" according to Zuckerman.

The little toddler we imagined, now painting her face with pollen and eating clover leaves, is hardly an extreme sports athlete. However, sensation seeking correlates very closely with a set of behaviors that are similar, but don't involve the same level of bodily risk. Getting out there and seeking sensations may also have to do with finding new information, not just the high that comes from flinging oneself off the peaks of the Dolomites in a wingsuit.

Litman and his colleagues posit that sensory curiosity relates more to an "interest in engaging in adventurous exploratory behaviors that involved relatively little danger." While we may scoff at the silly games of our little explorer in the park, she's on an adventure all her own.

FOUR

Some Awe Is Awesome

TALKIN' TRASH ABOUT A PRETTY SUNSET

And then, just like that, the little girl we imagined stops in her tracks. Maybe it's the angle of the sun, setting the trees ablaze in light. Maybe she's noticed a waterfall gushing and misting over mossy rocks that look to her like some primeval faerie kingdom. Perhaps she sees the peaks of distant mountains jutting up against the sky or hears the ominous thunder and beholds massive cumulonimbus clouds towering overhead. Her jaw goes slack. Her eyes widen. Time slows. Our little wilderness explorer is experiencing *awe*, one of the most profound emotions.

Across cultures, people are uniformly filled with awe by visions of the beauty and magnificence in the natural world. A blazing magenta sunset is awe inspiring both to the jaded New York City hedge-fund manager and the Andaman Islands fisherman in his dugout canoe. We share awe much the same way we share curiosity—it is central to the nature of humankind.

Awe is different from surprise or aesthetic appreciation. We feel awe when the sheer magnitude of stimulation is overwhelming, when what we perceive is vast and too much for our minds to get a handle on. But we try anyway. We strive and struggle to comprehend and understand the scene before us. We feel awe in the face of scenes or experiences that exist somewhere between terror and ecstasy, a deep appreciation that approaches joy and fright. Think of the terrible beauty of a volcano, and you start to get the picture: it is both stirringly beautiful and monstrous, belching forth fire and smoke while also lighting the sky with glowing embers.

Our intrepid, waddling little girl out in the woods is naturally open to awe. She's so small and the world is so big. But she is also outdoors, and this is where awe is most likely to find all of us. In Ralph Waldo Emerson's essay "Nature" he writes, "I am a lover of uncontained and immortal beauty." It is that word "uncontained" that we find at the heart of the wilderness. It is the corollary emotion of awe.

In the natural world—filled with vistas, storms, mountains, raging oceans, and vast forests—awe is easier to come by than the local strip mall. When we experience awe, we try to accommodate the experience. We literally interpret the world anew. We attempt to understand experience in a new way in light of this new information. Awe fundamentally changes us.

It also explains why the little pioneer girl in our imagination ignores us despite our repeated entreaties to get her back inside (since it's almost time for dinner!). Awe changes the way we experience time.

TEMPUS FUGIT

Humans have sought to subdue the unruliness of nature for about 10,000 years. From the time when the first farmers planted seeds, tended crops, and corralled grumpy goats to now, nature has been seen as the antithesis of progress. Vegetation is usually viewed in the Apollonian sense. We want order—neat hedges, carefully groomed and trimmed topiaries.

In the movie *Maleficent* (2014), starring Angelina Jolie, the wild, untamable nature of the faerie spirit herself is symbolically represented by a massive wall of wild, tangled thorns. Her warriors are beastly trees shaped like giants and dragons. Nature is fierce. Nature is unruly. Nature must be paved for progress.

But something in nature also inspires—its very wildness and vast, uncompromising rawness can invoke states of awe. When we're forced to reckon with the sheer majesty of nature—a mountainside lit up with alpenglow, a thundering cataract, the heaving seas—we begin to understand awe, which is an important piece in the puzzle of curiosity.

Anyone who has ever been trekking for a few days through the mountains will recognize instances where awe slows down time and allows us to access that frame of mind that's conducive to wonder. But to experience it, we first have to throw some snacks into a backpack and get out there to nature.

In a much-reported-on research paper, published in *Psychological Science*, authors Melanie Rudd, Kathleen Vohs, and Jennifer Aaker dial in on the relationship between awe and our perception of time. Not only did individuals who experienced awe feel like they had more time, or that time stretched, but they had more patience and possessed a tendency to be altruistic and volunteer their time for the benefit of others.

They had more time, and they gave more of it away. They valued experience over material goods and had an overall higher level of fulfillment and goodwill. They felt satisfied by life. The authors wrote, "Experience of awe brings people into the present moment, which underlies awe's capacity to adjust time perception, influence decisions, and make life feel more satisfying than it would otherwise."

Imagine you're walking through the Sierra Nevada mountains—back all sweaty and feet blistered—and there's a cloud of no-see-ums dive bombing your nostrils, trying to get as far up into your sinuses as possible. You can't wait to put the huge pack on your back down and eat a candy bar for dinner before falling into a grimy, exhausted sleep.

All of a sudden, you come over the hill, and there's the landscape in front of you. The air is so crisp and clear. You feel like you could reach out and touch the granite spires of rock stabbing upward in the distance. Alpine lakes dot the high country, and the rocky clefts of the high mountainsides are filled with last winter's snow. There's a hush, with only the winds shushing your ears. The sun is setting, blazing all orange and gold in the sky.

How long do you stand to take in the scene, and how does the moment impress itself on you?

It's always seemed to me that moments like this shift my worldview. Small, petty annoyances drop away. Big, important things come to the forefront. Life gets curated, and I think about people I love and things that matter. I feel more within myself, less a part of the daily world, and more in touch with something larger.

This isn't spirituality per se. I'm a fan of science, a firm Darwinian if ever there was one. But I think there is a subtle philosophical shift, and the research supports the notion that I'm not alone.

CASHING IN ON YOUR TIME-INVESTMENT PORTFOLIO

Travel writer Rolf Potts, whom we'll meet later in this book, often refers to the ability to live a life that maximizes opportunities for awe as *time wealth*. He actively constructs a lifestyle that fosters awe and invites time to slow down. One of the arguments he makes in his writing is that time is a commodity and one that is on par with more traditional forms of wealth. When I am up there in the mountains, I think about how Potts often talks about paying a "different kind of attention" to the world around me.

I've never replicated this experience in the classroom. I can admit that my lectures and activities don't inspire awe. So I've worked hard at creating experiences for students and myself that may tend toward awe as a possibility. Inevitably, this leads me back to the woods, into the mountains, and out the classroom door.

"That's all well and good," you may say, "but isn't creating awe a bit outside of what we can practically achieve as parents or teachers? What's the point? Aren't you just being some kind of Vermont mountain hippie?"

Maybe. But if Rudd and her research partners are correct, there's a huge amount to be gained by constructing experiences that could lead to awe.

We can inspire ourselves (and others) to be more community minded. We can be more fulfilled, more satisfied, more patient. These qualities— patience, self-sacrifice, and volunteerism—sound like the very virtues we seek to imbue in our children and students. Often, education is described as a means to create competent, engaged citizens. The qualities of selflessness and fulfillment seem to me to be of paramount importance for any decent citizenry.

IT'S A WONDER-FILLED LIFE: HOW DO COBRAS GET VENOM?

On the landing of our stairway I've hung some of my son Finn's artwork. Mixed in these treasures is a laminated photo of Finn mounted on a piece of construction paper. In the photo, Finn is looking happily into the camera, his chin clasped in his hand in the iconic pose of The Thinker. Below, in his kindergarten teacher's neat and careful handwriting, is a quote: "I wonder where cobras get venom?"

This little art project was great. His teacher quite literally took snapshots of her student's curiosity, providing a freeze-frame of what occupies the roving mind of a five-year-old. What's great about Finn's question of wonderment is that it leads to more and more glorious wonders.

To explain cobra venom, you'd have to get into evolution, predation, and herpetology, and the wonders would pile up faster than you had time to keep track of them. The thing that really captivates me every time I look at the photo is the use of the word *wonder*. How is wonder different from curiosity and awe?

In a 2015 article from *The Guardian*, nature writer Robert MacFarlane wrote about the rich glossary of words he's collected in his travels through the British Isles to describe landscape and weather: *pirr* is Sheltlandic for a light wind, *smeuse* is a gap in a hedge worn by small animals, and *crizzle* is the Northamptonshire dialect's verb for slow freezing water. To say nothing of all the various terms MacFarlane collects for the word "icicle": *aquabob, clinkerbell, daggler, cancervell, ickle, tankle,* and *shuckle*—words that come from Kent, Exmoor, and Cumbria.

Such a rich lexicon, and of course, if you've spent time enough outside in a place like Vermont, where I'm from, you know that this is not some overzealous anomaly. Leaves don't crinkle the same way underfoot when there's been recent rain or if they're tinged with frost. Aspen and birch make a different carpet than maple and oak. Freshly downed leaves are different than the rich mats of last year. There are worlds to be discovered by walking through the woods and kicking leaves.

The same must be said of our desire to know and discover the gamut of emotions and responses spurred when we're faced with the confounding natural world or the vast, infinitely wide reaches of human experience. From the mild tickle of curiosity at the way dandelion seeds dance on the air to the awe-induced terror of watching a volcano erupt, the way we see the world and experience the desire to know more is a vast and kaleidoscopic wonder in itself.

Bewilderment, astonishment, fascination, shock, adoration, veneration, delight, rapture— like MacFarlane's words for the rocky and fern-choked corners of the world—are ways of describing the endless quest for the new and novel.

Wonder exists on this scale. It is a close cousin of awe and curiosity, but there are marked differences. Awe, for example, can be tinged with fear. It is similar to wonder, but markedly different.

But wonder is slightly different from this at a lower and more available frequency. Like curiosity, wonder can be fostered. Also, like curiosity, wonder is fickle and transient. And while curiosity can exist to close knowledge gaps or reduce uncertainty, it is not *necessarily* a behavior or trait that is connected with pleasurable feelings.

But with wonder, we get this inherent sense of joy. Feeling wonder is an effusive, warming state to be in. A glow. Finn's face as he thinks his five-year-old thoughts of hooded cobras slithering around some green jungle is bright and open and full of wonder.

Wonder also has a strain of the unexpected running through it. We wonder at that which is outside our usual experience. We encounter something in our lives that is novel and spurs wonder and the concurrent joy that accompanies new, unexpected discoveries.

We may marvel or gape at such a thing, or be filled with wonder at its beauty, its very uniqueness. In "A Study of Wonder" from *Psychology Today*, author Neel Burton wrote that wonder is a "heightened state of consciousness and feeling brought about by something very beautiful, rare, or unexpected."

Awe can contain fear as well as wonder. But with wonder, we are pleasantly buzzed with the gift of astonishment, and there's almost this sense of reverence—not quite worship, but something like low-key homage that we pay to the wondrous in our lives. In an essay from *Aeon* magazine, Jesse Prinz writes, "science, religion, and art are unified in wonder." The thread of wonderment runs through all three.

TO SERVE, TO STRIVE, AND NOT TO YIELD

One of the relationships that Kurt Hahn, founder of the experiential outdoor education organization Outward Bound, understood clearly was the relationship between what people experienced and how they were able to apply that experience to difficult challenges. Authentic learning, he felt, necessitated actual experience.

In the case of the schools that he originally started in England, those experiences were often rigorous, outdoor expeditions. That tradition has continued in Outward Bound and similar organizations like the National Outdoor Leadership School. Such experiences challenge the body as well as the mind, and they take place out in the world. Hahn's original inspiration for the founding of OB was older sailors who had survived extreme circumstances because of the knowledge and the wisdom of accumulated experience.

But beyond simple survival, experiences in the great wide open change us in even more substantial ways. We have to create relationships. It has been remarked upon that Ernest Shackleton's failed Antarctic expedition aboard the *Endurance* should have killed everyone involved back in 1915, but in fact, everyone survived in part because of the culture Shackleton had created and the relationship he had with his crew.

This relationship building is essential; curiosity is a fickle flame that can be snuffed out easily by assumed hierarchical authority, oppression, and distrust. Curiosity doesn't exist well in a world of deadlines and grades and institutional expectations. And nowhere are those obstacles less relevant than in the untrammeled woodsy parts of the world.

Not only does unstructured experience in the outdoors foster curiosity, but it also nurtures the very relationships essential to learning and growth. (Watch a kid in a tide pool for a while, and it seems clear that structure has nothing on the multifaceted fascination present in interactions with the natural world.)

ARE YOU EXPERIENCED?

The influence of the outdoor world facilitates experiential learning in a way that simply can't be replicated in the classroom. The conditions for learning to occur are benefited by experiences in the wild. Unstructured, noninstitutionalized moments are ripe with learning. This type of learning—based on hard-to-forget, exciting and risky episodes—has a longer lasting effect than traditional, class-based instruction.

For instance, I may remember the time my canoe flipped during summer camp, but struggle to remember anything at all about pre-algebra. Studies have shown that learning of this type, when children are given the opportunity to experience novel situations and apply prior learning to new situations, stays within their long-term memory.

Classroom experiences just don't have the same shelf life. It is also quite possible that developing sensory curiosity of this kind could have positive benefits in other areas of personal development. Because we push ourselves and seek thrills in an outdoor environment, perhaps we become more willing to take risks creatively and professionally, even intellectually.

This is tricky ground, however, as fear can actually obstruct learning and memory. In cases where the fear or stress is chronic, long-term, and consistent, fear can lead to negative cognitive effects. This is often seen in returning military members who suffer from PTSD. A year of exposure to the constant, life-threatening stress of the battlefield actually erodes cognitive abilities.

We're not built physically for long-term, chronic stress or fear. However, fear is adaptive. Evolutionarily speaking, it's a useful and helpful behavior to have and, under very specific conditions, can help with both learning and even the way our brains are built. The most clearly defined environments that foster this positive learning outcome from short, intense bursts of fear is an outdoor one, where weather, animals, and exposure place us in a context that more closely resembles the environment we evolved to cope with.

This isn't to say that every outdoor experience needs to be fraught with terror. But mildly stressful, exciting, and thrilling situations do have a tendency to pop up in outdoor situations, and as long as they're within an acceptable risk limit they can provide excellent learning opportunities. Perhaps unstructured outdoor environments are so conducive to this type of learning because of the flip side of the coin: while there can be risky sensations involved, it's also more fun to be outdoors.

YIPPEE!

Learning has the most impact when it's dynamic, whether that dynamism comes in the form of fun or danger—and it's that sense of fun and danger that lends itself to growth. We can lose sight of the sense that fun plays in our students' lives—how the relationships we build with our students can be pivotal in developing experiences that change them and even ourselves. But the idea that we need to segregate play and learning is beyond ridiculous.

In the book *Play as Exploratory Learning,* a collection of research papers on how play relates to learning, editor Mary Reilly points out in an essay titled "Defining a Cobweb" that initially, our concept of school and teaching in the West was originally a more playful experience, compared with the 19th-century development of Dickensian-style teaching exemplified by characters like Mr. M'Choakumchild from *Hard Times*. The word for school comes from the Greek *schole*, which actually means leisure, according to Reilly. "Games, music, and mathematics were intimately related in the culture and were included under the word *schole*," she writes.

In a 2006 article from a journal of the American Psychological Association, *Monitor on Psychology*, the title says it all: "How Laughing Leads to Learning." In the article, Ron Berk, a professor and author of two books on humor in the classroom, *Professors Are From Mars, Students Are From Snickers* and *Humor as an Instructional Defibrillator*, offers the idea that using humor can help students remember, in part because humorous scenarios are memorable. He notes that humor "helps relieve fear and anxiety." This isn't to say that every class has to be a hoot, but rather that like anything else in life, humor and having fun should have a fair share in learning, just as it does in raising kids and hanging with friends.

Students have vast amounts of patience for learning as long as it's fun. Skateboarding is a great example of this. If you've ever watched kids at a local skate park, one of the things you may have noticed is the failure rate. Kids will try to nail a trick like a crooked grind or heelflip and fail hundreds, if not *thousands*, of times before achieving even a basic level of skill in landing it. But it's fun. The learning of that specific skill set is placed within a broader experience of careening around, carving and crashing, and hanging out with friends.

Many of our most formative learning experiences follow this pattern of failure and persistent attempts because they're fun activities (like learning to swim or to ride a bike). This is true for some of us with regard to intellectual learning as well. My stepdaughter has read J. K. Rowling's *Harry Potter* series multiple times because the books are fun—all the adventures of Harry, Ron, and Hermione and their battles with Voldemort and the Death Eaters. However, the skill set developed—reading long, complicated stories—has delivered dividends for her as a learner even now as she heads off to graduate school.

Our assumption is that students need level progression from one stage of learning or mastery to the next, but there is also the jolting leap of curiosity that allows them to switch gears. It's often because curiosity has led them into something they consider fun. They're just playing around.

When I was a middle school teacher in Los Angeles I used to take my students camping in Joshua Tree National Park. Students would spend hours climbing the huge dun-colored monzogranite rocks tumbled across the desert floor like giant Legos. Generally, I didn't create lesson plans for these trips. I intuitively felt that the adventure of being out there was reason enough to go.

These unstructured trips eventually started to bother some of my students' parents and other teachers. Shouldn't I be teaching something out there? I resisted at first. My reticence was born of the gut instinct I had that they were gaining *something* through the freedom to roam and explore. But in the interest of keeping the peace, I designed a sort of ecology scavenger hunt. Students had to find and draw the tree the park was named for, and locate and collect piñon pine needles. They were given notebooks to record their work and a handout with questions.

Before I'd gathered the students up to get them started on the work, they'd been playing and adventuring, their shouts echoing around the boulders. Once I'd started them on the assignment, however, they assumed the bored posture of the dutiful student with notebooks hanging listlessly from their hands. Some of them liked it all right, but there was a palpable change in the group dynamic and mood—and not a positive one.

After about ten minutes, a boy named Jack came walking toward me and asked, "Why do we have to do this stuff? Isn't it okay if we just play?"

More and more, research suggests that it is okay just to play. As psychologist Peter Gray notes in *Free to Learn*, play *is* learning, and it's often learning of the best kind. Kathy Hirsh-Pasek, a developmental psychologist at Temple University, noted in a 2011 *New York Times* article, "Play is just a natural thing that animals do and humans do, but somehow we've driven it out of kids."

Standing there with the sun blazing overhead in Joshua Tree, I sent Jack back to his work as gently as I could. But I could have just as easily—and with the potential for deeper, more lasting learning—taken the worksheet out of his hands and let him go back to playing.

John Dewey would agree. In *Democracy and Education*, he wrote, "In their intrinsic meaning, play and industry are by no means antithetical to one another as is often assumed, any sharp contrast being due to undesirable social conditions." Unfortunately, it seems at times that the "undesirable social conditions" are our schools.

In addition to this external stimuli in the form of risky, stressful, or fear-based experience, there is another dimension to unstructured outdoor experiences that is vital to learning: the incorporation of the body in the development of the mind.

In a way, it comes down to simple movement. Traversing a landscape, we're in a tactile relationship with our environment—feeling the path beneath our feet, feeling the wind on our faces, watching the horizon for weather—and yet we also are able to *draw inward*, focusing on that subterranean, running commentary from which springs so much inspiration.

Normally, that inward voice is drowned out by the competing noise of our world: the phones, our work chums, the television, and the constant cacophony of our daily life. When we get out and about in the natural environment, we finally get to tune in to the subaudible ramblings of our own minds. We all know this voice, and yet it's so hard to figure out what it is saying. If we try too hard to tune the dials and listen, it often fades away, ironically replaced by the very concentration we called on to listen to it. But if we are physically engaged in negotiating the landscape, we can enter a sort of reverie.

David Byrne, erstwhile front man for the seminal band the Talking Heads, talks about just this kind of thoughtfulness and contemplation in his memoir of two-wheeled transit, *The Bicycle Diaries*. And indeed, riding a bike is a great parallel for trekking through the terrain. It requires just enough attention to keep balanced, but frees up the brain for all sorts of interesting inward investigations.

But even beyond this contemplative, internal focus, the fact is that when we enter into the natural world *stuff happens*. Things happen to us: we fall, lose our packs somewhere, climb mountains, get our feet wet, get stung by a yellow jacket. And we also make things happen. We work together to haul each other up a particularly feisty slab of rock; we share our last Kit Kat with a friend; we mark our progress through a mountain chain by scanning the land from a high, windswept ridge and think, *Wow, I just walked that far?* It's both meditative and hyperfocused. We have the opportunity to listen to ourselves as never before.

NATURAL CONNECTIONS

Being outdoors in a natural setting instigates a deeper level of curiosity because it puts us in unfamiliar situations. We aren't able to depend on our normal social ways of negotiating the world. We're left with only each other, and while this can be stressful, it makes us more dependent and more invested in each other—and this can lead to a greater curiosity.

This sort of curiosity just can't be fostered in the same way in a classroom or in traditional settings. Within a classroom, or the workplace, we use the systems we've developed to negotiate our personal relationships. Hierarchical dominance, authority, being a wallflower—they're all part of a system of behaviors designed to navigate the weirdness of traditional academic or institutional settings. But by locating ourselves outside, by removing the artificial barriers to connection and interpersonal curiosity, we can reach a deeper wavelength with each other.

Additionally, experiences fuel curiosity. Remember, curiosity for a long time was thought to operate as a basic drive either as a solution to boredom or to fill in knowledge gaps that caused uncertainty. There's another type of curiosity, however, that I believe is reflective in nature.

We ask ourselves *why* this thing or that event happened. Because we're able to remember the event, thanks to fear, we can draw upon the experience and form questions about it. What, exactly, happened within a given memory is a cause for curiosity for all of us: why we chose certain actions and not others, made particular decisions, and said what we said at the time. We can be as curious about our past selves as we are about other people.

Curiosity plus experience equals learning. The thing is, like all good equations, this one can be flipped around and reordered. Just as 3 + 4 = 7, so too does 4 + 3 = 7. And sometimes, it's experience that gives rise to curiosity: *experience plus curiosity equals learning.* And nowhere does this happen more frequently than when we explore in the outdoor world, kicking up leaves and listening to the birds with each other. For it's in moments that we spend together when we can truly begin to connect. We can grow curious about one another.

FIVE

Empathy, Conflict, and Gettin' to Know Ya

"JE SUIS CHARLIE"

On January 7, 2015, heavily armed terrorists stormed the Paris offices of *Charlie Hebdo*, a satirical French magazine well known for publishing cutting, sometimes crude, cartoons attacking politics, society, and religion. The terrorists were radical Islamists who were angered over recent unsavory depictions of the prophet Muhammad in the pages of *Charlie Hebdo*. Twelve people were killed during the attack.

Global reaction was deeply supportive of the rights of the cartoonists and editors at *Hebdo*. *"Je suis Charlie"* (I am Charlie) became the slogan as millions took to the streets in the days after the attack in solidarity with the slain cartoonists and in solidarity with ideas of free speech. Outrage against the attack was international.

As the weeks wore on, however, a more nuanced conversation could be found. The cartoonists were certainly well within the rights of free speech as granted by the French government in terms of their frequent depictions of Muhammad, Jesus, and other religious figures, but many people began to question whether their often crude, one-sided denunciation and ridicule of religious ideology also suggests a lack of understanding and perhaps even blatant racism. At the least a cultural bias was present, many op-ed pieces claimed. The opinion war raged back and forth on the screen and page around the world.

With an event like the *Charlie Hebdo* shootings, it's difficult to untangle competing viewpoints, bound as they are to religious ideology, zealous protection of the freedom of expression, and outrage against violence. The same week, there was an attack by Boko Haram, the fundamental terrorist organization that operates predominantly in Northern Africa.

Terrorists killed an estimated 2,000 people in a horrifying massacre in Nigeria. For the spread of about a week, the world was forced to stare straight into the gullet of intolerance, fear, violence, and terror.

The power to ascribe meaning or explanations for these violent acts is beyond me. Most people are sickened and saddened and confused when they hear about them, overwhelmed by the scale of the atrocity. What people wonder is *why*—why it happens, why people fear one another, why that fear causes us to lash out.

Curiosity may be the very thing that moves us toward a more just world. The alternative—an incurious world—may be one where prejudice and misery reign. Curiosity may be one of the essential ingredients to empathy, something that we can all agree the world could use a little more of right about now.

Empathy is a funny thing. It's not necessarily just being nice to people and being a good listener, though those can be the outward expressions of empathy. And, unlike sympathy, it's not quite like pity. With sympathy, there's this kind of superiority that can rub some the wrong way. Finally, empathy isn't some idealized form of the old kindergarten rule of treating others how you want to be treated. Empathy is certainly recognizable with those behaviors and traits, but it is also something else.

Empathy is our ability to imaginatively project ourselves into another person's experience. It is to imagine we *are* another person, *feeling* what she feels, *thinking* like she thinks. It's not just feeling sorry for her; empathy is a higher level of understanding than just facts or figures. We can know all kinds of information about a person, but until we actually try to become that person, we aren't really being empathetic. Much like reading allows us to enter the world of a novel, empathy gets us inside the head and experiences of another person, not merely to poke around, but to look out her eyeballs and see the world as she does.

Let's say we have this friend Jane, and Jane's mom was killed in a tragic car crash. We'd feel terrible for Jane. We would console her. But for us to be empathetic, imagine *being* Jane. For the rest of our lives, every time we got into a car, every time we heard screeching tires, every time we drove by a pileup on the freeway, we'd be forced to relive the loss of our mother. We'd have to face the horrible incident again and again, relive the horror of the most banal act imaginable—driving in a car—resulting in the gut-wrenching loss of our mother. We would forever be altered and never look at cars the same way again. We might even give up driving completely.

To actually be empathetic, we'd have to not just wonder how it would feel to be Jane; in a way, we'd have to *become* her. We'd have to be curious about her. And in fact, there's a name for this type of curiosity: *interpersonal curiosity*.

Often called social curiosity, this behavior is defined by an interest in other people. It is noticeable in extroverts who seem bent on talking to everyone in the room. One of the characteristics of interpersonal curiosity seems to be the development of empathy and compassion. Just as people who are perceptually curious respond to visual and perceptual stimuli by investigating the world around them, people with interpersonal curiosity seek to explore the people around them.

DIPLOMATIC EMPATHY

Roman Krznaric is a founder of The School of Life, in London, and the author of *Empathy: Why It Matters and How to Get It*. Krznaric, a former Cambridge professor, has consulted the UN on empathy and is considered to be an expert on empathy and its social uses.

To be more empathetic, Krznaric claims, we need to be curious about other people. By seeking to understand those who exist outside our usual social circles, we broaden our perspectives of human nature. He claims we need to listen, be present, and most of all, be curious about other people, their experiences, motivations, and desires.

In an article from the *Huffington Post* in April 2014, Zubin Sharma, the founder of Project Potential, wrote an article documenting his experiences introducing a curiosity-based style of learning in rural India.

Project Potential is an educational program with the goal of empowering rural people in India through education. As its founder, Sharma was convinced that introducing curiosity would improve the lives of the people with whom he worked in the Kishanganj district of Bihar.

Sharma realized that there are obstacles to living a curious life for the people of Bishanpur. He notes that intense social obligation, inflexible mind-sets, and a lack of ways in which people talked about curiosity—a lingua franca of curious inquiry—all contributed to the incurious students he worked with.

But in working with the students to improve their curiosity, an interesting thing happened: interpersonal conflict between previously antagonistic individuals decreased. He writes, "[T]wo volunteers, who previously defined one another as "enemies" said they now consider one another best friends; the well-being language and interventions allowed them to empathize and see past their differences."

One wonders what the effect would be if a curiosity-based approach to education was tried. Would students be more empathetic? Tantalizing evidence says maybe. Sharma removed obligations and preconceived ideas, and introduced a language of communal inquiry. It worked.

THE ART OF SOCIAL CURIOSITY

Often, as we're driving to some party or function, my wife reminds me not to "ask people a million questions." She is right to do this—I've been known to corner people with incessant questioning. But sometimes I can't help myself—I like listening to others talk. I like trying to figure people out. She's very much the same way—curious about people's history.

For a brief time I was a newspaper reporter. My beat was the local municipalities, so I covered some intensely boring meetings: storm-water mitigation project updates, development review boards, school budget debates, city council. It wasn't exactly the UN.

In a town of about 18,000, the news of the day was often pretty dull. But I loved being a reporter because I got to interview people. I had permission to approach people I chose and ask them whatever I wanted. It was not only acceptable, but expected. I was always intensely curious about their *actual* motivations. Why this particular decision? What do they *really* think?

The human drama unfolded before me under layers of social nicety, professional demeanor, and the stultifying language of small-town government. But every once and awhile, embezzlement, revenge, capricious fate, or ugly opportunism would appear, and I'd have a front row seat.

Obviously, my wife and I rate pretty high in interpersonal curiosity. We've been married twelve years, and while we've experienced as many hiccups and messes as you'd expect over that time, we remain strong together and our relationship feels vibrant in part, I think, because we're still curious about each other.

But I'm not perfect. I can definitely slip into self-absorption and egocentric selfishness. I'm a writer, after all, and it's one of the pitfalls of the job. But I know that if I engender my interpersonal curiosity, it benefits my marriage, my friendships, and my life.

The benefits go beyond creating better bonds, however. I am more understanding, happier, and less quick to judge when I gear up my curiosity about other people. I am interacting with the world in a more fulfilling way when I indulge in my interest in others, try to figure them out, and allow myself to be curious about their motivations, thoughts, and feelings. I'm also less likely to respond with snap judgments.

In a wonderful little book called *The Art of Conversation: A Guided Tour of a Neglected Pleasure*, author Catherine Blyth notes that we often mistake good conversation for being able to hold forth eloquently on a given topic. Yes, but more than that it's about the give and take, the dance of getting others to open up and share their experiences.

THAI TENTACLES

As we've seen, curiosity can promote empathy, as demonstrated by Zubin Sharma. It also improves our relationships, promotes personal growth, and lowers aggression according to a series of studies done by psychologist Todd Kashdan.

Kashdan is an adherent of positive psychology, and his interest in curiosity seems to stem from a basic question: how can curiosity be used to improve our lives?

His attempts at answering that question provide us with some tantalizing stuff. Kashdan and his colleagues have found that those individuals with high levels of interpersonal curiosity create a feeling of closeness with those around them. Kashdan's work strongly supports the idea that curiosity isn't just a part of the individual mind-set; it's vital in building substantive relationships.

Furthermore, the studies also note how being curious, as part of a "positive affect," also means being open and adaptable to new or ambiguous stimuli, new places, people, and ideas. Part of that openness includes an acceptance of the unusual and unfamiliar. Kashdan and his colleagues wrote in the *Journal of Personality*, "Being open and curious to novel, complex, or uncertain elements in the environment includes a tolerance of differences."

Charlie Hebdo. ISIS. Boko Haram. North Korea. Syria. Ukraine. Ferguson. Baltimore. Acts of aggression get splashed across the papers every day. Kashdan notes that aggression can be a means to gain control. It's purposeful. It's also close-minded.

Being curious about others—customs, experiences, and mind-sets—reduces the fear and frustration that lead to aggression. Remember, people who are high in curiosity are not only open to eating that weird new Thai dish with the tentacles hanging out; they're also more open toward other individual's internal experiences. They're more open to other people, despite the fact—or even because—they may be different.

But how does it work, being curious about other people? Why do we find the mysterious dark stranger across the room so compelling? Interpersonal curiosity, like other forms of curiosity, can begin in states of boredom or to close a knowledge gap. Often it is the ambiguity of a person or social situation itself that not only spurs our interpersonal curiosity, but makes us like the people we're curious about.

I LOVE YOU BECAUSE YOU'RE ME

The mystery of why we find that stranger across the room so attractive and mesmerizing at first has an actual cause, and it comes to us from a researcher named Jeana Frost. Frost and her coauthors, Michael Norton from Harvard Business School and Dan Ariely from MIT, wrote a paper titled "Less Is More: The Lure of Ambiguity, or Why Familiarity Breeds Contempt," published in the *Journal of Personality and Social Psychology* in 2007.

The research addresses how people feel about potential partners in conditions like dating, where the initial contact is often brief and leaves a great deal of information unknown. In the study, ambiguity led to *more* liking, not less. The researchers found that when two individuals met, they filled in knowledge gaps about each other with information—guesswork and conjecture—and often presumed a level of similarity with the other person.

In these instances, ambiguity led to liking people more. Participants in the study projected positive attributes onto the other person in lieu of more definite information, in contrast to what many researchers categorize as deprivation states. Knowing less should mean liking less, but it doesn't.

Even weirder (or cooler) is that over time and with increased knowledge, this shifts. Frost and her colleagues wrote, "[W]ith the acquisition of more information, ambiguity is resolved and dissimilarity reveals itself, causing a decrease in liking."

I e-mailed back and forth with Frost about her findings, asking her if she thought ideas about ambiguity that held true in relationship studies could also be true for ambiguity about ideas and learning. Turns out, this beneficial kind of ambiguity can in fact be experienced not just in reference to people, but also to ideas and "places, products, or alternatives" according to Frost.

She categorized all of these things as "entities." Is this sort of pleasurable ambiguity something we could categorize as a state that exists either on, before, or after a spectrum of curiosity traits? Could it be true even for fictional characters?

I gave Frost this hypothetical scenario: Let's say I hear about a book with this really cool, witty main character who's totally punk rock. He drops out of school and cruises around New York City. I like this idea, and I already like the rebellious character. He resembles me in my imagination. We share tastes and personality traits.

But then, I actually get my hands on a copy of *The Catcher in the Rye* and discover that I'm not like Holden Caulfield at all. Not even a little. I soon realize that a depressed and whiny prep school kid has replaced my archetypical punk rock icon. In fact, I find him a bit annoying. Could this scenario, which is all taking place within my own head, have the same results?

According to Frost, the answer is yes.

"The argument is that we read similarity into ambiguity and without any conflicting information, e.g. before we read *Catcher in the Rye*, we hold onto it. Once we acquire something that conflicts with that image, disappointment can be the result," she wrote.

It seems that there are certain kinds of ambiguity that are pleasurable because we associate perceived similarity with information that is ambiguous, as Frost's research suggests. But in addition, there seems to be certain realms where ambiguity may be closely aligned with curiosity, awe, or wonder.

Think of religion, as an example, where there is a love of God and yet God remains unknowable. To know the face of God is to have your face melted like the Nazi, Major Toht, in the end of *Raiders of the Lost Ark*. This concept of not knowing while being in awe has some interesting correlates to teaching and learning that we'll get to later.

As we know by now, the commonly held understanding of knowledge deprivation or ambiguity, especially within the latter half of the 20th century, is that it causes uncertainty and discomfort. We don't like not knowing. But it's more nuanced and complex than that when you introduce context, situation, consequences, and individual personality into the mix.

We don't like ambiguity when the stakes are consequential and potentially detrimental (*Holy cow, I can't figure out how to do this stupid quadratic equation. Now I'm going to fail this test!*), but we *do* like wondering about stuff that's unknowable where the stakes are only our own epistemic curiosity (*I wonder if the universe is really infinite?*).

Basically, ambiguity isn't all bad. If novel scenarios or new information is presented favorably—meet someone cute when you're out for beers with your crew, go home and begin liking them more and more based on that fun, flirty, initial interaction—then we increase our liking *despite* the ambiguity. But if the initial introduction to ideas is a bit dodgy—picture a cranky teacher telling you that if you don't plot your *x*'s and *y*'s the right way or understand what *jurisprudence* means, you'll never get into college and will spend the rest of your life selling beef jerky at the local convenience store—then we have a tendency to associate everything to do with that sort of knowledge as unpleasant.

Frost wrote to me in an e-mail, "From the pattern in our results, we suggest positive information seen early on leads to this type of presumed similarity and liking and that negative information seen early on negatively colors all subsequent revelations."

As the old Head & Shoulders shampoo ad tells us, "You never get a second chance to make a first impression."

THE A-B-CS OF EM-PA-THY

Take a look at any syllabi or curriculum description. Most likely "empathy" has never been a learning outcome on any of them. We just don't teach empathy in school.

But we should.

Curiosity is not a subset of learning or some detached construct. It's an integral part of authentic learning and goes beyond the mere quotidian acquisition of knowledge for an arbitrary reward to something more comprehensive. It doesn't just help us become more open to people and ideas; it fulfills us in an important way, and this in turn positions us to learn more. It helps us grow as human beings.

It sounds cheesy to say it, but unless we're happy with ourselves it's difficult to be positive in our relationships. But if building empathy is part of teaching, part of education, then we just need to return to our basic formula: *curiosity + experience = learning*. Within this equation we can find a way to imbue our lives, both in and out of school, with empathy.

There is a fragile, complicated relationship between unstructured, out-in-the-world experience and learning. Under the right circumstances, allowing for serendipity, curiosity, and adventure to be the guiding force could fulfill us, teach us, and maybe even make us more compassionate and empathetic.

Travel and adventure seem to me to be an essential part of it—putting yourself in places in the world that fire up curiosity, demand experience, and foster learning. How could you not feel more in touch with other human beings than when standing at Machu Picchu, looking over the relics of a once great civilization, or standing amid the root-tangled ruins of Angkor Wat, or gazing over the tidal humanity of the yearly Hajj in Mecca?

The problem, of course, is that most of us are not in these places either very often or at all. I've never been to any of the aforementioned locations. Most of us are in line at post offices, shopping at grocery stores, and sifting through shelves at Kohl's looking for a decent birthday present. But we can still look at the relationship between experience, learning, and empathy and see whether there is any connection.

I called Rolf Potts. Potts is an inveterate traveler and author of two books, *Vagabonding* and *Marco Polo Didn't Go There*. I've known Rolf for a few years, and what always struck me about him was not that he would go on and on about the majesty of the Great Wall of China. It was Rolf's interest in his own birthplace of Kansas, his curiosity about the politics of the dining hall of the local college.

I asked Potts what he thought of the idea that awe leads to experiences that shift our perception of the world and maybe even make us more empathetic. "Awe is something that's built into travel. Travel puts you into a childlike frame of mind," he said.

The idea he suggested was that because of both awe and the unfamiliarity of the environments we experience when traveling—the different languages, foods, customs, people, and landscapes—we're rather like children in that we have to depend on others and take more at face value than we normally would. This childlike appreciation of the world, spurred by the swirling confusion and alien nature of a new place, may even help nurture awe.

Potts's book *Vagabonding* is about travel as philosophy, but also about long-term, immersive travel. Potts doesn't stay in the five-star resorts you see in *Conde Nast Traveler*. So I asked Potts, as a person who's spent the better part of two decades traveling the globe on a shoestring budget, whether he thought that by traveling, experiencing awe, and taking ourselves out of the familiar, we can begin to see other people differently—if we can become more compassionate, even more empathetic. Potts said, "Through other people you discover your own strangeness."

The scenario Potts offered was that of breakfast cereal. Highly processed bran wafers covered in cow's milk is a pretty normal way for me to start the morning, but it's not the case for many other places in the world. This shift in consciousness, this swing from the perceived normality of our own experience and the ability to see it through the lens of another culture or perspective, is the seedling of empathy, of understanding.

Back to *Charlie Hebdo*. I asked Potts what he thought of the shootings and the backlash of anti-Muslim sentiment. Potts has traveled widely in the Middle East and spends summers in Paris teaching, so I figured he'd be able to explain the situation to me and give me some perspective on what he thought the events could tell us about Arab and non-Arab relations in the world. Potts responded that what happened at Charlie Hebdo was not useful to understand Muslims the world over, nor was it indicative of some generalized Islamic ideology—it was the abhorrent act of a few isolated killers, not in any way instructive in understanding a vibrant, complex, and nuanced religion like Islam.

"There isn't a monolithic Arab or Muslim identity," he said.

He wasn't just spouting off typical multicultural jargon. He'd been there, met people, hung out with them. He'd hitched rides from Muslims and walked with them through the desert, shared food and water, and haggled over the price of a new pair of shoes. Potts wasn't just regurgitating what he'd seen on CNN. He had absorbed a deeper understanding through experience.

SIX

"Call Me Ishmael"

IN DEFENSE OF SMALL, BORING MUSEUMS

I used to be a rather grim museum goer. Truth be told, I spent inordinately more time reading the accompanying text for each work than I did looking at the art and displays. Not only did this undermine my own enjoyment, but it caused me to pass on my particular brand of museum neurosis to my students as well.

The whole experience about visiting museums and zoos and galleries hit home with me finally when my family and I were hanging out with my good friend Adam and his kids and wife. We were at a tiny, dusty museum housed in an old brick federal building in the little town in Vermont where I grew up. As we walked around looking at colonial spindle back chairs and old letters and diaries under glass cases, Adam said to me that he could imagine writing an essay titled "In Defense of Small, Boring Museums." I laughed, and asked what he meant.

Adam said that the thing about small, boring museums and long, dull dance performances is that they change the way you pay attention. As teachers, writers, and researchers, both of us are always trying to get something from the experience. We're analyzing, synthesizing, cogitating. Measuring and being critical.

But there are certain experiences when those trusty skills just don't work or where we view an experience through the wrong lens. It is sometimes better to engage with a different sort of attention. It is sometimes better to remove agenda and expectation and allow for surprise, serendipity, boredom, distraction, and the slow ferment of initially benign meaning to develop into something more potent and frothy down the road.

GREEN HAND

When I read, I often consider myself to be a flaneur. According to the German critic Walter Benjamin, a flaneur is someone who sort of just wanders around the city, window-shopping, people watching, and soaking it all in. Reading is a low-key, ambling, and pleasurable exploration that happens all in your head. The image that comes to mind is poking around a bookshop without anywhere to be.

The thing about this analogy is that it's not goal driven or achievement related. Reading for pleasure sits outside the normal equation of commodified accomplishment. The satisfaction that comes is not in finishing the book or receiving praise for reading it. The pleasure is almost like a luxurious stretching of the self, hatha yoga for your head.

While reading, we have the wherewithal to enter into dialogue with the writer and the text, and while the scope of the experience is channeled through the book, we maintain this level of control. We can shut the cover whenever we wish. But the experience of entering into the vision of someone else's head is so unusual. Film comes close at times, but nothing can match reading's strange allowance for another person's internal world to be superimposed over our own.

It's a peculiar kind of curiosity precisely because it's so hard to understand, or even explain. Imagine a place in the world with no name that doesn't appear on any maps and you don't know exactly how to get there. The only way you can remember your own journey there is when you meet someone else who's been there too, and he describes it to you. "Yes, yes!" you will say. "I recognize that place!" But it exists outside of maps. That's why curiosity compels us, again and again, to go forth and try to find it anew.

"A SUBSTITUTE FOR PISTOL AND BALL"

Let's begin at the beginning.

> Call me Ishmael. Some years ago—never mind how long precisely—having little or no money in my purse, and nothing particular to interest me on shore, I thought I would sail about a little and see the watery part of the world. It is a way I have of driving off the spleen and regulating the circulation. Whenever I find myself growing grim about the mouth; whenever it is a damp, drizzly November in my soul; whenever I find myself involuntarily pausing before coffin warehouses, and bringing up the rear of every funeral I meet; and especially whenever my hypos get such an upper hand of me, that it requires a strong moral principle to prevent me from deliberately stepping into the street, and methodically knocking people's hats off—then, I account it high time to get to sea as soon as I can. This is my substitute for pistol and ball.

This, the first paragraph of *Moby-Dick* by Melville, stands as one of my favorite chunks of writing of all time. I've read it dozens of times—maybe hundreds—and I have yet to grow tired of it. It reminds me, every time, of why I love books. They transport me.

It's also a helpful example of understanding curiosity, particularly the I-type, low-wanting but high-liking scenario.

The lines above begin one of the greatest American novels of all time, *Moby-Dick*. Melville's great work was published in 1851. In just the last half dozen years or so, there have been a number of works that deal directly or indirectly with *Moby-Dick* and Melville. *Moby-Duck*, by Donovan Hohn; the novel *The Passages of H.M.*, by Jay Parini; *The Art of Fielding*, by Chad Harbach; and in 2011, Nathaniel Philbrick's *Why Read Moby-Dick*. All reviewed in the paper of record, the *New York Times*, all more or less favorably.

In addition, an article in *The Chronicle of Higher Education* stated that there have been over 5,000 academic papers on Melville since 1960. Obviously, there is some stuff here that hoards of academics, students, and writers feel need further exploration.

To put things into perspective, the editors of *Bartlett's Familiar Quotations* wrote the following caveat under the list of quotes from *Moby-Dick*:

> The editors of Bartlett confess the complete inadequacy of these few quotations from *Moby Dick*. For that great book there is no substitute; it cannot be represented in excerpts; to attempt that would require a Moby Dictionary.

Get it?

And then *Bartlett's* tells us: "He [Melville] is too dense with intuition to be parceled out in clippings."

All of this is to say that I'm quite confident that I have nothing scholarly or new to add to the conversation about *Moby-Dick* or Melville. What I would like to do is look at how books foster curiosity of a specific sort and give us intellectual agency. How they are activators and how certain books operate as a yeasty agent of change in a learner's life. They lead to experience.

We read to get closer to our inner self, to hear our interior voice echoed and substantiated by the words of the author. At least I do. But we also read because if what is written on the pages is compelling, the book acts as its own breath to spark into life the flame of our curiosity. We wonder what's on the next page and where the characters can take us.

And the very best books—the ones we return to again and again or that affect some sort of sea change in our view of ourselves and the world—have that echo of our deepest self within their pages. *Moby-Dick* is such a book for me.

Melville himself had a similar experience. Writing to Richard Henry Dana Jr. in 1850, Melville talked about the feelings that Dana's *Two Years Before the Mast*, an autobiographical tale of life aboard a ship on the open sea, had wrought: "those strange, congenial feelings, with which I after my first voyage, I for the first time read 'Two Years Before the Mast,' and while so engaged was, as it were, tied and welded to you by a sort of Siamese link of affectionate sympathy."

A *Siamese link of affectionate sympathy.* It's a great line because what it suggests is that in reading certain books we are linked with the author. This line of thinking, it turns out, is born out by modern linguistic research within the social sciences.

Shirley Brice Heath, a linguistic anthropologist and researcher who has done a lot of work on reading and readers, has investigated this triangulation between reader, book, and author. While being interviewed by Jonathan Franzen for his now famous *Harper's* essay "Perchance to Dream," Heath describes this experience as usually having a root in children being social isolates. "What happens is you take that sense of being different into an imaginary world. But that world, then, is a world you can't share with the people around you—because it's imaginary. And so the important dialogue in your life is with the authors of the books you read. Though they aren't present, they become your community."

I began, in my interest in Melville, to discover more than a few weird coincidences between the two of us. We were both born in Manhattan. We both struck out for the West, imagining fame and adventure, and returned with neither. We both were teachers at a young age. Melville went to sea for the first time aboard a ship destined for Liverpool; I sailed around the Florida Keys where the Atlantic meets the Gulf of Mexico. According to many reports, we both dress slovenly most of the time.

The discovery of these convergences was, in a way, haphazard and random, but it excited something in me as a reader and writer. I felt close to Herman, felt like I understood him. Our relationship became intensely personal. I was having conversations with someone who died 124 years ago. This was curiosity in action—I was pleasurably compelled, for no reason that I could logically explain, to seek further and further afield for information about the writer and his book.

So what was happening here? Why was I engaged in this writer so, and why did I feel like there was this weird convergence between us? And why did I sense some ill-defined pressure to *do* something about it? Because what I felt compelled to do was take the next step. But what could that next step be?

For many, the next step they take upon being caught up with a writer is to become a writer themselves. But for me, there seemed to be something else that needed doing. I was unsatisfied. And not just unsatisfied; Melville and *Moby-Dick* and the secrets hidden within its 135 chapters plus epilogue plus etymology plus extracts—somewhere in there was the answer to my discontent. Somewhere in *Moby-Dick* I might discover what exactly it was I *do* want to do.

What happens when the social isolate—Ishmael—me—you—gets deep in at the 500th page? We begin to see that ultimately, the world in our heads is ours and ours alone. The operative word here is *alone*, not *ours*. For it is singular in us, and we are alone in it. The aloneness of the deep reader is not an enviable position. Like Ishmael on the *Pequod*, we are truly afloat on a vast sea of our imagination, and getting our bearings is a struggle.

BIG, BORING BOOKS

Writing does things *for* you; novels do things *to* you. Literature edifies and educates and informs. It even inspires. But novels transform; they modify. Novels mess with the wiring in a way that other types of writing can't. This messing of the wires, altering of the course, taking of a "new tack" is essentially complex imaginative projection. We'll come back to that term and flesh it out later in this book, but essentially, complex imaginative projection is the manner in which novels—*especially* novels, and particularly big, ambitious novels—change us in both internal and external ways. It's also connected to the way interpersonal curiosity and daydreams make us better empathizers and more able to connect with our fellow humans.

Taken a step further, this process of complex imaginative projection is what happens when we read. What is imagination? Author Sven Birkerts wrote in the literary magazine *AGNI*:

> Imagination—artistic Imagination—is of its very nature an act of independent volition, the initiative of an individual. It is private, not public. It repudiates political coercion. And it is not to be assimilated to networks, mass systems, or demographic pie charts. Without it there is no art.

What does imagination actually do? And how is curiosity connected? Much has been written about this connection. It seems clear that curiosity, among many things, allows us to ponder probabilities and alternate futures in a way that more straightforward, task-oriented thinking perhaps does not. There is another, connected reality about reading, which is that it can, quite literally, "project" us into the world in various ways. Reading curiously, in this way, fits neatly into our equation where curiosity gives rise to experience, which in turn stimulates learning.

In her review of Philbrick's just in time for Christmas *Why Read Moby-Dick*, Kathryn Harrison wrote in the *New York Times* that "Melville challenged the form of the novel decades before James Joyce and a century before Thomas Pynchon or David Foster Wallace." She goes on to say how "Melville substituted dialogue and stage direction for a chapter's worth of prose. He halted the action to include a parody of the scientific classification of whales, a treatise on the whale as represented in art, a meditation on the complexity of rope, whatever snagged his attention. He introduced himself as author within the novel, sort-of inventing meta-fiction."

Metafiction, modern and postmodern structural experimentation—Melville did it all. But *Moby-Dick* shares something in common with those other doorstop novels by Joyce, Proust, Pynchon, and Wallace. At times, it is mind-numbingly boring.

All those books have passages that are boring. They force you to sit up straighter on the couch or to brew an extra pot of coffee to get through them. But I've come up with a theory about the boredom of these big novels. It's a theory that I think Fowler—who, if you remember, connected boredom with curiosity in the mid-20th century—would perhaps agree with.

One of the more recent boring big books that I read was David Foster Wallace's *The Pale King*. In her review of Wallace's posthumous and incomplete novel in the *New York Times*, Michiko Kakutani writes, "Not surprisingly, a novel about boredom is, more than occasionally, boring. It's impossible to know whether Wallace, had he finished the book, might have decided to pare away such passages, or whether he truly wanted to test the reader's tolerance for tedium."

Wallace very well might have been aware of the challenge he was putting before the readers, but he could have been up to something else as well. Wallace was definitely interested in writing books and stories that were hard to read and was equally interested in the idea that such reading, though challenging, provides a real pleasure for a very small number of people.

Considering boredom and reading and why these ambitious, totalizing novels often have vast desiccated plains of boredom stretched between verdant valleys of lush prose, a possible answer emerges from Walter Benjamin, whose own posthumous book, *The Arcades Project*, is long and tedious. In his essay collection, *Illuminations*, Benjamin writes, "[B]oredom is the dream bird that hatches the egg of experience."

I think that is why these large, seriously undertaken, ambitious books so feed that complex imaginative projection in our lives. The boredom of them somehow pushes us beyond ourselves. There is work being done of which we aren't even aware when we're slogging through a big, thick, complicated book that actualizes itself in our experiences. It comes out later, when we least expect it. Some lingering effect of the novel stays with us in the form of language, appreciation for complexity, patience, or recognition.

Not all of us have books in us. But some of us can go out and find one if we are willing to look hard enough. But to understand Melville—to come to some resonance with his worldview and his genius—I desperately desired to see what he saw, go where he went. Only by tracking his restless path through the blue waves of the world's oceans could I discover the man behind the leviathan.

Moby-Dick is prescriptive, in a sense. The book provides a framework for how to categorize the world, how to handle the position of "outcast," like Ishmael, like Heath's "isolates," and maintain some sense of order— more than order, how to dry your wet Novembers. Maybe even how to live a curious life. After all, our narrator is curious about everything, even dedicating an entire chapter to discussing the color white.

VARSITY NOTICING

The answer that we get through *Moby-Dick* is from Ishmael. We handle the role of outcasts—which, really, all readers of the kind we're talking about are—by becoming observers.

Once our outsider status has been noted, two choices remain: become the introvert, looking within, or look outward, becoming the ethnographic anthropologist of the entire human condition.

One of the common themes of all the books mentioned so far is that they are written by the world's great noticers. One thinks in our modern era here of Wallace, whose noticing was almost overwhelming. But as Melville tells us, during his chapter on fossil whales, "Since I have undertaken to manhandle this leviathan, it behooves me to approve myself omnisciently exhaustive in the enterprise not overlooking the minutest seminal germs of his blood, and spinning him out to the uttermost coil of his bowels."

This level of noticing is salvation. But we must be in a place conducive to notice what we notice. One of the great things about the modernists— Proust, Joyce, Woolf—was how well they observed. Think about Wallace and Pynchon, how robust their books are with noticing.

I worry, at times, that the combination we've sort of roughed out here—social isolate, reading, hypersensitivity, and a world that couldn't care less about your literary leanings—is a recipe for disaster. We've all seen cases where it can be. But it actually doesn't have to end up that way if we commit ourselves to noticing—and noticing *everything*.

One of the complaints lodged against *Moby-Dick* and other large, totalizing novels is that they're so dense. The description is too long. They read like 800 pages of adjectives. But that misses the mark. Melville was a particular kind of writer. He was a writer who went forth, a writer who ventured out to find his book, and his book was the world.

Like most working adults, my opportunities for exploring the watery reaches of the world, with the gale and sea spray lashing my face, are nil. I have a mortgage, a job, and a family I love, and being away from them is agonizing. The tough thing is now that I've imaginatively projected myself into the world of *Moby-Dick*, it's very difficult with my head full of the sea to fill out a spreadsheet correctly and watch colleagues Power-Point presentations at work.

What do I do with this powerful curiosity?

It is, as Loewenstein stated, *intense*. But Melville himself experienced the same thing transitioning from a young wanderer and roustabout to eventually becoming a customs house employee. How do we handle this moment in our lives where the reading becomes unattainable as an actualized experience?

This is the classic Don Quixote conundrum. No one wants to be the fool, charging windmills. This predicament is sadly known as the onset of middle age. Children who are still vibrantly in touch with their imaginations happily enter into this world of make-believe to satisfy this urge. They pretend to be Batman, or enter into role-playing games, or dress up.

After he'd written *Moby-Dick*, Melville, an unscrupulous note taker and poor keeper of his own legacy, did continue to write. And he did keep a journal, particularly on one trip. I'm not sure how, but in his note taking, I find myself relieved. I may not part the waves or stand shoulder to shoulder with Queequeg, yet I still can be an observer, like Melville, like Ishmael. I can still actualize the knowing by actualizing the noticing.

My salvation is not like Bartleby, the Scrivener, who preferred to do nothing, but the noticing of Ishmael. My leviathan is not in the South Pacific, but under my very feet.

How do we actualize the reading of a novel that is so important to our personal mythology? How do we follow the curious path we've been set on without becoming lost? Melville himself answered this very question.

In 1856, at the age of thirty-seven, Melville traveled abroad to visit locations in Europe, the Levant, and Constantinople. He wrote a journal on the trip, and it's an intense record of how curiosity works. Melville's curiosity can seem almost pathological through the lens of *Moby-Dick*. The minutiae of sailing, the details of whaling, what people wore, ate, sang—it's encyclopedic and suggests a roving, voracious curiosity, both intellectual and perceptual.

But nowhere can we find a better example of perceptual curiosity incarnate than in the journals of Herman Melville. Remember, the people who are perceptually curious seek out new and interesting stimuli in the world; they may not be the best at sitting still in a classroom taking notes, but set them loose in the world, and they'll take it all in.

Perceptually curious people also *notice* more, and they use that noticing to inform themselves. They need to see, hear, feel, and experience the world to understand it; intellectual abstractions are not their forte. Melville was a master of this. In his journals, he records a visit he took first to Greece and then to Constantinople.

Everywhere he goes on this trip, he sees, records, *ingests* the scenes around him with an astoundingly precise level of both description and interest. He's fascinated by just about everything: "Streets of stairs up the Old Town. As if made for goats. The donkeys climb them. All round barren and tawny hills, here & there terraced with stone. Saw a man ploughing with a piece of old root."

It's the "old root" part that gets me. How often have we, as teachers, parents, and educators, overlooked the random, tangential noticing of our students because it didn't fit the lesson? Or distracted all of us? Melville sees the little and the big.

David Foster Wallace once famously said when asked what the purpose of fiction was, that is was to figure out "what it is to be a fucking human being." I would say that it goes beyond that; fiction helps us figure out what it means to be a *curious* human being—and what to do about it.

The leap we make from Melville's sharp, observant eye in his journals to the deep understanding he has of our inner thoughts that he brings to the forefront in *Moby-Dick* is the very trajectory that the experiences we have in the world, fed by perceptual curiosity, can lead to a nuanced and complex understanding of what Wallace was talking about.

And so to the question: how do we reconcile the pain of living through the novel and its inherent curiosity—of wanting to actualize it in our own experience—when we cannot? The answer, for me, is in the breadth of vision, the scope of imagination, and in taking that same watery plunge in the ambitions of our own lives.

Rather than a conversation in my head with young Herman, rather than remaining the social isolate, the act of complex imaginative projection can be outward bound. No, perhaps no *Pequod* for me, but in watching my son play in the shallows of our local lake, I see in that moment a chance to capture everything—the mineral taste of the water, the glint of sun, his high-stepping dash through the shallows, the gleeful abandonment with which he runs—and notice it, notice all of it, and be inspired to keep on noticing.

SEVEN

Finding Our Direction (with or without the GPS)

Technology has been much ballyhooed as the saving grace of education for a long time. When I was in high school, I got to watch the birth and introduction of Channel One, an educational broadcast network that promised to give public school children equal access to the best educational programming possible through a TV set in every class.

Since its inception in 1989, Channel One has been sold four times. It never really took off, while partnerships with everyone from NBC to publishers like Houghton Mifflin Harcourt bred hopes that Channel One would become a viable educational alternative, the enterprise struggled.

In my current job as a professor, the looming presence of MOOCs (massive open online courses) has threatened to unseat us mediocre professors and teachers and replace us with content from the world's leading institutions, classrooms, and scholars. But that hasn't yet happened. As Steve McQueen says in *Papillon*, "I'm still here, ya bastards."

Even outside of education, the past few decades have seen digital technology and the Internet rise as a panacea for all that ails us, while at the same time being demonized for making us all just a bunch of salivating, mouse-clicking Pavlovian dogs.

The Atlantic's 2008 article "Is Google Making Us Stupid?" goes head to head with Carl Zimmer's 2009 piece in *Discover* titled "How Google Is Making Us Smarter." Silicon Valley scions like Nicholas Negroponte want "one laptop per child," while Waldorf schools eschew computers in favor of knitting needles.

Despite the raging battle, it's estimated that in 2013, the world spent about $13 billion on educational technology according to PR Newswire.

Certainly in the United States, giving students access to digital technology is widely seen as the way to increase student performance, improve curriculum, create more competitive job seekers, and make more efficient the delivery of instruction and personalize learning, allowing students to interface with the software at their own speed and comfort level.

The question remains though: is all this typing, screen swiping, and mouse clicking making kids smarter?

Clive Thompson seems to think so. Thompson is a well-respected journalist and blogger who's written for publications like *Wired* and *The New York Times Magazine*. In his highly readable and great book, *Smarter Than You Think*, Thompson claims that the Internet particularly, and search functions like Google especially, create an opportunity for more learning. He writes:

> When humans lecture at us, it's boorish. When machines do it, it's fine. We're in control, so we can tolerate and even enjoy it. You likely experience this effect each day, whenever you use digital tools to remind yourself of the lyrics to a popular song, or who won the World Series a decade ago, or what the weather's like in Berlin. You get the answer—but every once and awhile, whoops, you get drawn deeper into the subject and wind up surfing for a few minutes (or an entire hour, if you vanish into a Wikipedia black hole). We're seduced into learning more, almost against our will.

Thompson describes with grace the situation I find myself in every day as I peck away at the keyboard, trying to get stuff done at work. The only bone I have to pick with him is that last bit about being "seduced into learning more." I don't think that reading stuff on the Internet in and of itself is learning. Or at least, not the kind of authentic learning I'm interested in—the kind that's concerned with curiosity.

Thompson is talking about content-based learning, which is an important aspect of developing intellectually. Facts, figures, data, and the various opinions and online sources I choose to ingest certainly help with learning, but ultimately it's not the same type of learning as that which occurs when we engage with other people, experiences, and places.

Authentic learning has curiosity as its starting point. Remember, curiosity is defined by transience, intensity, and impulsivity and can only be born from moments of ambiguity. Maybe if your modem is still a tortoise-slow dial-up kind, you can indulge in curiosity while you wait for web pages to load, but most of us can get answers to our curious questions in a matter of seconds.

The kind of learning this book is concerned with includes this sense of unknowing and the propulsive motivation of curiosity—that which gets us up and moving into the world to discover things.

Thompson's first chapter is fascinating. He writes about the well-known battle between Garry Kasparov, world champion chess player, and IBM's Deep Blue, a supercomputer designed to play chess. In 1997, Deep Blue beat Kasparov, signaling the triumph of cold-calculating digital power over human cunning and ambition.

What sort of era we've entered is up for debate. We can now build computers that can win at chess against the world's greatest Grandmasters. This suggests that we could build computers that could outperform humans in any number of intellectual games or challenges. A new age has dawned, at least in the world of chess, where being the greatest is not the same as being number one.

Thompson gives us an insightful tour of the world of chess in this dawning age of computers. Players like Kasparov started to play collaboratively with computers, each human player paired with a computer that was running chess strategy software and with a databank of hundreds of thousands of chess games, millions of individual moves. "Together, they would form what chess players later called a centaur: a hybrid beast endowed with the strengths of each," Thompson writes.

With Kasparov's creativity and a computer's merciless number crunching, a superior chess player had been built. Games of chess were now more challenging, more complicated, and more competitively daring.

Thompson writes, "Which is smarter at chess, humans or computers? Neither. It's the two together, working side by side."

Some other writers believe this sort of thing to be a harbinger of the apocalypse, a time when machines will begin to make obsolete human endeavor and creativity. I understand their fears, but don't share them. On a very basic level, I agree with Radiohead's Thom Yorke, who said, "I'm not afraid of being taken over by computers though, because the thing is, computers cannot resist. You can always smash 'em up, and they're totally defenseless. All we need are more people with hammers."

But more than that—and on a more serious and fundamental level—I'm not worried because technophiles like Thompson and Zimmer and Negroponte have it wrong. When they talk about computers helping us "learn" or as making us "smart," they are leaving out the essential factor: curiosity.

Curiosity will never be a programmable trait. It is too human—undeniably so. Curiosity is radical and impossible to duplicate with artificial intelligence. Additionally, curiosity is part of building meaning. Investigating why we are curious and about what is helpful in plotting our passions and determining the course of our interests. Which, in turn, plays a big part in how we live our lives.

No computer program, no matter how artificially sentient, could access the well of memories, proclivities, and idiosyncratic desires that feed into the way in which we navigate our own lives. And really, who would want it to?

So Kasparov got beat by Deep Blue. What of it? To strip chess down to the moves on the board only, to algorithms and probability, is to forget what chess is. Without that tension that exists between two minds, using the board as a physical sphere for their mental wrangling, it ceases to be chess. It loses that essential meaning that human relationships and curiosity provide.

In his wonderful novel *The Yiddish Policemen's Union*, Michael Chabon opens the story with a tale of chess. Landsman, the novel's bitter, alcoholic, hard-boiled detective, is working the seedy streets of the imagined Jewish settlement of Sitka in Alaska. We find him investigating a homicide in a run-down hotel.

At the crime scene there's a chessboard with pieces paused in what appears to be midgame. Landsman takes a Polaroid of the board as the murdered body lays sprawled across the room. He studies the Polaroid later while downing Slivovitz in his room. He's reminded of his father, a good chess player himself, who once played a visiting champion to a draw when he was only a teenager.

Landsman's father played chess grotesquely, his contorted body movements and reactions to developments in the game making him look like a man with "hemorrhoids." Chess assumes a central role in Landsman's relationship with his father, a metaphor for the battle sons have with their fathers as they move through life, contesting each other for tiny squares of personal sovereignty and dominance. This is not a game, then, that is mere numbers and probability. It is a cultural artifact; it is the very struggles of life reduced to a game.

Chess has always been rooted in numbers and strategy when stripped of its context. Of course a computer could beat a human. If we developed a robotic arm to chuck basketballs from the three-point line, with enough Swiss engineering I'm sure we could build one that would drop the ball into the bucket 100 percent of the time.

But that's not the point of basketball—it's contextual and historical and allegorical, all things computers are not. Think of it this way: we're not at all offended or shocked when our calculators are faster at computing our compounded mortgage rates than our brains.

ACHILLES'S RETIREMENT

The game of chess is a beautiful example of the meeting of two minds, the intellectual struggle. It is not the perfection of the game that draws us into the drama of chess, but the way players seem able to rise above the very deficiencies that make us human—distractibility, boredom, stress, error—that holds us in thrall.

But beyond that, it's the perfect example of D-type versus I-type curiosity. Depending on how competitive a player is, he can either feel an intense D-type curiosity about the opponent's next move or a more relaxed I-type curiosity, content to muse about the game itself and simply "play to play" rather than "play to win." The ambiguity of chess—not knowing what your opponent will do next, nor what her strategy is, or even necessarily how good she is—is fundamental to the game. *It is the game.* Deep Blue isn't playing chess, really, not in the way we imbue the game with both personal and cultural meaning.

This is why at some level we watch professional sports. The very reason we watch is to watch players transcend our human fallibility, our inherent weakness. It is not that players like Michael Jordan are simply amazing, but that they are amazing *despite* their humanity, their hubristic pride, petty inconsistencies, and imperfection.

Watching players at the top of their game, in their prime of life, is incredible, but I've always been more interested in how they hold on, even as their bodies begin the sad decline of middle age during their late careers.

I remember when I lived in Los Angeles I saw a Lakers game when Kobe Bryant was in his prime. He was like some mythical demigod, a slicing and dicing immortal among men. Wiry and unstoppable, he would put up two-dozen points a night or more every game, cutting through players in the paint like a scythe. In one game, Kobe leapt over the outstretched defensive hands of his defending player, the 7'6" Chinese-born Yao Ming.

While that was awe inspiring (Yao Ming was no chump), I found the denouement of Bryant's career much more captivating, particularly his last year or two in the NBA. His body, so solid and unstoppable before, began to fall apart. He snapped his Achilles, tore a rotator cuff, and broke his leg. He didn't play nearly as well, *couldn't* play as well. But watching him hang on after years of holding aloft an ego the size of the sun, showcasing a Machiavellian competitive streak that alienated him from his peers, demonstrating his capacity for violence and repulsiveness by sexually assaulting a nineteen-year-old girl, and winning five NBA championships, he looked tired and worn and consumed by his own pride and ambition.

It was like Macbeth in real life. He still had waning talent, but his team was awful and the tragedy was so piquant. But he was still playing, despite his best years being behind him. It was so *human*, so tragicomic. Michael Jordan with the Wizards, Iverson playing in China, the list of players fighting the descent into irrelevance goes on and on.

Yes, we could create that robotic arm that dumps in 10 out of 10 three-pointers every time. But how much more interesting is it to watch players battle time? How much more nuanced is our appreciation of sport and competition? We don't get the same Shakespearean drama with Deep Blue. Had Bryant been given cybertronic parts and able to keep dunking on other players for infinity, what would've been the point?

Mid-20th-century media critic Marshall McLuhan famously stated, "[T]he medium is the message." While a simplification, it bears on the relationship between curiosity, experience, and digital technology. When we write by hand, for instance, it triggers different reactions in our brain; it helps us learn. To try to divorce the physical environment from the experience of learning is a tacit rejection of what science and our own experience has taught us—learning is a mind *and* body experience.

When the medium is a screen and we are passively absorbed in swiping and clicking our way through its directives, we have become an obedient follower of rules rather than an active creator of connections.

I'm not antitechnology. Far from it. The Internet is where I publish my writing, where I do my research. It's where I pay for my son's school lunches, where I pay my bills. I schedule travel online and e-mail my aunt in Irvine. I'm on Twitter, Facebook, and LinkedIn. I have a website.

I'm not a technophobe, but I'm also not interested in giving technology, the Internet, and computers some form of agency they don't deserve. They don't make us smarter. They don't make us better, deeper, and more thoughtful thinkers. And they sure as hell don't make us more curious.

KILLING SEA HORSES

There is an insistent push on teachers to digitize their instruction. On multiple fronts, the message is clear: incorporate digital platforms into your teaching or suffer the rapid encroachment of irrelevance. No one is praised for teaching students calligraphy, much less cursive. A new age has dawned where machines—the digital computer, laptop, tablet, smartphone—have become the primary tools for learning.

Sort of.

In my son's first-grade public school classroom, the old school rules still apply. He does spelling tests based on good old-fashioned spelling lists every week; he walks around the house singing "when two vowels go a walking, the second does the talking!" He reads aloud to his teacher and writes little books that he illustrates with his own pictures.

On the far end of the spectrum, here at the college where I teach, I allow (and even encourage) students to turn in work written by hand. Frequently, students express one of two reactions: relief at not having to upload yet another digital product of their learning to somewhere in cyberspace or surprised at how "out of practice" they are at writing with a pen or a pencil.

Despite these examples, though, there can be little doubt that the concept of learning has more and more to do with digital devices. I'm not finger pointing here: I use blogs and social media in the classroom and within my assignments. I am conversant (or can pretend to be) in the online language of my students and can relate to their experiences on Tumblr, Yik Yak, or Tinder. I get what they're up to, somewhat, and I believe this has, at the very least, offered some interesting variety in how the classroom works.

Colleges have multiple platforms for assessment, grading, event planning, advising, and storing common documents. Every day, like most people in the professional world, software regulates much of what I do.

The most insidious notion that pervades the embracing of digital technology for learning or even for socializing is that it creates connections. This is the argument from Silicon Valley and from folks like Negroponte and his One Laptop per Child campaign and from revenue-hungry tech companies like Coursera or Knewton—more technology equals more connection equals more learning. But what we're doing when interfacing with a screen rather than with another person isn't connection—it's something else.

When we're engaged with a computer instead of a person, even when we're chatting or texting or Skyping or posting back and forth, we're not connected in an *authentic* way. We're responding to electronic stimuli. Connection, at least as it relates to learning, isn't actually "connection" at all. It's relationships. It's friendships.

How we learn and react—physically and cognitively—with a person face-to-face versus how we react and respond to a screen are radically different scenarios.

For starters, perhaps the most important piece of this comes down to sharing space with other people. Being with other people in the same room makes us healthier. In her book *The Village Effect*, Susan Pinker brilliantly argues that face-to-face contact makes our lives better in lots of ways, but one of the most crucial is that it improves our cardiovascular, immune, and nervous systems—it even can make us smarter over time if we have complex, overlapping, and supportive friend groups. (Not Facebook friends, mind you, but real friends.) The key to this benefit is physical proximity; virtual experiences, such as through screens, don't have the same effect.

The converse is also true. Research on populations, including prisoners in solitary confinement, show that lack of social connections atrophies the brain. It actually causes neurological damage.

In her book, Pinker discusses a program initiated at Boston City Hospital in the late 1980s where physicians began prescribing face-to-face reading time for parents and children as part of their overall pediatric treatment. Unsurprisingly, those kids who were read aloud to as part of Boston City Hospital's program did better in school and developed better vocabularies.

But there's a subtler piece here too. More interaction leads to better learning, which increases self-esteem, which is healthy.

When we *feel* good, all sorts of positive chemical reactions occur in our bodies as a result. After all, the Boston City Hospital program wasn't started by teachers interested in improving literacy and test scores; it was started by medical professionals who saw a distinct connection between getting kids to turn off the TV and interact with those around them and kids being *healthy*.

This isn't to say that online communities can't be supportive, nurturing places where individuals find a sense of belonging. For instance, Tumblr has become the de facto home for many younger people who identify as LGBQT, and the anonymity and relative physical separation offered by online communities has been helpful as they explore their identities.

Other claims include that digital interfaces like Twitter remove the baggage of having a body, so people can connect on an intellectual level. These examples, however, differ slightly but importantly from what the proponents of digital learning would suggest.

These forums for self-realization are vital for some people, especially adolescents. Not to say that self-knowledge isn't vital; it is. But it is a difficult claim to make that sitting in a room, staring at a screen, and receiving "likes" and "shares" is as nurturing, supportive, and physically and emotionally beneficial as being in contact with another empathetic, compassionate human being.

When kids are hurt or scared, a parent or caregiver scoops them up and hugs them. It's the physical touch that matters, the proximity.

There is a robust community out there in education that would disagree. Some claims have been made that the interconnectedness of digital platforms, the real-time ability to work on documents, and the transparent nature of open software spur an attachment to and investment in learning from students. These systems, called "hybrid pedagogy" or "open digital pedagogy," are exactly that: systems.

The arguments in favor of these technologies are alluring. A simple example would be Google Docs, where multiple authors can edit and work on a document in real time, communicate via a comments window, and see changes as they occur. Supporters of this type of learning would argue that it flattens traditional hierarchies and allows students and teachers to work more collaboratively. I can see this being true, but again, when the experiential bit is left out—and by experience, I mean the interaction of self and other people, or self and physical environment—something is lost.

In my early twenties I wanted to be a short story writer. I was reading Raymond Carver, Dorothy Parker, Ernest Hemingway, Cynthia Ozick, Jack London, and Alice Walker stories like a second grader devours birthday cake. I wrote a story and sent it off to the editor of a well-respected literary journal whom I had met briefly when I was in college.

Shortly thereafter, I had a chance to attend a dinner party where the venerable editor would be in attendance. I gathered my courage and sidled up to him as he stood sipping wine and munching crackers and cheese. I asked him if he'd received the story. He said he had. "What did you think?" I asked.

At the time, I felt like my life depended on his answer. In my visions of grandeur, he'd publish the story. I would get a six-figure advance from a publishing house and begin my ascent to the top of the American literary landscape. It all hinged on this moment. The editor smiled, not unkindly. "It's hard to be critical of a friend," he said. "But absolutely none of it works for me."

Oh, the agony! I sheepishly slinked away, tail between my legs, and spent weeks plagued by self-doubt, rage, depression, and the sort of self-loathing only the very young can afford. Then a bright idea occurred to me—write another story and try to make it better.

I don't know of a digital platform out there that could replicate the kind of learning that took place at that time—the way I had to gauge what I thought of the editor, myself, my writing, my goals, and his magazine. How I had to take that long walk across a crowded room and receive feedback in person. How I had to deal with the shame and embarrassment, but more importantly, come to the realization that I just had to keep trying. The lessons learned from that *experience* reverberate to this day.

CONSTRUCTING MEMORIES

So what does this have to do with curiosity and technology in schools? More accurately, perhaps, we should ask what the interconnectedness of the web has to do with curiosity.

The Internet is often heralded as this infinite treasure trove of information, an egalitarian library available to any and all. Shouldn't the Internet, with its billions of ideas and facts and globs of information, spur our curiosity? Shouldn't it drive us toward discovery and exploration? Well, no, not really.

Earlier, we saw that curiosity functions, at least on one level, on *not* knowing stuff. Curiosity as motivation drive theory posited by George Loewenstein states that curiosity thrives on ambiguity, on the inability to close a knowledge gap. In fact, curiosity is patently not knowing stuff, but wanting to.

This letdown we feel when we are curiously striving to discover answers and then actually discover them was best summed up by British writer Charles Lamb in the early 19th century: "Newspapers always excite curiosity. No one ever lays one down without a feeling of disappointment." Disappointed, perhaps, that the entertainment provided is over or that the curiosity sated through reading wasn't all that satisfying after all.

In a 2009 study by Veronique Bohbot, a researcher from the Douglas Mental Health University Institute in Canada, it was determined that the use of global positioning satellite (GPS) devices for navigation had direct correlations to activity in the hippocampus, the part of the brain researchers believe deals primarily with memory.

A brief released by the Douglas Mental Health Institute in December 2010 regarding the study states:

> When we find our way in the world, we rely on one of two strategies. One is spatial strategy, in which we build cognitive maps using relationships between landmarks to help us determine where we are but also help us plan where we want to go (for instance, you will memorize the spatial relationship between the market, home and school such that you can take shortcuts when going to novel destinations). The other one is a stimulus-response strategy, which is kind of an auto-pilot mode (after some repetition, you make a series of right and left turns out of habit like going to work every day using the same route. Sometimes you get there out of habit without knowing what you saw on the way). When you use a GPS, you don't necessarily use your spatial memory.

The study claims that those who use spatial strategies—the folks who ramble around town figuring out where to go based on landmarks, memory, and cognition—had a significant correlation with a robust hippocampus. Basically, when the researchers stuck people in an fMRI machine and read their brains during virtual navigation tasks, only those who used spatial strategies had fireworks in the hippocampus. The GPS users had no such activity.

The research suggested that use of GPS, or any activity that limits or replaces spatial strategies, can "weaken" the hippocampus. Granted, this is a rather old paranoia, that some new technology will rot our brains and make us stumbling morons incapable of putting on socks or finding our keys. Plato wrote that books will ruin our memory, because people will be "calling things to remembrance no longer from within themselves, but by means of external marks." The difference in this study is the ability to actually measure the physical response of the brain, a rather important distinction.

The hippocampus is a funny little part of the brain. It's older than the flashier cerebral cortex, evolutionarily speaking. It hangs out underneath the big swirl of our hemispheres, a little glob of neurons. It's named after the Greek word for *sea horse* because it looks a little like one.

While it helps us navigate the landscape, it also plays a role in building meaning from experience. Learning, really. Neuroscientists generally agree that the hippocampus is important for the formation of new memories about events and experience. Damage the hippocampus either through Alzheimer's or brain injury, and new memories don't get formed as easily.

Think of the character from Christopher Nolan's *Memento* and you have an idea of what role the hippocampus plays. In the film, the protagonist, Leonard, is a former insurance claims investigator who received a traumatic brain injury that makes it impossible for him to form new memories, a difficult situation made even more sticky since Leonard is trying to solve his wife's murder.

The structure of the hippocampus is relatively consistent in mammals, and most vertebrates have a similar structure in the brain called *pallium*. Taking evolutionary history into account, it seems that the hippocampus has played a vital role in navigation—a key adaptation for our hunter-gatherer-scavenger hominid ancestors over the past five million years or so.

It works like this: for the sweep of primate evolution, our ancestors learned to navigate the landscape in a similar fashion. We'd be plodding along, looking for juicy berries or grubs or maybe a nice carcass to gnaw on, and we'd get thirsty wandering around primeval Africa. It's hot, after all. We'd remember that to get to the water hole, we have to pass by that big baobab tree on the right, go through that rocky cleft where that leopard almost got us that one time, and track the ravine down to that big boulder, underneath which is a little seeping spring.

Our brains have evolved to interpret terrain and direction in this way—to "read" landscape and remember location based not only on physical features, but by incorporating what we experienced in various locations as notational memories. It's hardwired into how we navigate in the world.

As we continued to evolve, we also developed a similar capacity to navigate events in our memories. Instead of baobabs and boulders we assigned a similar internal cartography to our lives—the time our older brother clobbered us over the head and stole our gazelle leg or the memory of the whack we received when we accidentally interrupted the alpha male during his nap. One of the correlative symptoms of damage to the hippocampus is difficulty processing relationships and new information. It's hard to learn when you can't remember new experiences.

When we use GPS to find our destination, we find it in the same way, by following the little car icon as it travels down the highlighted path on the screen, following the instructions spoken by some generic voice. But when we find our own way, we call upon memory, intuition, and experience in a way that is wholly individual and personal.

Nicholas Carr puts it this way in *The Shallows*, his book about the digital revolution's effect on our lives: "But the growing body of evidence makes clear that the memory inside our heads is the product of an extraordinarily complex natural process that is, at every instant, exquisitely tuned to the unique environment in which each of us lives and the unique pattern of experiences that each of us goes through."

Is it possible that a similar degradation occurs when we use the Internet as a means of navigation—either navigating the social or intellectual realms—and as a means of satisfying curiosity?

Curiosity is propulsive; yet when we search the web we just sit there. The equation of curiosity leading to experience leading to learning is negated. There's no experiential aspect. You're just sitting there, staring at a screen, clicking or scrolling or swiping. We've undermined the very conditions hardwired into our brains and bodies for learning. When we depend on technology to navigate the world—both geographically and intellectually—we have truly "lost our bearings" and are directionless.

EIGHT

Snorting Lines of Ed Tech

CRUMBS IN MY BEARD

Prior to learning about quadrilaterals, the definition of *oligarchy*, the lyrics to a Taylor Swift song, or how to use a semicolon, the most vital information we gathered in our primate evolution was about the world around us. Where to find food, water, and protection from the elements and predators, and determining territory were vital adaptations.

As our primate ancestors became more and more dependent on social structure as an evolutionary advantage, the ability to remember events and individuals, and imbue experience with meaning may have contributed to our success as social mammals. Navigating terrain and finding, caching, and using resources are key—so is memory and experience.

If Bohbot's research is at all indicative of the effect GPS has on reducing stimulation to the hippocampus, it makes sense to wonder if relying on the Internet for learning—surfing the web and looking up stuff on Google—has a similar effect.

Prior to the Internet, information or learning came primarily from three sources: books, people, and direct experience (such as going to see a film or play). If you wanted to know more about Samuel Beckett, you could read his books, talk to someone about him, watch a film, or go see *Waiting for Godot*.

The commonality in all those experiences—reading, having face-to-face relationships with others, and moving out into the world to find theaters and DVDs—is that they stimulate the hippocampus.

They're also interrelated: learning is taking place both internally and externally when you try to decipher the maddening Library of Congress catalog system after decades of Dewey Decimal. There you are, searching for the book, scurrying around in that weird half-crouch, neck bent at an awkward angle to read the spines of books, exploring the hushed and dusty rows, and the whole time you're mentally exploring as well.

Tech companies—including ed tech—depend more and more on creating products that are experienced as pleasurable to the consumer. One of the quickest biochemical routes to pleasure is through the production of dopamine, a hormone that creates a pleasurable sensation in our bodies. It's the chemical released by the body when snorting cocaine or smoking cigarettes. It forms the basis for those addictions.

Aside from sharing the same neurochemical response as that produced by Bolivian marching powder, ed-tech companies create games that have a built-in "compulsion loop." Just like gambling, many ed-tech products offered on sites like coolmath-games.com and mathplayground.com utilize research on games that capitalize on getting the compulsion loop spinning and the dopamine pumping. It's why when you play the slots in Vegas, you'll often get two out of three matches. "Damn," you think, "almost!" and then you quickly start plunking more of your kid's college fund into the slot machine in the hope of victory. That elation you feel at the moment of "almost!" is dopamine coursing through your veins.

Despite this confluence of learning and addictive behavior, ed tech and "digital education" are the rule rather than the exception nowadays. Gary Small, a neuroscientist at the University of California in Los Angeles, was quoted in an article in Reuters in 2008 as saying that people who were constantly online were better complex decision makers and more adept at certain kinds of reasoning. "The brain is very specialized in its circuitry and if you repeat mental tasks over and over it will strengthen certain neural circuits and ignore others," Small said.

But it's exactly this kind of deliberate "decision making" that runs counter to how curiosity functions. Curiosity has as its wellspring indecision or ambiguity. By creating faster neural circuits for decisions and reasoning, heavy Internet users atrophy their ability to foster the very unknowingness that gives rise to creativity and innovation. A speedy ability to reason doesn't allow for contemplation of unreasonable ideas such as the theory of relativity or quantum mechanics.

Part of the reason for this ability to function faster as the result of increased exposure to online environments, which Small goes as far as to call an "evolutionary change," is that *young people spend an average of nine hours a day exposing their brains to technology*, according to the article.

What happens when we subtract nine hours—or over 35 percent of our day (or 56 percent if we don't count the eight hours of sleep we're supposed to get every night)—and replace it with a virtual, screen-based interaction? Well, for one, we're sitting on our butts a lot.

I speak from experience here. There have been many an afternoon where I've come up for air out of a deep Internet-induced fugue state after clicking for hours and noticed my body: slumped in a chair, butt tingly and asleep, crumbs in my beard.

In *The Shallows*, Carr writes of this experience: "And what the Net seems to be doing is chipping away my capacity for concentration and contemplation."

While it's sort of horrifying to think about how many mornings I've spent idly mouse clicking and half reading, it's far more terrifying to think about what I *haven't* been doing. Walking the dog through the woods. Playing checkers with my son. Having a cup of tea with my wife. Reading. Dreaming.

Instead, I've robbed myself of experience. I've replaced the circumstances in life that lead to serendipity and discovery, to boredom and inspiration, to love and authentic connection with a comatose state where nothing—other than zillions of electrons flying back and forth between my screen and a server somewhere—has happened. I am bereft of actual experience.

Carr wrote in his 2014 book *The Glass Cage*, "When software reduces our engagement with our work, and in particular when it pushes us into a more passive role as observer or monitor, we circumvent the deep cognitive processing that underpins the generation effect." Even though an observer would say that I'm engaged there at my desk, clicking and clacking and scrolling and swiping, I'm not.

You'll say that I *did* learn. I read Wikipedia, I read blogs, and I read articles on Facebook. I boned up on my bona fides as a professor, reading Slate, Gawker, *The Guardian*, *The Atlantic*. But in reality, I collected information. Learning is connected to experience, or more accurately, *learning is experience*.

OMG

In 2012 a couple of researchers from Harvard decided to figure out why the infernal social media loop was so addicting. Particularly, they hoped to expound upon our propensity to disclose mundane details about ourselves on Facebook, Twitter, blogs, or elsewhere. "Scrambled the heck out of some eggs this morning #breakfast," we write, or "Look at all this sunshine #beachday!" or whatever other mindless dreck we've assigned some importance to.

The article, published by the Proceedings of the National Academy of Sciences, suggests that every time we engage digitally in selfies, posts, and tweets we get a little burst of dopamine. The very same reaction a kid has playing Mario Kart is what happens to us when we send an article on workflow management to our colleagues. We feel good, like we're contributing. It's actually the same burst of happy hormones we get from sex or exercise.

This lovely shot of neurological cocktail doesn't come with other forms of learning or participating. Reading novels, for instance, doesn't bring about the same shot of dopamine. It can, of course, but due to the time it takes to read the new Zadie Smith tome, the experience is markedly different.

Oddly, however, in higher education, there has been a trend in adopting strategies that engage in reward loops like social media. Novels are, if my own experience at an institution of higher learning is at all representative, falling out of favor—which is weird.

The novel remains the most consistent if stubborn purveyor of curiosity in education. Its potency to produce a low-level curiosity endures. Remember Jordan Litman's scenario of low wanting, high liking? We don't really seek our reading as a stimulation, but once we read, it gratifies on some level. But the value of the novel in education is depreciating. Why read *Moby-Dick* when you could learn how search engine optimization (SEO) makes tech-hungry future employers drool?

Give a kid a bowl of quinoa and a bowl of Coco Pebbles and the choice to eat whichever she wants, and we all know what will happen. Give a kid a moth-eaten copy of *Old Yeller* and an iPad, and you'll get similar results.

The problem, of course, is that we're all like kids now. Shiny new toys that promise to captivate, expedite, and connect are hard competition for the muted rewards of reading. I recently had a librarian visit one of my college classes. He had a live stream survey projected in the class.

He'd ask questions, and students could text their answers. A cool infographic responded to their answers, the data transforming right in front of their eyes. As someone who is both annoyed and seduced by technology every day, I found myself itching to text my own answer and see the column grow in response to what I thought. I wanted to feel irate and talk about reflection and time and the importance of complicated ideas and why we shouldn't make education like an episode of *The Voice*.

But regardless of how we try to bend technology to the task of education and learning, it will always default to a plaything for kids. I don't think it's a coincidence that the operating system for Negroponte's globally equalizing laptop is named "Sugar."

As noted earlier, neurobiology isn't everything. Some of the smartest people I know are online all the time and work in the tech field. Some of the best articles I've read are on blogs. Joyce Carol Oates is on Twitter. But at the end of the day, when we are using technology to learn, we're sitting in a chair, isolated, while the world, with all its potential for experiencing, passes us by.

THE WISDOM OF OSKAR

In Günter Grass's 1959 novel *The Tin Drum*, diminutive Oskar lives his life as an emotionally and mentally mature person in a three-year-old's body. In recounting his education, Oskar relates that he was deprived of having a lot of books, but depended on a partial copy of the writings of Rasputin, the semi-mythical mad healer of Russian history, to help him navigate the world and develop intellectually.

Perhaps when we overlearn—are overwhelmed by the sheer mass of new information and stimuli available on the web—we dampen our dopamine receptors (like drug addicts do) and new information no longer gives us the same jolt. It certainly makes us less curious, for curiosity lies in the shadows, not in the harsh glare of the screen.

Maybe the key to fostering curiosity in part is to learn less, but more potently, more experientially. If it is in non-knowing and ambiguity that we most directly engage in curiosity, perhaps it is in specific, experience-activated learning that we truly gain knowledge and understanding rather than in the voluminous slurry of information that is the web.

LA RÉVOLUTION!

Not everyone is in step with the ed-tech companies, however. There are entire movements (such as Waldorf schools) where technology is verboten, at least in the early years. And there are plenty of folks like Carr who are rightly skeptical of all that technology—and by extension ed tech—has to offer.

One of the most dynamic members of the insurgency against the dominance of ed tech is Audrey Watters. The author of the popular blog Hack Education and the book *The Monsters of Education Technology*, Watters describes herself on her website as "an education writer, a recovering academic, a serial dropout, a rabble-rouser, and ed-tech's Cassandra."

"The education part of ed tech has a troubling history," Watters pointed out to me when we spoke. She was talking about what she called the "lack of attention to social justice around talking about educational technology."

In her research, Watters has unearthed troubling links between ed tech and assessment, which she claims has roots in earlier eugenics-driven educational policy. The simple fact of the matter is that ed tech is a multibillion-dollar industry in the United States, and where there's money, there's power. That means, as usual, that the folks without money are left out of the equation.

"Government is working hand in hand with capitalism" to make ed tech a priority, according to Watters, and creating a dangerous imbalance where access to fancy digital tools can widen the gulf between the haves and the have-nots. In my own well-heeled New England town, all junior high and high school students are given an iPad. This is not the case a few towns over, where farms dot the primarily rural landscape.

Why is there so much support for ed tech then? Former president Bill Clinton pledged millions to Negroponte's One Laptop per Child campaign. The line items for technology grow every year in school budgets. Meanwhile, kids don't seem to be responding by transforming into little Steve Jobs; they are still the same old confused bunch of hormonal adolescents.

When I asked Watters where she thought this situation came from, she responded, "Technosolutionism is a really powerful new form of magic. There's so much cheerleading that's uncritical. Technology means progress."

Watters's point rang true in many ways, particularly in the context of history. Modern technology—and in our conversation "technology" implicitly meant digital software, web-based programs, and devices like iPads and laptops that implement them—shares much in common with many older technologies.

In fact, every new technology—the printing press, the steam engine, the automobile, the television, and the telephone—has been trumpeted as proof positive of "progress." Since the Industrial Revolution in particular, this embrace of new technologies has gone hand in hand with capitalism, and new products for new markets has been a difficult logic to overcome. Current digital technology–based ed tech isn't going anywhere until newer and flashier products replace them.

But the argument that's been made by ed-tech companies is that the software and machines that they create deliver content that students want at a faster and more efficient rate. The problem with this scenario is that, as we now know, content is not the name of the game. Watters agreed. "There are learning experiences beyond content."

But what of curiosity? In wrestling with the idea that machines may or may not help with spurring curiosity, I asked Watters what she thought about the way technology affects learning. "We used to support and honor humanness," she said. "What makes us human is that we're messy, and stumble around in our different ways."

When I told her that the boosterism that I'd experienced as a teacher in multiple institutions came down to the idea of ease of access to the infinite amount of information available through the web and technology, Watters offered, "Information doesn't flow through people anymore. It flows through devices." She then went on to describe what the effects might be of a scenario where we get our information—our experience of learning—from a screen rather than from another person.

The point she brought up is that with humans, we get to argue, ask questions, respond to tone and body language and implied meaning—all that nuance and subtlety is gone when interfacing with a device. We can't ask complex questions of machines, she pointed out, questions that are in and of themselves ambiguous. We can't get answers that are contradictory. We can't live in ambivalence when wired into a screen. Binary code doesn't suffer uncertainty well.

And curiosity is killed in the glare of a screen. This much seems clear, at this point, and the reasons are that while there is perceptual, sensory, intellectual, and epistemic curiosity, most of us also have a healthy dose of interpersonal curiosity in us. We pique each other's interest. And there is something crucial in the human connection for us to really learn.

Watters is no Luddite living in a mud hut "of clay and wattles made." She's about as tech-savvy a person as ever existed, with a robust social media presence. But even she agrees that with access to digital technology, there's a price. "We do have really powerful machines at our disposal."

It's not for nothing that her book is titled *The Monsters of Education Technology*. The title is a direct reference to the cautionary tale of Mary Shelley's Frankenstein. "He (Dr. Frankenstein) created this creature that he then abandoned, and *then* he became monstrous. I think that's what we face with Ed Tech."

In a later chapter we'll discuss learning as a journey; Watters may be the living embodiment of it. Her own path in life is littered with false starts and accidents. She's a folklorist by education, but has dropped out of both high school and her PhD program. She was a mother very early on in her life and is a widow. If learning is a journey, then hers has been rich with experiences that have led to a deep understanding of what it means to be human—and how to think about our place in the world.

For Watters, who values social justice and the pioneering spirit of intellectual exploration, the digitally cluttered classroom isn't progress. It's the reverse of the way we grow, intellectually, personally, and developmentally, as human beings.

"The way we do school isn't natural," she said.

NINE

Paying Attention without Trying

THE EMPTY PROFOUND

Helping ourselves, our students, and our children find creativity and discover inspiration is the ultimate challenge. Creating circumstances where curiosity can be given free rein to grow and bloom and given the liberty to spread where it will is essential for learning. In fact, it could be argued that it's essential to living a fulfilling life.

Ensuring that we create the *time* for curiosity to take root and also the right kinds of *environments* is tricky, but can result in fertile, rich imaginations for all of us. Which is all well and good, but in the daily chaos of the world, how can we actually *accomplish* this?

One of the most often-used phrases in education—usually in descriptions of curricula, competencies, and learning outcomes—is "learn how to learn." However, it's somewhat empty in its profoundness—sounds cool, but there's a question as to its actual substantive meaning.

Boston College has an entire office dedicated to the concept called the "Learning to Learn Office." It's a program "designed to improve student's critical thinking abilities." The Association of Waldorf Schools of North America published a brochure titled "Learning to Learn," a collection of essays by graduates talking about how Waldorf inspired them to become lifelong learners.

I always took the statement to be referring to study skills, intellectual aptitude, reasoning and argumentation, and something I'd call stick-to-itiveness, the ability to plow through things that are boring and seem pointless. Whenever I used the phrase and insisted that part of my job was teaching students to "learn how to learn," what I felt I was talking about was instilling a sense of diligence, of rigor.

Learning is wonderful, but underlying the fancy, brochure-friendly stuff, I secretly nurtured this understanding that what I meant was some vaguely defined Puritan-esque sense of toughing it out—the image was of the shivering schoolmaster, threadbare jacket pulled over hunched shoulders. The literary example that comes to mind is Jude from Hardy's novel *Jude the Obscure*, who saw learning as an epic quest rife with sacrifice. The other image has lately become Casaubon from *Middlemarch*, fruitlessly whittling away the years of his life in empty, useless study.

My understanding of lifelong learning wasn't all that unusual, and it was a direct corollary to how schools have been modeled since the Middle Ages. The way we run schools now—with students progressing in the same-age groups through the years, learning blocks of information at appropriate times—has been often compared to an assembly line.

Unsurprisingly, as many studies of the history of education show, that is exactly the model developed in the 18th and 19th centuries. Schools ran like factories, producing obedient citizens. The mistaken belief that learning is best served through sacrifice and denial is a hangover from the school's roots in the church.

Germany, in particular, developed many of the structures we recognize in schools hundreds of years ago. One of the primary purposes of school, prior to being a secular state-run enterprise, was religious instruction (Christian instruction in Western Europe). What that meant was the reinforcement of Christian hierarchy and the concept of only *one* right way to read the scriptures, only *one* right way to be a devout Christian.

Putting the selfish desire of the individual aside was paramount and accepting earthly suffering, as well as the dominance of the church, was central in how early schools formed. One can't be curious about the nature of God—or if God even exists—within the confines of dogmatic religious instruction. Questioning is dangerous; disobedience is sin.

Learning to learn was, in a sense, putting aside childish things and embarking on serious study. Salinger once wrote that he liked people who "read and run," and while the sentiment seemed to strike a chord of truth somewhere deep within my bones, when asked what my end goal was as a teacher, I'd often respond with the expected answers: to develop my students' critical-thinking skills, deep reading, logic, literacy, and numeracy. It was focus, it was structure, it was concentrated effort.

I was wrong.

CURIOSITY: A PERPETUAL MOTION MACHINE

It turns out that if by learning we mean being receptive to new information and incorporating it easily—remembering it, absorbing it, and being able to do so with lots of information of different kinds—then the old process of shutting ourselves up in the classroom and repeating *laudo, laudas, laudat* a million times isn't the way to go. It's not even close.

I mean, it can work, but there are other ways that work too. If what we're talking about is learning, then engaging with curiosity is the best trick there is. Recent studies indicate that there are neurological under-pinnings to curiosity that provide some tantalizing answers to not just how curiosity works, but how being curious may in fact *be* "learning to learn."

In a 2014 article in the journal *Neuron*, Charan Ranganath, a University of California at Davis researcher in psychology, and his colleagues used fMRI of the brain to investigate what goes on in our noggins during heightened states of curiosity.

What they found was that individuals who were curious displayed increased activity in the brain when curious about novel information and the activity was located primarily in the midbrain and hippocampus. The research also addresses how dopamine, the happy hormone, is produced during those states.

Ironically, this is the same chemical that is released during the "compulsion loops" designed into video games used by ed-tech companies mentioned earlier. Dopamine is the all-purpose reward system built into our bodies; whether you're pleased at performing well on trivia night or snorting cocaine, dopamine is your body providing itself with a little biochemical reward.

This begs an interesting question—can curiosity be addicting? If other activities that spur dopamine production are any indication, then yes, in theory, curiosity could be addictive. I haven't found any studies that conclusively make the correlation between curiosity and addiction, but I would argue that of all the addictions one could have, an addiction to curiosity has got to rate more on the positive side than blowing your life savings on drugs.

I called professor Ranganath at his office at UC Davis. Friendly and affable, he walked me through his findings. One of the more interesting bits to come out of his research is that when subjects were in a heightened state of curiosity, not only were they more attentive to discovering the answers to trivia questions during the study, but they also retained more incidental information. The authors wrote, "Behavioral results from two studies revealed that states of high curiosity enhance not only learning of interesting information, but also learning of incidental material."

The core of Ranganath and his colleague's research focused on the idea that when we are studying something we're super excited about, we become sponge-like and able to soak up all kinds of information that isn't even related to what we're invested in. Ranganath pointed out that we filter out all kinds of stimuli and information. If we took in everything that was happening all around us all the time, we'd go nuts at trying to process the information.

There is a state we can be in, though, where not only do we pick up more information, but we remember it better too. When we're learning about something we're excited about, things change in our brain. "Curiosity is changing the state of the brain, making it better for learning," Ranganath said. "It definitely seems to improve our ability to remember later on."

The trick to all this is the dopaminergic circuit—basically rewarding ourselves via a little hormone boost when we are curious. But what also happens is that we become more attentive. It's a different, more specific kind of attention.

The state we experience is a little hard to describe though. "In psychology, we don't have a great way of talking about these things," Ranganath admitted. What he was getting at is that there is a state, a relaxed but attentive focus, that seems to coexist with a certain kind of curiosity. But pay too much attention, and we lose the periphery—both literally and figuratively—and are only able to see the task at hand. "Attention is kind of a funny thing," Ranganath told me.

In the research, it seems pretty clear that from a purely scientific point of view, generating a learning experience based in curiosity would be a good thing for students:

> We found that curiosity had large and long-lasting effects on memory for interesting information. Although effects on memory for incidental information were more subtle, it should be noted that our trivia question paradigm might only *weakly* approximate the effects of an individual's idiosyncratic interests and motivation to learn. If anything, it is likely that our results may be underestimating the effects of curiosity on learning in daily life.

We can't have boring, standardized experiences if we want to learn—both in school and out. The research seems to suggest that if we truly want to learn, we've got to engage with our curiosity. We've got to nurture that appreciative, attentive state that accompanies learning about cool stuff. Otherwise, we're doomed to rote and boring work.

Ranganath and his colleagues offer a suggestion at the end of their research: "Stimulating curiosity ahead of knowledge acquisition could enhance learning success." Also, if you want to get across the content that is important, you've got to do it in an environment where students are already primed for learning: "Teaching of detailed material that may not be of broad interest might be best done in the context of instruction on topics that students are highly motivated to learn."

Reading through the research, I'm reminded of my students in class. They are motivated and excited when we discuss or write things that are important to them. I often eschew content and focus on structure in my classes. (Just because I'm interested in Claude Lévi-Strauss's definition of kinship doesn't mean a nineteen-year-old will be.)

We often mistake rigor for excellence and persistence in the face of frustration for achievement. Hard work is necessary, but we also have to pay attention to ourselves and to what we love to learn. Michel de Montaigne, the great French Renaissance thinker, said it best, perhaps: "If I encounter difficulties in reading I do not gnaw my nails over them; I leave them there. I do nothing without gaiety."

WHY WE WRAP PRESENTS

A significant amount of curiosity research focuses on the relationship between curiosity and motivation. Loewenstein and others posited that gaps in understanding create uncertainty (an unpleasant feeling), and we're motivated to close those gaps. The reward we receive comes in the form of dopamine, the neurotransmitter that functions as the brain's reward system.

Only that might be an oversimplified version of how our brain works. Sometimes, a spike in dopamine production and the firing of associated neurons does in fact signal that certain parts of our brain's networks are jamming along. For instance, those networks associated with seeking behaviors, evaluating, and understanding *value*.

Think of a kid looking at a Christmas present under a tree. There's a little box all wrapped up the size of a matchbox car, and one as big as a full-sized air-hockey table. The kid will be ferociously evaluating the potential award value of each present based on size, and the particular part of his brain associated with motivational value will be lit up like the Christmas tree itself.

But there's a whole other system of neurons that respond to different circumstances. These little guys encode what's known as "motivational salience," helping the brain develop networks for orienting and cognition.

Ethan Bromberg-Martin is a researcher at Columbia University who explored these neural networks with colleagues such as Masayuki Matsumoto and Okihide Hikosaka. In a series of research papers, Bromberg-Martin has explored the diverse ways the brain uses the neurotransmitter dopamine to build different networks for different types of conditions.

What he and his colleagues discovered was that although these two systems respond to different cues, they both transmit an "alerting signal" that might respond to events or stimuli that have the potential to be important—a slight difference that matters, as we'll see.

Regardless of the scenario, research strongly supports the argument that dopamine transmission encourages and motivates us to seek rewards.

But here's the weird thing Bromberg-Martin and his team discovered: the key to dopamine production—and the associated building of neural connections—is not knowing what *value* the reward has.

Remember the little kid under the Christmas tree? The core of this scenario is that the presents are *wrapped*. The kid doesn't even know what's in there.

What the researchers have found is that when the value of a reward is known (little Jimmy sees it's just a rinky-dink matchbox Pinto under the tree) and fully understood, there's no real response from the dopamine neurons.

Basically, we don't get excited about what we already know. It's the *not* knowing, or ambiguity, that amps us up.

The research points to a much more sophisticated system of dopamine neural networks than previously thought. We're not just Pavlovian dogs, drooling when we hear the dinner bell. Our neurons don't just fire in response to stimuli—they help us make predictions about the "structure of the world" based on our "sophisticated beliefs," according to Bromberg-Martin and his team.

All of this research suggests some funky stuff. If our neural reward system is capable of motivating us to seek rewards, but also to orient ourselves as a response—to think about what the reward may be and to predict what may happen—it's a much more finely nuanced system than we previously thought. It means that our dopamine neural systems may be tightly connected with what the researchers call "predictive learning"—thinking about possibility, multiple answers, and the diversity of outcomes. Basically, figuring stuff out.

An important distinction that emerges from the research is that this isn't just a matter of basic reward-motivation scenarios. For instance, there's a large, flat, square box with a delicious smell coming out of it, and we're motivated to open up the box to gobble up a few slices of deep-dish pizza. But some cues are more complicated and may not appear to be immediately connected to reward, or the reward may be ambiguous. We've got to figure out a lot of stuff to determine their *value*. In this case, the dopamine signals are much more muted and gradual, and occur over longer periods of time. There's a longer burst of dopamine as we learn more and more about the potential reward.

Knowing that a reward is coming and figuring out what type of reward it may be signals the dopamine neurons. But here's where things get turned around. Turns out, it's not just rewarding events that fire up our dopamine transmitters. It's aversive events too—things and experiences that we expressly *don't* like—that spark similar systems in our brains.

Huh?

Not only do aversive events that we try to avoid spur our dopamine levels, but when we engage in behaviors that are behaviorally averse, the dopamine starts pumping as well. So dopamine isn't all about pleasure, but can also have something to do with the motivation to avoid discomfort.

As if that wasn't confusing enough, there's another set of circumstances that spurs dopamine responses. These sensory events are not necessarily reward or aversive-experience related. The response could be related to surprise or new or novel stimuli, or even simply the *act of paying attention* can cause a burst response in the dopamine neurons.

Bromberg-Martin calls these types of factors "alerting signals." He and his team, in a 2010 paper in *Neuron* titled "Dopamine in Motivational Control: Rewarding, Aversive, and Alerting," define an alerting event as:

> An expected sensory cue that captures attention based on a rapid assessment of its potential importance, using simple features such as its location, size, and sensory modality. Such alerting events often trigger immediate behavioral reactions to investigate them and determine their precise meaning.

What seems possible is that the ambiguity of curiosity is its own reward. Dopamine neurons respond to multiple signals in specific ways, and according to the *Neuron* article, "some reflect detailed predictors about rewarding and aversive experiences, while others reflect fast responses to events of high potential importance."

Whether we're figuring out what might happen or evaluating which events are more important than others, we're spurring dopamine production. It's when we *don't* have all the answers—when life gets ambiguous—that our brain really lights up.

In addition, there seems to be an intrinsic reward for indulging in impulsive curiosity. The *Neuron* paper states, "Alerting signals are generated by a neural process that motivates fast reactions to investigate potentially important events." Of course we're all distracted—our brains want us to be.

YOU SMELL LIKE A MONKEY . . .

The problem with all the aforementioned research is that much of it was done on animals, not humans, and the time spans measured in most laboratories last only milliseconds. When I spoke with Bromberg-Martin, I began to see just how complex the relationship between motivation, reward, environmental factors, and behavior really is.

Bromberg-Martin's enthusiasm is infectious, and in the course of our conversation, my inbox filled with study after study of how dopamine responds to cues in various laboratory settings.

My questions were those of an amateur enthusiast, but as Bromberg-Martin explained, simple answers about the neurological underpinnings of motivation and reward are anything but.

For instance, despite our various proclivities for bananas, catnip, and cheese, we are not monkeys, cats, or rats, respectively. Many of these studies carried out on the relationship between dopamine bursts and cognitive functions are done with animals. A cat swiveling her head and "orienting" herself in response to a novel sound is not quite the same as a junior high kid entering a crowded school dance and "orienting" herself close enough to the cool kids to maybe be considered part of the in-crowd.

But still, one of the most intriguing aspects of Bromberg-Martin's research seems to me to be the idea that, given a certain state of attention, stimuli of unknown value evoke a response that includes orienting, cognition, and dopamine bursts. This suggests that in certain instances when we are confronted with ambiguous cues, we respond by trying to figure out the value of the cue. We get curious, and our curiosity fires dopamine neurotransmitters.

Basically, we're wired for curiosity. It's the *not knowing* that engages certain neural structures, and our response is to orient, to cogitate—to alter our position and thinking to better evaluate and figure out what the initial stimulus is all about. Curiosity is the propulsion that leads to experience.

Because he's an excellent scientist, Bromberg-Martin was hesitant to sign on to my wild speculating. Most of these studies are carried out on less complex life forms in scientific exactitude, measured in dense little graphs and repeated endlessly to ensure accuracy (not really like the chaos and one-offishness of the real world). Curiosity about the lack of aesthetic appeal of Soviet architecture couldn't be the same type of phenomena, neurologically speaking, as a monkey anticipating a sweet gulp of juice. As humans, we're just too complex.

But as we chatted, I realized there are scenarios where the studies could at least point us in a direction for further inquiry. Think of a kid in a classroom, in that quiet-alert state (not unlike boredom). He hears a sound, notices some unusual visual stimuli, or smells something peculiar (if you've ever taught elementary school, you know that your day is a veritable minefield of strange smells).

The kid will orient toward the cue, focus on it, and theoretically fire off a dopamine burst. When I asked Bromberg-Martin if a hypothetical scenario like this was representative of the *idea* behind the research, he said it was, but in concept only. The research is highly specialized and has way too much specificity to be transferrable to our own weird, curiosity-driven lives.

But he did allow that curiosity is connected to our brain's reward system. "It may well be that there is a dopamine release when we're curious," he said.

Neuroscience—as amazing as it is and as much as it tells us about how our brains determine our behavior—is only part of the equation. The curiosity response a rat shows when a novel object is dropped into its cage is not the same curiosity we experience about other people, the world, and the meaning of our own existence. But it can point us in a direction that helps us frame how we've evolved responses to stimuli, how we are motivated to seek rewards, and how we orient ourselves when we're given new information. What these neurological studies can't do is help us define meaning or explain the way in which we assign meaning to our actions and our lives.

FINDING MEANING THROUGH SMEARING AND MANTLING

On January 14, 2015, Tommy Caldwell and Kevin Jorgeson completed an epic first in the world of rock climbing by free climbing El Capitan's Dawn Wall in Yosemite National Park. The 3,000-foot sheer face had never been climbed in a single shot before, and the news spread across the world with the speed of a dropped carabiner.

The odd responses from those who felt the endeavor was foolhardy, not all that impressive, or just plain stupid (*What's the point of climbing a big piece of rock?*) seemed to be the main criticisms in the comments sections of multiple online articles.

One of my guilty pleasures is reading the blogs of mountain runners, folks like Anna Frost, Kilian Jornet, and Anton Krupicka, who race hundreds of miles through the windswept peaks of the world. I find their words and stories both inspiring and motivating. As someone whose favorite deadly sin is Sloth, I need to read about their exploits and watch videos of them sprinting up the Grand Tetons to force myself to get my butt off the couch and go outside.

In a blog post from January 2015, Krupicka responded in a thoughtful way to the debate over the historic climb of the Dawn Wall. He wrote:

> I don't get especially worked up about this kind of stuff, probably because over a decade ago, when I was studying for a degree in Philosophy, I found myself mostly in agreement with the notion (with significant encouragement from the likes of Kierkegaard, Camus, and Sartre) that the universe is basically an indifferent, meaningless place.
>
> On the surface, this can be a frightening prospect, but it is also a freeing one in that it accords individuals with the responsibility and agency to create meaning. Instead of allowing us to devolve into nonstop pillaging and murdering (as it seems some would have us believe is the logical conclusion), I think it instead suggests that it is incumbent

upon the individual to go out into the world full of curiosity, searching for experiences and emotions and knowledge and in the process inevitably happening upon instances of beauty and joy, and maybe even moments that feel disturbingly close to something like truth.

And this, I think, helps us see how curiosity, while empirically an instinctual, neurological, and psychological behavior, is also something else. We are the only species that ponders our own place in the world, that seeks to find meaning in our experiences. We are the only species that wonders about the nature of the universe—its size, age, and content. We are desperately curious about what happens when we die, and our curiosity has driven us to try to answer that question through religion, science, superstition, and empiricism—Scientology and *Ghost Hunters*.

Curiosity is an observable trait. The observation of its existence and causes is empirical. Scientists like Bromberg-Martin are paving the way to understanding what the neurological underpinnings may be to some of our behaviors—curiosity included. But the way we think about ourselves is beyond anything that can be studied in a lab. Our self-mythologies, our internal landscapes—our destinies—exist beyond the bounds of MRIs and microscopes.

Curiosity is as much about pondering the nature of God as it is about trying to figure out what's under the Christmas tree. It's about wonderment and awe.

NEUROMYTHOLOGY

Potentially, one of the reasons for all the debate around learning is that it is so highly personal, and therefore everyone involved in the discussion is coming from an understanding of learning that is subjective. Common Core, No Child Left Behind, assessments, and learning targets are all institutional responses to this highly complex and individualized experience.

Teachers, educators, and policy makers are constantly looking for some level of guidance in creating and implementing institutional solutions in education, and the success they get is at times tepid and at other times has transformed countless lives. The only commonality it seems that learners have is that they all have a brain.

Often, research from the field of neuroscience is used to substantiate claims made about the efficacy of educational packages or programs. Indeed, much of this book is based on findings in neuroscience, particularly in relation to dopamine production and its relation to curiosity. But studying curiosity and figuring out how it works is different from using highly specific neuroscience research to teach twenty-five students in a room.

Using neuroscience as a means to make helpful changes in the class-room may sound like a good idea, but a close analysis of the current research—and statements from the neuroscientists themselves—suggests that while neuroscience can tell us a great deal about curiosity and how we learn, to depend on it as the *primary* means of crafting impactful learning experiences is overreaching the mark.

One of the theories that gained ground in the classroom was the bene-fit of assessing which learners were "right" versus "left" brained. The idea gained ground in the latter part of the 20th century as researchers began to identify that the two hemispheres of the brain were responsible for different abilities.

The left hemisphere was in charge of logic, the right creativity. The myth that arose from this was that lefties were rational, math-oriented people, and righties were more artsy. However, most of the initial studies that were used to develop this theory came from research on people who had had their corpus callosum severed. The corpus callosum is the big bundle of brain fibers that connect the two halves of the brain.

Of course, most of us don't have separate brain hemispheres, and current research suggests that both sides of the brain are active in many tasks that used to be deemed hemisphere specific. In a 2013 article in *Popular Science* debunking the left-brain/right-brain myth, Larry Alferink, professor emeritus at Illinois State University, stated, "The hemispheres are not completely specialized."

Even before Alferink got started in parsing out the finer points in the brain-based education debate, Usha Goswami, of the Centre for Neuro-science in Education based in the United Kingdom at the University of Cambridge, wrote an overview of misconceptions about brain-based edu-cation for *Nature*. The 2006 article touches on the three greatest "neuro-myths" plaguing educators. Goswami's take on the left/right brain debate is similar to Alferink's: "This neuromyth probably stems from an over-literal interpretation of hemispheric specialization."

Neuromyth-buster Goswami goes on to suggest that learning pro-grams such as Brain Gym, Posit Science, and Lumosity use spurious claims based on cherry-picking data within brain research. Learning styles—identifying children as visual, auditory, or kinesthetic—are also based on tenuous evidence, claims Goswami, as are programs that pro-mote synaptogenesis, or brain growth. "These neuromyths need to be eliminated," Goswami states in the paper.

The point the article makes is that the brain is incredibly complicated, and factors at play in the classroom, including various learning disabil-ities, have a far more substantial effect than trying to apply neuroscience theory to educational practice. "Owing to placebo effects, these pro-grammes may indeed bring benefits to children in the short term. How-ever, such programmes are unlikely to yield benefits in the long term, and so many will naturally fall out of use."

The list of books based in the latest theories and research of cognitive neuroscience, biology, and other scientific disciplines that attempts to get a handle on how we learn based on how our brains light up when we have an fMRI scan is getting longer and longer. *Why Don't Students Like School? A Cognitive Scientist Answers Questions About How the Mind Works and What It Means for the Classroom,* by Daniel T. Willingham, is one such example. *The Art of Changing the Brain: Enriching the Practice of Teaching by Exploring the Biology of Learning,* by James E. Zull, is another.

And then there's the counterargument, voiced by authors like Sally Satel and Scott O. Lilienfeld in their book, *Brainwashed: The Seductive Appeal of Mindless Neuroscience.* While both sides of the argument—the pro "brain research explains everything" side and the "no it doesn't" camp— have valid points, for teachers who are in the classroom every day, the argument between theory and application, research and practicality, can start to sound like the background hum of a lawnmower on a lazy summer day: nap inducing.

There is so much to be gleaned from research on the brain for success both in the classroom and in the wider scope of education, but no understanding of bundles of neurons will ever replace a learning journey based in relationships and experience. Neuroscience can help teachers become better. So can evolutionary biology. So can getting eight hours of sleep. Eating more kale probably wouldn't hurt either.

There are so many facets to learning that the desire to oversimplify and come up with baseline solutions is well nigh irresistible. However, by looking at the nature of our learning, of how our lives are lived alongside the books we read and the people who mentor us within a changing world, we can start to grasp how learning functions. How curiosity is not a product of learning, but something that inspires it. How learning is not just a result of massed tangles of neurons, but of our own journey through the internal landscape of our own experience.

An argument to be made is that certain interventions in education pay off later, that neuroscience-based teaching can have wide impacts down the line.

But our minds—our sense of self, our personas, tastes, proclivities— are not reducible to neurons and dopamine. Again, we're just too complex for that kind of analysis. Yes, the brain is important and holds many of the keys to behavior, particularly in terms of how and why we learn. I mean, it's our *brain,* for gosh sake.

As noted previously, a decent portion of this book draws on the field of neuroscience. But psychology, culture, biology—all these play a role too. So does self-mythology, environment, social settings, institutions, and parenting. The factors that add up to our personal and intellectual growth are a tangled web. There's no silver bullet solving the mystery of learning and curiosity—it's more like a hundred blunderbusses firing grapeshot.

TEN

Learning as Journey

HITTING THE TRAIL

Learning is a personal journey, an experience unique to each individual. How we learn, what we learn, and the place where we do so are dependent on highly subjective experiences. To try to capture some generalized definition of what learning is—much less how to engender it in students—is challenging business.

Not only is learning a multifaceted experience, but the results of learning are not easily codified. I can learn to make an omelet; I can learn to fix satellites during space walks. There are corollaries between situational learning experiences—skills, memorization, analysis, and conceptualization being just a few.

I learn one skill set, conjugating Latin verbs, and other related languages become a bit easier to understand. But there's another kind of learning that exists as well. Contemplation, self-reflection, and reverie, these too are learning experiences or modalities, but difficult to explain and even harder to teach. Not to mention almost impossible to commodify. They have more to do with curiosity than with institutionalized, transactional education.

That's why we struggle sometimes as parents, teachers, and students to figure out what exactly we're learning. I know that when I taught middle school math, I was a fractions, decimals, and percentage guy. No matter what, I was going to cudgel those kids into understanding those languages and make them conversant in changing them back and forth.

But as an English teacher, although grammar, argument, and concision are important, it's not as easy to define. Maybe part of it is because when we look at our own learning, it's difficult to figure how we know what we know. For a brain surgeon, there are lessons in how to slice into gray matter that one can describe. But what of the artful way a painter expresses an idea, or even the artful way one particular brain surgeon saves a life while another bumbles the operation? It's harder to figure out this other dimension of learning.

In an attempt to understand what it means to learn and the relationship with curiosity, it's helpful to look at the usage and meaning of the word itself. It pops up fairly frequently in syllabi, course descriptions, curricula, and policy, and with students, parents, and colleagues. What do teachers mean when they talk about *learning*?

The etymology of the word gives us a good place to start. The history of the word *learning* actually resonates with how learning happens in the world. The etymological roots are in harmony with the most direct and practical way to learn. To learn is to become curious and explore. To learn is to head off on a quest into the unknown.

According to *Origins: A Short Etymological Dictionary of Modern English*, by Eric Partridge, "to learn" derives from Middle English *lernen* and has similar roots with the Old English word *laeran*, which means to teach. There are multiple cognates in Middle Dutch (*leernen*), Old High German (*leren*), and others.

What all the words for learning have in common is their oldest and truest meaning: "to teach is to cause to understand (literally), to lead someone on his way." Both learning and teaching are born of this idea of movement, of the teacher's leading the student on a journey, a trek, a trip.

Multiple cognates exist that further emphasize this idea of learning as a journey. Old English has the word *laest*, meaning a track, like a well-trodden trail through the woods. The cognate *Last* is also a term used by shoemakers, as in the German *Leisten*, or the Middle High German *leis*, a *track*.

From an etymological perspective, to learn is to strap on some boots, hit the trail, and hike into the mountains.

ARISTOTLE ON HORSEBACK

Compulsory education has lost touch with the adventure of learning and is instead mired in bureaucratic debates and institutionalized rhetoric. The very core experience of learning is one wherein we enter the wilderness of the unknown, both literally and figuratively. Again, it is the *not* knowing that is important—the seeking and the journey are the truly transformational experiences. Arriving at answers and destinations is always a bit of a letdown, for it's in traversing the landscape that we see the world and come to understand ourselves in relation to it.

In an essay called "What's a Story?" Leonard Michaels wrote, "The problem with storytelling is how to make transitions into transformations, since the former belong to logic, sincerity, and boredom (that is, real time, the trudge of 'and then') and the latter belong to art."

It's not too much of a leap here to insert the word "learning" for storytelling. If learning is a journey—a narrative of our development as thinkers, an exploration of the world of ideas—then we want it to transform us. Rather than just transition from grade to grade, from world history to algebra, from student to employee, wouldn't it be something if we sought transformation in education, if teachers and students headed off on a journey together?

This isn't just philosophical poppycock. When we change our physical location or even when we experience the idea of other places and experiences, it makes us more capable of handling challenges, more able to intuit connection.

Psychologist Lile Jia at Indiana University designed an experiment to see if exotic places and experiences—even if only experienced through the imagination—could have an effect on student learning. He broke students into two groups and asked them to list all forms of travel they could think of. One group was told to list travel possible for students studying abroad in Greece, the other group told they were compiling a list of possible transportation alternatives for right there in Indiana.

The students who were designing for Greece had a longer, more unique list. It included normal forms of transportation like cars and buses and bikes, but also Segways and horses. Jia performed a number of similar experiments, all pointing to more or less the same conclusion: when we think about things that are psychologically distant, or situations that are removed from our immediate area or locus of concern, our minds take flight and we make intuitive leaps. We solve problems. We think freely, unencumbered. Perhaps we allow curiosity to play a larger role in considering not just what is probable, but what is possible.

The reason for this phenomena is that our brains are efficient at dealing with the here and now, and equally as efficient at cutting out all the other creative, intuitive, and unlikely scenarios that may exist. We're constrained by the familiar and the local, and unfettered when we introduce distant lands and release ourselves from the onus of the present and obvious.

How much of this kind of interior journey does compulsory education give students? If learning is driven at least in part by creativity and problem solving, one of the best ways to encourage it is to release students from a trajectory of assignments and skills and information designed for nothing more interesting than a standardized test.

The journey of learning must be one that takes students to distant lands. When learning is based not on the exotica of faraway places or fantastical, chimeric tales of other worlds, we get mired in boring expediency and practicality. *Learn this*, we tell our students, *because it will help you get into college. Learn that, because it will help you get a job.* Important achievements no doubt, but surely not the only results we hope for from our learning.

Learning in school usually gets delivered in distinct chunks: Russian Revolution, Pre-Algebra, Western Religion, Institutional Equities, Renaissance Painting. And yet each of us has been on a distinctly unique journey as a learner, one that started at a young age when we began to parse our meaning in the world and that continues to this day.

While there have been stages and disciplines, for the most part learning is a kinetic and chaotic quest, full of all the boredom, hair-raising fear, exhaustion, and exhilaration that comes from journeys into the unknown spurred by impetuous curiosity. Recognizing that fact, and capitalizing on it in the classroom, is a step toward making learning in school reflect the authentic learning we do in life.

Learning in our own myriad fashions isn't seen as valuable. Schools have defined a "better" way to learn and therefore undermine our own internal logic. Learning outside of school is configured according to each person. Ultimately, learning can happen in groups and institutions and communities, but each individual's learning is rooted in her own private, internal narrative.

THIS TIME, IT'S PERSONAL

Learning is an intimate experience. One of the arguments in favor of school is that it "socializes" students. One of the arguments I'd make about learning is that it can take place in social environments, but is ultimately a private act that depends in large part on how curiosity manifests itself.

No matter how many group activities, discussions, or workshops students participate in, and no matter how engaging and dynamic those may be, everyone learns within the confines of his own subjective experience. Learning is an external journey that shapes our interior selves. It defines our personal narratives and mythologies, and it is difficult to predict the effect large-scale institutionalized curricula will have on students.

We literally travel through space and time to learn: change towns, schools, and classrooms. Our bodies move. But concurrently, there is an internal journey that is happening as well, and it's the interplay between these two poles that begins to shape our learning experience. Curriculum detail, content, delivery, skills, and assessment—not how the material and ideas may shape the student's sense of self. How our experiences etch themselves onto our internal templates is a matter of highly individualized context. Much of that context derives from where our curiosity takes us.

In this way, learning is similar to going to church or the movies. While we all sit together in the pews or in our plush chairs eating popcorn, we are sharing a public experience, but our perception of the event is entirely personal. In fact, our associations in connection with what is being said or performed in front of us is highly defined by our personal experience.

To put it simply: your Jedi is not my Jedi, and my Bruce Willis is not your Bruce Willis. Yet within schools, we assume that learning is somehow this group activity, done in clusters of 10, 20, or 100 students, when in actuality it is happening on an individual level. Every student experiencing her learning privately.

Students must be given agency in their own learning, and this begins within relationships. Personalizing content, both in terms of the learner and the material itself, is vital for the student to approach learning as one would a friend, with inquisitive trust. Authentic learning is not overly concerned with content or skill sets—though that's part of the equation, to be sure—but rather is more about developing the personal mythology of students, ensuring that they see themselves as an active character with agency within the greater narrative of knowledge seeking.

That agency is the right and choice to pursue curiosity, in terms of what they're curious about, but also *how* they're curious, be it epistemic, perceptual, interpersonal, or sensory. Education can, at its most impersonal, present information and ideas and concepts as foreign entities to be besieged or cryptic codes to be cracked. Learning occurs best when learners create a relationship with ideas that disregards decorum and hierarchy. Learning is a humble enterprise.

The best kind of learning is when we feel able to sit across the table from Shakespeare and try to understand his choices or walk in the woods with Schrödinger and listen as he prattles on about cats. But the only way to get to that place—to assume an informal, convivial familiarity with the world of ideas and concepts—is to move away from the oppression of content and allow students to engage with learning in a relationship-based way. Just as they seek out their friends, they'll seek out connections and resonances with ideas according to their own tastes.

When learning is personal it removes absolutes, introduces complexity, and offers students the chance to change their minds. This is no small feat. An example: I had always considered Céline's novel *Journey to the End of the Night* to be one of the most formative books in my life and revered it for the way it helped me understand art, literature, and my own confused self-mythology at the age of eighteen when I first read it (coincidentally, Céline's novel was given to me by a mentor—my high school French teacher—who clearly saw how abysmal I was at learning a foreign language and chose instead to capitalize on my curiosity about books and movies by introducing me to various novels and French art films).

Then, in January 2010, critic Wyatt Mason (a mentor of mine from graduate school) wrote an article for *The New York Review of Books* titled "Uncovering Céline" in which Céline is exposed as a virulent antisemite. Everything I had learned changed. When it comes to the question of whether the person behind the book matters in terms of appreciation of the writing, I realized I fall firmly on the side where it does.

Reading Mason's assessment of Céline's bigotry I had to reconfigure my appreciation of the novel, question my own ability to suss out finer modalities in literature, and discard this previously important monument in my own creative and intellectual life. I took the whole thing rather personally, as I had placed the book as an important marker in my development as a thinker and a human being, and was horrified to learn that its author was a hateful bigot.

I was learning, and it was messy. Curiosity had driven the context of my understanding of Céline, and now I became curious about other authors, my own proclivities as far as their values were concerned and whether any of it mattered.

THE SHEER BORINGNESS OF INSTITUTIONALIZED "SPLAININ'"

English class is an arena where this personal context becomes more prevalent. I remember bridling when a teacher in high school started diagramming *Lord of the Flies*, by William Golding, on the blackboard: the conch was order, representing democracy; Jack and the hunters represented the fascism that Golding faced as a naval officer in WWII; and so on. All done in yellow chalk with neat little boxes.

While all those dissections are interesting and very possibly true, what I felt at the time was disappointment. It was almost as though I could hear the flatulent sound of a balloon deflating in my brain. As a student I had read the book twice through in a matter of two weeks, wide-eyed and panting as Ralph battled for control of the island. It spoke so directly to my own experience in high school that I wrapped the very fibers of the narrative into my own and wanted to be Ralph, built "like a boxer," so that I could be the one to stand up to the bullies.

It wasn't that this teacher was wrong or that any of the contexts she provided were untrue; it was that I wasn't given any time to reckon with the novel as part of my own story. She had provided labels and meaning in spheres that didn't matter to me at all, when before, it had mattered very much. What I needed was help in figuring out *why* I had sped through the pages twice in a row with such passion.

Relationships play a key role in learning—both the learner's relationship with the material and content and ideas, and real-world relationships with mentors, such as my friendship with my French teacher, with whom I'm still close to this day.

In Dante's *Inferno*, Dante would be lost without the guidance of the shade Virgil, who gives him a tour of the different levels of hell. It is partially Virgil's knowledge of the topography of hell that is useful—his knowledge of its inhabitants, their transgressions—but part of any successful equation of learning is Dante's admitting that he is lost, that he needs help: "Midway upon the journey of our life / I found myself within a forest dark, / For the straightforward pathway had been lost."

It is this sense of being lost, the place where the *Inferno* begins, the very first lines of the first canto, that is the perfect analogy for learning. It is within this dark wood of ambiguity that curiosity can take root.

CURIOSITY KILLED THE CAT, THEN GOT HER INTO HARVARD

There are multiple kinds of learning (shooting free throws versus quantum mechanics, for example), and an understanding of how the brain incorporates new information and trains new behaviors is helpful if our goal is to create an engaging classroom. However, the neurological underpinnings of learning are only part of defining what it means to learn.

Equally important is reviewing educational theory to find out just what sort of conceptual implications exist behind practical lessons, and even then we get only a piece of the picture, as applying theory to the pell-mell rush of the modern school day is a hit or miss proposition. The experiences of novelty, curiosity, risks, boredom, motivation, community, and stakes are just a few of the additional pieces of the puzzle of what it means to learn, and consequently to teach.

Learning, when it's derived from the wellspring of curiosity, can be fun. It's exhilarating and exciting. Maintaining the thread of fun is important, especially when undertaking requisite activities that aren't as enjoyable to further learning. Learning is fun because it's an expression of the joy of discovering novelty.

The default view of learning is that of the student bent over a book or listening to a lesson or working away steadily at a desk. Despite incredible gains in introducing group work, more activity-driven lesson plans, and self-motivated exploration in the classroom, most of us still consider learning to be a passive reception of information rather than an active, curious search for questions.

This is not to say that this style of learning—whether by rote memorization, drills, or repetition—is not valuable. It is. In fact, for most students, it is the easiest way to deliver the goods promised by education: numeracy, literacy, some understanding of social/historical continuums, and civics. But it is not the only way.

Not only do other modalities exist, but other kinds of learning exist, which are activated in ways not embraced by most schools and not easily assessed through standardized tests. Traditional learning functions on deliverables: you ask a student to memorize the presidents, to change fractions to percentages, or to memorize the spelling of words like *aesthetics* and *Uruguay*. But there is a different kind of learning that can take place that is equally valuable (if not essential) for students to understand themselves and develop a tacit understanding of their corporeal existence and the nuances of the world around them: learning through active experience.

One of the most authentic forms of learning is the product of unrestricted curiosity. For curiosity to be given free rein, a premium must be placed on getting the students to be propulsive in their desire to explore, to adventure.

Even though his writing predated much of contemporary research on curiosity, John Dewey knew a good thing when he saw it. In *Democracy and Education*, he wrote:

> Children proverbially live in the present; that is not only a fact not to be evaded, but it is an excellence. The future just as future lacks urgency and body. To get ready for something, one knows not what nor why, is to throw away the leverage that exists, and to seek for motive power in a vague chance. Under such circumstances, there is, in the second place, a premium put on shilly-shallying and procrastination. The future prepared for is a long way off; plenty of time will intervene before it becomes a present. Why be in a hurry about getting ready for it? The temptation to postpone is much increased because the present offers so many wonderful opportunities and proffers such invitations to adventure. Naturally attention and energy go to them; education accrues naturally as an outcome, but a lesser education than if the full stress of effort had been put upon making conditions as educative as possible.

Dewey's quote underscores the importance of impetuosity, capriciousness, and the pinballing excitement kids feel when their curiosity is given full rein. It's a feeling that never goes away, though as students mature, those that matriculate and do well have learned to temper it.

Instead, they carry on rational and steady arguments with the content of their learning. *Yes, yes, it is very important and good to know this. This information is functional and meaningful, and assessing its meaning is a valuable enterprise,* rather than, *Here, here! Look at this! Listen to this! What's up with that?*

Researchers from Yale have recently argued that curiosity is a particularly human trait. A paper by Yale psychology professor Laurie Santos tried to find whether capuchin monkeys would engage in "causal reasoning" (thinking for its own sake) in the absence of food rewards. Turns out, for the most part, they won't, whereas young children will.

An article in the *Yale Daily News* from March 2014 reviewing the research states that "previous research has demonstrated that young children are often curious regardless of other benefit." However, this seems to be at odds with the findings of other researchers that suggest that even birds like the great tit can have curiosity.

What the Yale study seems to demonstrate is that how we define curiosity and the conditions that give rise to it can affect studies like the one above and give us conflicting results. This serves as a valuable reminder that individual studies are useful, but only to a point. Bringing in history, culture, and our own experience is important to define any behavior.

Reading the Yale study, I struggled with the term "causal reasoning." While the capuchins may not have exhibited exploratory behavior, who is to say that at the neurological level they weren't assessing, contemplating, and figuring out their environment?

When I watch my dog as we ramble around the woods and fields, I see her constantly sniffing out her environment. When new people come to our home, she's all over them, greeting and sniffing and rather overenthusiastically engaging with them. Her behavior appears deeply curious, which is one of the reasons I think we have a tendency to anthropomorphize dogs so readily—we see in them our own propensity for relationships and exploration.

Ultimately, humans don't have anything "special" about them as a species. We evolved from the same system of genetic and environmental factors as spiders and toads and wildebeests. Our curiosity may be more prominent as an adaptive function, just as whales and arctic terns have adapted a highly evolved navigational ability to transit the globe every year. But it doesn't make us special, only different.

It certainly seems that adventure and curiosity become us. It behooves us as a species to explore new foods, be curious about other people, poke sticks into cracks, and turn over rocks. It also benefits us to toss aside that which doesn't keep our attention. Beyond that, the research suggests that we gain some intrinsic benefit from being curious and thinking about stuff. It may be one of the traits that has made us so successful as a species.

THE BENEFITS OF SLIGHTLY NEGLIGENT PARENTING

Curiosity is also born from boredom. It was Fowler who explored this idea most completely, postulating that boredom was one of the "prerequisites" to curiosity. Boredom has a way of first widening the net of our attention. We have the ability, because there's nothing immediately claiming our attention, to notice things and to notice what we notice.

When I'm being a particularly neglectful parent, trying to vacuum up dog hair or send off e-mails, my son will become bored and start climbing the walls, driving us both crazy. But if I can restrain myself from intervening in his boredom, he eventually wanders away, and inevitably I find him some time later absorbed in a task or game or outside, deeply immersed in some imaginative landscape. To find his curiosity, I must first give him the space and time and boredom he requires so that his innate curiosity can be given free rein to find a course to pursue.

Teachers can't prescribe curiosity. We simply can't make students curious about one thing or another. I teach undergraduate writing, but find that by making slight adjustments I can engage students in what they're curious about. I'm lucky in that rhetoric/writing is inherently interdisciplinary. We can read and write about whatever we want. But like everyone, I can be a stick in the mud.

As teachers we can be dogmatic about content. I know I am. I force Montaigne's essays down my students' throats. But even when I try to play it cool and use Twitter feeds or clips from Tosh.0 to demonstrate some rhetorical strategy, sometimes that doesn't work.

Students find their way into various activities and ideas in ways I would never expect, and with better results than I could gerrymander. By following their own curiosity they have a more authentic learning experience. I only try to give them time, space, and the tools to navigate the landscape.

But by allowing students and ourselves to capitalize on that feverish desire to know, that impulsive quest for answers, we're connecting with a kind of learning much deeper than just dutifully following instructions.

ELEVEN

Impulsivity and the Need to Know

YOU KNOW YOU WANT IT

For the most part, impulsivity is seen as an aberrant behavior. It's often used to describe actions such as aggression, substance abuse, and suicide. In fact, in the *Diagnostic and Statistical Manual of Mental Disorders*, the book published by the American Psychiatric Association that classifies mental disorders, most behaviors lumped under the impulsivity banner are listed as personality disorders. Which is accurate—an inability to control dangerous impulses is a serious issue.

But what if the impulse is toward something good?

Impulsivity is really just an umbrella term that includes lots of different behaviors. For instance, "sensation seeking" is a part of impulsivity. There's a similar trait called "venturesomeness," which is often seen as related to, but distinct from, impulsivity.

Donald Lynam, a psychologist at the University of Kentucky, framed this more complicated understanding of impulsivity in a paper titled "The Five Factor Model and Impulsivity," which appeared in a 2001 issue of *Personality and Individual Differences*. Lynam (who co-wrote the paper with then doctoral student Stephen Whiteside) stated: "Given the pervasive importance of impulsivity in psychology, it is somewhat surprising to note the variety of current conceptualizations of impulsivity and the inconsistencies among them." This is academic speak for "What the hell, guys?"

Lynam then goes on to discuss various traits that have been lumped under impulsivity, including boredom susceptibility, risk taking, novelty seeking, boldness, adventuresomeness, and messiness. And this is where things get complicated, because some of those traits are kind of cool. In fact, combine a few of them together, and you've got Indiana Jones.

107

I called Lynam at his office, now at Purdue, to get a better handle on how impulsivity plays a role in curiosity. Remember, according to Loewenstein and others, curiosity can be defined by intensity, transience, and impulsivity.

The first thing we need to understand is what, exactly, impulsivity is. We use the word to describe a whole host of behaviors and actions, and oftentimes we aren't really sure whether impulsivity is the cause of an action or the result of some other intrinsic drive.

Lynam describes traits such as sensation seeking, desire for novelty, lack of premeditation, and others as *impulsigenic* behaviors—aspects of our personality profiles that give rise to impulsive behavior. Some of Lynam's research concerns substance abuse and the way in which individuals can't think through the negative effects of poor behavior; they just do it. This is what we usually think of when we describe someone as impulsive: the shopaholic who spends more than she should, the binge drinker who gets totally trashed on a Tuesday night, the friend who has multiple one-night stands.

All of these behaviors are impulsive and lead to bad consequences: hangovers, missed work, debt, sexually transmitted diseases. But there is another side to the story. There are some impulsigenic traits that are actually beneficial when they're combined in the right ways and at the right level.

Take Reinhold Messner. Messner is an Italian-born mountain climber whose achievements in mountaineering are staggering: first climber to summit Everest without supplemental oxygen and the first climber to peak all fourteen mountains over 26,000 feet—the guy is a risk taker. He is also, as of this writing, seventy years old.

Messner has that particular cocktail of sensation seeking and venturesome behavior, but it's balanced with premeditation. No one climbs mountains without careful preparations. It requires training, experience, equipment, and organization. It also requires a risk-taking trait that is potentially impulsigenic.

When I asked Lynam by phone if there was the possibility some combinations of impulsigenic traits (Lynam's term) could actually be beneficial, he readily agreed. If, like Messner, a person has a high level of sensation seeking, but combines that with premeditation, according to Lynam, "That's probably not a bad thing. It lets you do new stuff, and find things out." He went on to note that "being willing to take these risks" was essential for behaviors that resulted in positive experiences, exploration, and learning, but the risk taking had to be at a level that was kept in check by a counterbalance of premeditation.

Basically, if you want to go all Acapulco style and go cliff diving, go for it, but first learn how to control your dive, break the surface of the water perpendicularly, absorb the impact with your hands and arms, and check the depth of the water before you leap.

POSITIVE RECKLESSNESS

Some of the research Lynam mentioned during our chat concerned the idea of *negative urgency*. Folks who experience this find that at times of emotional upheaval, they're no longer able to control their impulses. The example Lynam gave me was of people who binge eat. They've got a gallon of chocolate ice cream in the freezer, but are able to go through their day just fine without eating it. Not to say it isn't there, the knowledge of the ice cream, but they are able to control the impulse to rip open the top of the carton and gorge.

Then, however, they get in an argument with a colleague, something stresses them out, and *boom!* they're all over that ice cream. "They lose some inhibitory control," Lynam stated. "They can't hold themselves back."

If the above example seems alien to you—*good on ya*, as the Aussies say. For me, and for most people I know, it's a variant of pretty typical behaviors. After a particularly stressful day or one filled with conflict and contention, I'll often have a generous pour of Vermont microbrew (or three) with dinner, even though I still have work to do and have to get up early the next day. Now, the double India pale ale has been there all along, but when I have that sense of negative urgency, my ability to control the impulse to get buzzed so I'm not so stressed is at its lowest ebb.

Lynam pointed out that there has been some work done around helping individuals with negative urgency problems. It comes down to "mindfulness." Lynam suggests that even recognizing that stressful, emotionally heated moments inhibit the ability to control impulse is a step in the right direction. What basically happens is that those individuals "lose the ability to control that impulse" Lynam says, and there has been some success in developing the ability to control impulses in these situations.

This scenario made me think of my students. Imagine you struggle with writing. Maybe you're dyslexic or have ADHD, and you're in a classroom with a strict but caring teacher. Maybe there's some social pressure not to look stupid, maybe your parents have really pressured you to improve your grades, maybe your current boyfriend has just broken up with you, maybe your family is struggling with money issues. In any case, that environment—the tough class, all the stuff swirling around in your life—is right there in front of your face.

You get the impulse to be disruptive, to sneak a cigarette, to skip school, to try drugs, to drop out. Whatever the impulse is, there's a good chance that if you suffer from negative urgency you're going to obey the call of impulsivity. It's almost like you can't help yourself. All of this certainly points to impulsivity as a negative aspect of behavior, but then how can impulsivity be so closely tied to curiosity, which is so closely connected to learning? And can the type of impulsivity or its effect be changed for the better?

What do teachers do to help the situation? Or more broadly, how are schools construed to handle these types of situations? Not well, I'm afraid.

The structure of the typical academic situation—learn these salient facts, memorize this data, take this test, get that grade—is fraught with the kind of stressors that could very well lead to negative urgency on the part of someone who struggles with impulsivity. Kids act out in class, and we come down hard on them, when the behavior could very well be the final act in what has been building for some time.

I asked Lynam if it was possible to "coach" folks who suffered from impulse control issues to become more like Indiana Jones, whether bad impulsivity—wanting to try drugs, for example—could be replaced with good sensation seeking like backcountry skiing. Lynam said that it was possible, and the key was "being aware of what the trait does, and using the information to get the message in better."

He mentioned that public service announcements aimed at potential drug users that used a high-energy, quick-cut editing style had a greater impact than the usual boring old PSAs. "You can use sensation seeking in interventions," Lynam said, and he reasoned that teachers could use the same techniques. "It's possible whenever you have individual differences that you can appeal to them with different kinds of arguments. If you can use that trait to inform the way you teach, you're better off."

This made a huge amount of sense to me. I asked Lynam what that would look like, particularly with students with attention disorders like ADD or ADHD. Lessons that came in "short, shiny bursts" would work, he thought, because it fit with the behavioral motivation of the student.

There's a whole counterargument, of course, that we can't teach every single kid in a special way. We just don't have the time or resources. But if what we're after is fostering curiosity, and an inherent part of curiosity is impulsivity, then understanding how impulsivity works and letting it inform our daily practice as parents, teachers, and learners seems worth doing.

Even our friend Eysenck had to reconfigure his understanding of impulsivity, eventually coming up with the idea that being impulsive was, yes, still a part of psychoticism, but being venturesome was part of being an extrovert. The trouble comes with deciding where one stops and the other starts.

Part of this gray area relates to how the brain develops. It depends on where the person is at with the development of the prefrontal cortex and his consequent ability to manage the impulsivity. It could be that curiosity is well-regulated impulsivity, at least as far as Eysenck's definition goes.

And in this place, where the various subjective distinctions overlap, we can begin to close in on how impulsivity plays a role in curiosity, as Lowenstein proposed. Let's take the ability to stay on task and not be distracted. Being able to resist the temptation to open up YouTube and watch the latest Amy Schumer sketch or see how the Lakers are doing is seen as a positive trait.

But there is a contextual question to be asked: what if the task is dull? What if it's not only boring, but also lame, compulsory, and useless? Is heeding the call of distraction a bad thing in that circumstance? Certainly, if it means nothing ever gets accomplished, yes, it's bad. But in terms of learning, when the stakes are not practical tasks being accomplished to keep the trains running on time, but rather the exploration of novel concepts, exciting ideas, and the fostering of an interest in discovery, then perhaps there is usefulness to getting distracted, as long as we're being distracted by something we're curious about.

THE OPPOSITE OF IMPULSIVITY

A hypothetical scenario: I get home from work. I know there's that bag of Chips Ahoy in the pantry, but I promised myself earlier that I wouldn't eat any until I worked out and swallowed my cruciferous vegetable and my omega-3s.

But I'm so tired, and I've spent the whole day at my exhausting job.

Think about it. Those cookies don't stand a chance, do they?

Why is this? Why do we give in to our impulses more easily when we're tired? We explored this earlier, but there's another dimension we should look at for a fuller appreciation of how impulsivity works in relation to curiosity. And what about our students when they're trying to learn? They're struggling through a particular lesson or task, and some of them just stick with it better.

I was always amazed at the alacrity with which Kathy, a classmate of mine in high school, would dive right into conjugating a worksheet of French verbs during class. I'd make it through the first two or three, then just kind of . . . give up. I'm sure she didn't find it to be the most exciting thing in the world either. She just had more self-control than I did.

Self-control could be argued to be the opposite of impulsivity. It's the power to persevere through a difficult task, to not give up, to resist the temptation to throw in the towel. The most popular example of the power of self-control is Walter Mischel's famous experiments from the 1960s at Stanford. Children were offered either a single marshmallow immediately or a couple if they could wait for fifteen minutes.

Some kids were able to hold off and wait for the bigger reward; others gobbled that first marshmallow the second the researcher left the room. Tracking those kids through their lives, it was found that those who could delay gratification, practice self-control, and wait were more successful later in life. And the impulsive ones who went for the immediate score of a single marshmallow instead of delaying gratification? They didn't attain the same societal rewards over time.

Self-control is a primary aspect of conscientiousness. Students who perform well in traditional academic programs usually have a pretty high level of self-control. They'll wait for the metaphoric equivalent of the two marshmallows instead of being impulsive and gobbling it right away.

Self-control is a bit different from what Angela Duckworth, a researcher at the University of Pennsylvania, calls "grit." According to Duckworth, grit is the ability to maintain effort toward goals over a long time period versus self-control, which is helpful in modulating behavior in the moment.

For instance, spending the morning working on a mind-numbingly boring presentation for work without slipping into a little YouTube reverie is due to self-control; making it through a decade of medical school and residency to become a surgeon takes grit.

Curiosity, given its impulsive, spontaneous nature, can often be in direct conflict with self-control. For instance, a medical student may hear her classmates gossiping about some mercurial professor and find that her curiosity compels her to stop studying and join in the conversation. She may lack self-control, but have grit, meaning that despite her momentary lapse in focus, she'll still go on to finish her MD.

There's little doubt in the research community that self-control has positive dividends. In fact, it's not too far out to suggest that self-control is vital for success in school, careers, and life. Controlling impulses and exerting restraint is how we manage to get through our day, work through long and difficult problems and scenarios, and achieve results. If we gave up whenever we got a little tired, we'd never get anything done.

Roy Baumeister is a psychology researcher who has contributed to the study of self-control. A fair amount of his research looks at patterns in addiction and how they relate to self-control and impulsivity. Baumeister and others have done research to overturn the outdated notion that self-esteem leads to success.

What they've discovered is that self-control is the key, especially in school. Self-esteem comes later, once you've completed the task and can rest on your laurels. To get the job done, however, self-control is necessary.

Baumeister's theory is basically that self-control is like a muscle. The more you exercise it, the stronger it gets. The stronger it is, the more you're able to exert self-control in challenging situations. However, like a muscle, it also tires, so it can wear out and become weak with overexertion.

Those of you who are able to hold off on eating the Chips Ahoy are probably also able to study for long periods of time for the bar exam, get a job as a corporate lawyer, and drive a way nicer car than the rest of us. But, just like us, if you find yourself tired at the end of the day when you've had to work with a frustrating challenge at work, and you have to get up ridiculously early the next day, you may still heed the call of the Sauvignon blanc in the fridge. Your self-control "muscles" are tired.

But things aren't quite that clear cut. For instance, let's say you're a closeted, functioning alcoholic. You make sure to drink only in private, you keep a load of Altoids in your pocket, and you are very aware of your proximity to people all day so they don't smell your breath. You hide your bottles in the neighbor's blue recycling bins.

You're practicing a high degree of self-control, even though most would put alcohol addiction under the umbrella of impulsivity. This scenario shows that while self-control is certainly a positive attribute, it can, given certain instances, be a way to reinforce detrimental behavior as well.

Which brings us to our first question: why did humans adaptively evolve both impulsivity *and* self-control? Or is self-control a psychological, rather than adaptive, behavior? What seems clear is that it's highly dependent on context.

For instance, impulsivity benefited those young and crazy vervet monkeys. But self-control also benefited my high-school friend Kathy, who went on to make a boatload more money than I ever will. If impulsivity is often a part of curiosity, then self-control would appear to be an incurious behavior.

It's not quite that simple, however; highly intellectually curious people are often conscientious, which is a trait similar to self-control. Again, determining whether self-control versus impulsivity and curiosity is either negative or positive comes down to context.

EXCUSEZ-MOI, MONSIEUR, VOS PANTALONS SONT EN FEU

Let's stick with learning French and try to shed some light on how impulsivity and self-control are not bad versus good, but depend on environment. In a traditional classroom environment, self-control is an excellent attribute: Kathy did great in French class. I didn't. But impulsivity may benefit the French learner on the streets of Paris while she's trying to figure out how to catch the train to Chartres. Making guesses, trying different words, and impulsively tossing out potential words in the hopes that their meaning is properly construed to get a point across can be, in certain circumstances, a way to learn.

In fact, research suggests that the sort of experience that language learners have abroad is conducive to learning in ways that a classroom may not be. In addition, having a healthy sense of interpersonal curiosity would naturally lead the learner to engage more with others, which is vital to learning a language in context.

Natasha Tokowicz is a researcher from the University of Pittsburgh who studies the cognitive processes involved in learners of other languages. Tokowicz has identified that it seems likely that those who study abroad—the ones who *experience* their learning firsthand—may have a higher level of perceptual curiosity versus the traditionally intellectually curious classroom denizen. They may also have a good "working memory capacity" and are often willing to attempt answers in conversation more often than their classroom counterparts. Basically, rather than not answering, or saying *je ne sais pas*, they'll give an answer a shot. Whether right or wrong, they'll make the attempt.

This is a minor difference, but an important one. And it's where we return to curiosity, after a circuitous route.

What Tokowicz's research suggests is that study abroad programs elicit effort from students. The students try to figure stuff out. I e-mailed back and forth with Tokowicz about the nature of language learning to see if there was a relationship between ambiguity, impulsivity, and learning within the context of language learning. The jury is still out on that one.

However, when language learners experience "translation ambiguity"—which is when multiple word meanings create ambiguity during the context of experience (travel)—the individuals may learn better. They may have more success, simply because they're able to activate their learning in the real world. "I'm guessing that the learner just has more chances to fill in those gaps. And strengthen existing knowledge," Tokowicz wrote to me in an e-mail.

And it seems likely that the impulsive individual on the streets, fumbling through these knowledge gaps, who's willing to gamble at some words to get directions to the subway, may in fact learn more, or at least as well as, a more traditional learner who practices self-control.

The question, then, is how can our schools reward not just students like my friend Kathy, but also the rambling, guessing, intuitive, impulsive language learners who are strolling down the Champs d'Elysee? Intellectual curiosity is a good fit for school, but what of the *perceptually* curious individual? Where does he fit into the traditional structure of school?

YOU PUT YOUR DIRT IN MY YARD

If our goal as teachers is to nurture lifelong learning in our students—to help them *learn how to learn*—then we must be honest with them, and ourselves, about what that means. Learning isn't about refining organizational schema and neatly cataloging skills and information, but rather embracing disorder and recognizing (even celebrating) failure, ambiguity, and doubt.

In reality, to be a true learner is to disavow the central tenet of education: that learning is a unidirectional transaction that will result in ever spiraling levels of acceptance into AP classes, then college, and ultimately delivering the holy grail of gainful employment. The learning our students do is often described in terms of material or social reward; rarely do we talk about the disordered process of internal evolution.

When we usually talk about learning, there is a finish line of pomp and circumstance and quantitative reward. But when we're addressing this path, what we're really talking about is school, not learning. While related and overlapping, they aren't the same thing. School is an institutionalized progression determined by age, economics, and at times, skill and knowledge. It is neatly divided and demarked. While learning can and does happen in school, it doesn't have to. School marches students along a predetermined course.

It would be nice if learning had that kind of neat, linear path, but it doesn't. Learning is messy, multidirectional, ambiguous, and malleable. It's driven by curiosity, even defined by it, which makes it a transient, intense, and impulsive experience.

To be a lifelong learner means not just learning new skills—deciding at the age of forty to learn Anglo-Saxon or take up volleyball with zeal—but also revisiting old assumptions and altering them. It's recognizing that some ambitious intellectual projects will never be finished, and that there are some things that you'll know only a little bit about, and that some of what you know will be utterly useless and impractical.

This can be a terribly unsatisfying state, and one that doesn't translate well to catchy slogans or neat marketing copy. This isn't to say learning can't be fun—it often is and should be—but it also acknowledges the work involved in understanding the world and our needs in a more complex framework.

Being a lifelong learner is like living in a house that is constantly being remodeled. Some people can't deal with the mess and clutter and "unfinishedness" of the place. Most of us want to live in a perfectly finished home, wainscoting and plumbing all up to par. Curiosity doesn't work well in this scenario, as we can be temporarily curious about one thing, then disregard it in favor of something else.

Lifelong learning is often described as this grand arc of constant achievement and advancement. But the reality of learning is far more quotidian, and it rarely feels like the clouds are opening and the angels are singing. Learning can feel like the scene in *Cool Hand Luke* where Luke (played by Paul Newman) is forced by a sadistic prison guard to dig a deep hole, only to have the guard tell him upon completion, "You put your dirt in my yard." Luke shovels it back in and then digs the dirt out again and again, Sisyphus-like, until exhaustion overtakes him.

Learning can be like that, defined by obstinacy and perseverance even in futility. The interesting part of that analogy, of course, is that Luke is having a unique sort of fun the whole time. Pulling a fast one on the guards, he convincingly acts the part of the submissive prisoner while gleefully planning his next escape. Sounds like some students I've taught.

This sort of work, which is its own reward, is important, but must be buttressed by adventure and excitement. Otherwise, it becomes a drag. The kind of arduous labor we ask students to perform to develop skills and informational acuity is most helpful when we place them within the larger contextual narrative of an adventure, or more appropriately, the type of journeys—both real and imagined—mentioned earlier.

IDEA FORAGERS

Remember Kurt Hahn, founder of the experiential outdoor education program Outward Bound? Hahn was a German Jew who grew up in the early part of the 20th century under the oppressive cloud of fascism in Germany. Hahn spoke out against Hitler and eventually had to flee the country.

Hahn would go on to found Outward Bound, the experiential outdoor program that was founded on the principle that when people are pushed beyond their comfort zones, they are able to access reserves of strength, courage, and compassion that had previously been untapped. Outward Bound would go on to become a pioneer in the latter half of the 20th century, developing programs across the world and taking adults and youths on adventures like mountaineering, white-water rafting, kayaking, sailing, and rock-climbing.

One of the threads that ran through Hahn's philosophy was the acceptance of difficulty and boredom. To climb the mountain and experience the exhilaration of the summit, we must first slog for days. It's boring and hard, and yet it is simply a chapter in a longer narrative of adventure. For Cool Hand Luke, the adventurous narrative was one of fighting against oppression, and he was willing to do the ugly work of mindless acquiescence because secretly it served a greater purpose.

With students, it pays to be more transparent. Let them know that the summit is within reach if only they are willing to trudge a few steps more. Learning is also more about fear than accomplishment, and while based in the vitiating thrill of adventuring into the unknown, it can be a frustrating experience.

A few summers ago my son learned how to ride a bike. As he wobbled about, he discovered he could do it, but he got tense and anxious. He was fearful of falling. He was fearful of *failing*, and when he inevitably did fall, he got upset at me, himself, the bike, and the world.

This process of learning wasn't what I'd call fun, though it's clear now that he loves the fact that he can ride a bike. He loves the *idea* of riding it. It's the act of doing it, or more precisely, of learning to do it, that he found scary. However, the eventual goal—to go rocketing down the sidewalk with his friends, wheels spinning, wind in his face—is fun incarnate.

It is similar to how I feel, as a teacher, whenever I compel myself to read dense theory. I'm out of my depth in the twisting labyrinth of postmodern texts. I find reading these books to be intensely un-enjoyable, yet later, upon reflection, I like that I have read them. There is a sense, not of accomplishment necessarily, but of relief and giddy escape, like I just outran a swarm of hornets.

The fun part comes in relating the story later. There is an element of fun when I am in conversation, or reading something else, or having an experience, and some piece of what I read pops into my head, and my understanding gains another notch.

This is the truth of learning that we don't usually embrace in education. Students read assignments, do projects, write papers, and earn grades. They don't have to exist in the limbo of not knowing or almost-knowing. It's a cafeteria conveyor belt education, whereas real lifelong learning is more like hunting and gathering; sometimes you kill the mammoth, but most of the time you're scrounging to fill your belly and trying not to get eaten by saber-toothed tigers. You're in a state of hopeful attentiveness and cautious curiosity.

I've read *Pilgrim at Tinker Creek* by Annie Dillard twice and still have no clear idea what 80 percent of the book is about. It's the same with William Gass's novel, *The Tunnel*. Reading ambitious, challenging literature is a good way to get comfortable with being lost. That "lostness" is a lot like the ambiguous state that often precedes curiosity.

You read a book like *The Tunnel* and you wander around for weeks, months, maybe years afterward, wondering what it was about. You seek answers and find only more questions, and eventually begin to realize that complexity and perspective, personal associations and internal connections, matter just as much as codified interpretation. But that makes you wonder about the objective truth of anything, which just sets the whole uneasy wheel of doubt spinning again. You are like Dante, wandering around in the woods, looking for help.

In an essay in the *New York Times*, Phillip Lopate digs into the role doubt plays in his life as an essayist and our discomfort in admitting doubt through the door in education:

> According to Theodor Adorno, the iron law of the essay is heresy. What is heresy if not the expression of contrarian doubt about communal pieties or orthodox positions? This is sometimes called "critical thinking," an ostensible goal of education in a democracy. But since

such thinking often rocks the boat, we may find it less than supported in school settings.

My own official title is Assistant Professor of Rhetoric, and one of the functions of my job is to teach students how to construct an argument. Of course, any argument is founded on the principle that the person writing the position has qualified that there is a right and a wrong answer—that things are black and white. At least, that's the basic idea of arguments, this side versus that. That idea doesn't sit well with Lopate, who writes:

> Argumentation is a good skill to have, but the real argument should be with oneself. Especially when it comes to the development of young writers, it is crucial to nudge them past that self-righteous inveighing, that shrill, defensive one-track that is deadly for personal essays or memoirs, and encourage a more polyphonic, playful approach.

The use of the word "playful" is important here: writing can be fun too. Indeed, most disciplines—science, math, history—all share that kinetic potential for joy. Accepting that learning is an end in and of itself is the key to becoming a lifelong learner.

To live in that fearful state of darkness, of hard work and ambivalence, is to embrace learning in its truest form. The rewards may be vague or even nonexistent. It is the search for understanding itself that is the payoff. As the poet Rainer Maria Rilke once wrote:

> I beg you, to have patience with everything unresolved in your heart and to try to love the questions themselves as if they were locked rooms or books written in a very foreign language. Don't search for the answers, which could not be given to you now, because you would not be able to live them. And the point is to live everything. Live the questions now. Perhaps then, someday far in the future, you will gradually, without even noticing it, live your way into the answer.

LEARNING TO FLY

Without the incendiary spark of curiosity, learning falls flat and becomes something that students *have* to do rather than what they're compelled, through passionate inquiry, to do because they *want* to. We rob students (even the youngest of them) of their agency when we define what is to be known and what content should drive learning. We are telling them that their discovering isn't valid, that their knowledge is ancillary to the more codified information we present. No wonder they get their backs up.

Learning in its contemporary, goal-driven guise doesn't allow room for complexity, for multiple answers. Imagine a test where there isn't just one correct answer for a question, but multiple ones. Introducing this idea of a complex, often contradictory world runs counter to our market-driven education where subtlety and nuance are replaced with data and assessment.

The 19th-century Swiss historian Jacob Burckhardt thought that the 20th century would be the great age of oversimplification—analysis rather than contemplation would bring about a black-and-white, rather than polychromatic, world. "The essence of tyranny would be the denial of complexity," he wrote.

Not only that, but learning is about embracing ambiguity. It's about not knowing what will happen, but wanting to know. Memorizing and cataloguing information has its place, but it usurps a hard-to-define, but vitally important, scenario—when students are forced to enter into the unknown and do so deliriously and bravely.

In my weaker moments as a parent, when the weather is too awful to go outside and I've run out of ideas, I sometimes watch nature videos with my son. We watched one that focused on a nesting pair of eagles and their young, and what captivated me was the way the young eagles learned to fly. While the parents were away hunting, the young eaglets would flop and flap around the nest. Eventually, the first one took a leap of faith. No parents around, no safety net—the eagle launched from the nest and flew.

Here's where I became riveted: when the second young eagle tried it, it fell. All the way down to land in a feathered heap on the ground. The video delivered the requisite drama—would the eagle survive down there? What would happen?

Eventually the young eagle regains the nest. But it was that moment of uncertainty that really galvanized my own interest. A step to the edge and a leap. Learning to fly isn't easy even for the best flyers out there. And once they learn to fly, it isn't long before they fly away from their parents, off on a journey of their own.

So if learning is a journey, undertaken by each person on her own, but supported through mentors, how can we practically maximize students' exposure to conditions where learning occurs?

The answer lies in two places, one metaphoric, the other concrete. Lessons, if we must call them that, should be driven by student interest, and facts, figures, and required content eschewed in favor of the hunt for ideas that have been imbued with the light of curiosity by the student. The easiest way to do this is to get students out of the classroom and into the world. Nothing forms our intellect more than the experiences we have.

In the book *Buddha's Brain: The Practical Neuroscience of Happiness, Love, & Wisdom*, Rick Hanson writes, "Much as your body is built from the foods you eat, your mind is built from the experiences you have. The flow of experience gradually sculpts your brain, thus shaping your mind."

Experiences can come in many forms—adventures in far-off lands, the challenge of reading a long Victorian novel, or re-grouting the bathroom tile. What is clear is that what we do with ourselves, how we project ourselves into the world, determines how deeply we're able to explore the terrain of our own imaginations. Larry Alferink, the psychologist mentioned earlier, noted in an article for which he was interviewed in *Popular Science*, "The wiring of the brain depends upon the experiences we have."

After Hahn had fled Germany in 1933, he settled on the storm-beaten coast of Moray in the north of Scotland. Hahn had tried to turn Germany's youth against the growing threat of Nazism and failed. In fact, he'd been jailed for a time because of his antifascist activities.

There, on the coast of Scotland, Hahn felt depleted and exhausted. He hung around the docks and wandered the coast. He met a fisherman named Danny Main, who told him stories of sailors who'd survived terrible storms, shipwrecks, and weeks adrift in lifeboats. Hahn began to notice a common theme—while older and not as physically strong as younger sailors, it was the more experienced men who survived.

Despite the advanced technology of the newer generation of seamen and without the same highly programmatic training that the newer sailors had received, the older sailors were able to draw on knowledge and experience to problem solve and survive in conditions that claimed others' lives. The key, Hahn felt, was learning through experience.

And the best kinds of experiences, as we all know, are those fueled by curiosity.

YOU GOTTA FEEL GOOD TO LEARN GOOD

As I write these words, it's winter in Vermont. It's cold today, just a few degrees above zero, and we've had pretty decent snow. This was the first year I took my son, Finn, alpine skiing.

We went to a little downhill area about thirty minutes away a few weeks ago. I signed him up for a lesson, and Finn dutifully spent the morning listening to instruction, wearing the brightly colored "ski school" bib, and doing his best to earn the hot chocolate they give kids at the end of the two-hour lesson.

When I picked him up, the instructors said Finn wasn't ready to hit the slopes quite yet. They'd kept him on the bunny slope, and he hadn't even worked up to riding the rope tow. He'd definitely need more lessons before he was ready to take the chairlift and ski, they said.

Finn wasn't into it. He said he didn't like skiing, but I wasn't sure what to believe. Finn, like his mother and me, doesn't like structure. The second someone tells us to line up, we step out of line.

As we sat together in the lodge eating lunch, I watched my son as he thoughtfully chewed a peanut butter and jelly sandwich. He's always been an observer who carefully looks at people and watches scenes unfold. He was looking out the window that faced the big chairlifts to the top of the mountain. He was watching people come slicing down the trails, snow glistening in the trees.

Finn was curious about skiing, and deeply so. His whole body seemed to be taking in the scene. The thought of shooting down the hill, wind in his face, zooming down the wide, snowy trails—it was right up his alley. The sort of thing he loved.

I didn't need to say anything. He just started asking questions.

"What if you fall?"

"How long does it take to ride the chair to the top?"

"Why can't I use ski poles?"

"How fast can you go?"

"How do you stop?"

He was bursting with curiosity. Finally, I casually mentioned that I'd be happy to take him up the big chairlift if he wanted to try a run. Granted, the kid had yet to *actually ski*. He'd only stomped around the base of the kiddie slope. Finn looked me right in the face, smiling. "Yeah, I want to."

I won't lie, it wasn't pretty, our first run or two. He was scared and stiff, and I had to ski holding on to him the whole time. There were wipeouts and tears. Luckily, I grew up skiing and have taken many, many kids skiing for the first time, so I knew how to get him down the mountain safely. Basically, I tried to give him as few pointers as possible and let him figure it out. And he did.

By the end of the day, we had ridden the biggest chair to the very top of the mountain and skied down. Finn had a blast. He was exhausted, exhilarated, and hooked. A few days later we went again, this time with a family whose kids had been skiing for years. Finn did his darndest to keep up, and he did.

One of the preeminent researchers on curiosity is Todd Kashdan, mentioned previously. Kashdan—a well-known TEDx speaker, author, and researcher at George Mason University—approaches his study of curiosity as a means to well-being. In his book, *Curious? Discover the Missing Ingredient to a Fulfilling Life*, Kashdan lays out the following trajectory for how curiosity can lead to fulfillment and happiness:

> By being curious, we explore.
> By exploring, we discover.
> When this is satisfying, we are more likely to repeat it.
> By repeating it, we develop competence and mastery.
> By developing competence and mastery, our knowledge and skills grow.

This is exactly what my son experienced on that snowy mountainside. His pride in being able to keep up with his friends is so fundamental to a kid's sense of self that he quite literally beams when he skis now.

In many ways this may seem to resemble how school is supposed to work. We introduce concepts or skills, let's say long division, and we practice and practice until we get it right. We feel good that we've gained this competence, and that boosts our self-esteem. Seems like the same continuum.

Only not so much. Finn came to the place where he wanted to get back out there *himself*. I created the space and the time for him to *want* to explore the slopes. It was his autonomy that led to it. All he wanted to do was keep up with his friends, so I let him establish what competence and mastery looked like. Finn doesn't care what his technique is like or what he looks like; he just wants to *have fun*.

Kashdan's equation works only if we have the time and space to explore, spurred by curiosity. With the onus of expectation—the inertia of criteria and rules and the deadly standardization of experience—this amazing learning experience wouldn't happen. It didn't happen in the ski class with the other kids. Finn had to get there on his own.

This isn't to say that ski school is a bad thing, or that lessons don't work, or that any structure is the coup de grâce of learning. But it's a helpful story for us to see how curiosity can be a vital tool that leads to *experience* that leads to learning. It's helpful to remember that learning can work this way, too, if we're willing to let go just a little bit.

If learning blooms from experience, then fostering curiosity—letting it bubble and ferment until it's ready—is key.

TWELVE

Curious Failures

HUNGER FOR EXPLORATION

How curiosity affects school performance is not as simple a question as it might seem. Due to the various types of curiosity such as epistemic, perceptual, sensory, and interpersonal—and the various factors that contribute to them—a picture of how curiosity affects different students is essential to understanding how it can be used positively in schools.

Sophie von Stumm is a researcher at Goldsmiths University of London whose work on curiosity and its relation to school performance uncovers some interesting facets of curiosity and how it can predict academic performance.

Once my math-belabored brain had figured out how to calculate the time difference between Vermont and London, I gave von Stumm a call. A good chunk of her research has been about defining what it is, actually, that makes us intelligent.

In general, the IQ test has been the most widely accepted metric to measure intelligence. But it has been criticized for measuring only a certain type of intelligence, and students' aptitudes and abilities may not be accurately represented by their scores on the IQ test. Intelligence is not just knowing what bubbles to fill in. Von Stumm believes that it may be a bit more nuanced than that.

In her research, von Stumm establishes that curiosity can be broken into a few categories, each with its own relationship with learning and school performance.

First, von Stumm explained to me that there are three basic categories of curiosity: intellectual, perceptual, and social (remember, in the research, the term *social* is often used interchangeably with *interpersonal*). These line up pretty well with what Litman taught us—intellectual curiosity is more on the D-type side of the scale, whereas perceptual would more often be aligned with I-types of curiosity.

Von Stumm's research explains what we would expect—that intellectual curiosity is a marker of academic success. Other factors, like intelligence and conscientiousness, also play equal roles. But that "hunger for exploration," as von Stumm puts it, is as vital a piece of the puzzle as to how smart a student is or how likely she is to remember to bring her trigonometry book home and crack it open at night to finish assignments.

Revisiting intellectual curiosity at this point will help us see how differing types of curiosity mesh (or don't) with school.

GETTING SCHOOLED

Intellectual curiosity is exactly what it sounds like. It's the drive to know more, to pour through the book you're reading to get at some nugget of information that will connect with other pieces of information. Typically, it's a trait that pays dividends in school. How do quadrilateral equations work? What was the Magna Carta? What's a blastula? These are all questions that spur the intellectually curious individual to find answers, make connections.

Of course, the intellectually curious person can then start spinning off in new directions as well, dealing with complicated questions like who is the more postmodern American dance choreographer—Alvin Ailey or Mark Morris?

Then there's perceptual curiosity, which fits more comfortably within the I-type category. With perceptual curiosity, there is often the prerequisite of boredom. "It's the tendency to explore things with your senses," von Stumm said.

You know the perceptually curious student or child if you've seen her. You stand there patiently explaining the fascinating intricacies of percentages to fractions pre-algebraic equations, and she's toying with some blocks or bits she's grabbed from around the room, looking out the window. The perceptually curious person is the one you want to travel with—he'll get the most out of the bazaar in Marrakesh, fingering the rugs, trying on shoes, gobbling food from market stalls, and listening to the muezzin call people in to pray on the loudspeakers. Conversely, the intellectually curious person may have her head buried in a map or be scrolling on her smartphone looking for the best way to say, "Where's the bathroom?" in Arabic.

Which, as we've established, brings us to the *socially* curious person, the social butterfly who also (usually) rates highly on what has been categorized as "emotional intelligence." This is an individual who's interested in other people. Not necessarily extroverted, but someone for whom relationships and people represent a world of stimuli he's curious to discover. You don't find many narcissists in this category, and this type of curiosity may or may not line up with I-type or D-type necessarily.

Of course, we almost all have some combination of these traits in varying strengths. It'd be pretty unusual to find someone who is all one way or the other. In academia, you meet more than a few folks who definitely have the intellectual curiosity part down, but score pretty low marks on social curiosity, as they're tucked away in their labs and offices, more comfortable with facts, figures, and experiments than with grabbing a pint with friends. But then there are the gregarious, outgoing types as well, happy to chat with students and colleagues as they bounce around campus.

To be sure, if we examine our own lives we can see which of these types of curiosity feed into our behaviors and affect how we navigate the world and our degree of success personally, socially, professionally, and academically.

Von Stumm defines perceptual curiosity as "purpose-free" and intellectual curiosity as "related to achievement," which fits pretty well with what we understand so far. This also correlates to Litman's scale of I-type versus D-type, respectively. What von Stumm was interested in was how these traits may determine success in school. What I am interested in is how school values and encourages those traits.

The important note here is this: traditional school really favors and rewards only *intellectual* curiosity. In fact, both perceptual and social curiosity can result in behaviors that are seen as detrimental to learning, when in fact they are simply different ways of learning.

The socially curious student wants to chat with friends. The perceptually curious student just wants to play in the woods next to the playground. As we know, there are other types as well, such as sensory curiosity. For the sensory curiosity seeker, sitting in a classroom may be a torturous experience, like some kind of sensory deprivation experiment. (It's hard to find thrills sitting in a chair.) These other types of curiosity don't receive the same support and encouragement as intellectual curiosity.

I asked von Stumm her thoughts about compulsory schooling potentially being at odds with fostering curiosity—either intellectual or perceptual. She responded that the correlation between success in school and intellectual curiosity was clear: the more curious a person is, the more likely she is to do well in school.

I ventured the idea that compulsory schooling (and I was painting with a broad brush here) and the way it's structured doesn't *actually* nurture curiosity, but awards it as a default by nurturing acquiescence to policy and conscientiousness. Von Stumm responded, "That is an absolute possibility."

Her work, which has dealt in part with reviewing research of a similar ilk to come to some of these large-scale conclusions about curiosity, has pointed to some interesting connections. Because school is a place where adherence to schedule, routine, and promptness is at a premium, it may not be conducive to fostering curiosity. This isn't to say that schools in Western Europe, the United States, and many Asian countries aren't places where curiosity can take hold and fire the imagination and learning of students. That happens, all the time.

It is suggestive, however, that the structure of compulsory schooling—the tests, the quasi-factory settings, the way expectations are framed from a transactional perspective rather than from an epistemic one—may not be the best environment to spur creative, innovative, and curious habits of mind for as many students as possible.

After all, the Forster Act in England in 1870 and the similar efforts of Horace Mann in the mid-19th century in the United States created the basis for our contemporary compulsory school system. But for all its virtues, and there are many, one of the common complaints was that the system adopted was similar in many ways to the factory models of the Industrial Revolution. After all, if you're providing free education for as many children as possible with limited funds, the best model to turn to is industry, where we attempt to create the greatest number of goods at the lowest cost possible.

Basically, train kids to sit still and learn, dammit.

We've come millions of miles from this blueprint, of course. Schools are often places of dynamic, exciting learning. But old ghosts are hard to kill, and much of our educational systems are still derived from the idea that all students will learn the same stuff in the same way.

While we move toward more personalized education models and get away from what is clearly not a friendly approach to individual learners, questions about qualities such as curiosity become more and more pertinent. Although intelligence and conscientiousness still reign supreme in the common understanding of how schools and students and learning work, there is a growing body of evidence by folks like von Stumm that points to more contextualized and nuanced approaches to understanding learning.

One of the biggest challenges in education is that it's set up to measure only intelligence and how dutiful a student is to her studies. It isn't gauged to measure curiosity per se, though intellectual curiosity can be a useful tool for a student.

The problem with including personality types and traits in the continuum of determining how "smart" someone is, is that people are messy, complicated creatures living in a complex, rapidly changing world. Many folks in education, psychological research, and policy may not want to open Pandora's box and include personality traits in discussing student achievement. Personality is "much more difficult to assess," von Stumm said. But, she added, "IQ shouldn't be everything."

Von Stumm's work got me thinking about whether schools even bother to teach curiosity. While many schools highlight curiosity as an eventual outcome of their pedagogy, and curiosity is clearly a trait desirous in a student, it's not necessarily implicit in how traditional schools are structured.

Much of schooling is designed to produce citizens who are capable of making rational decisions, voting, and being productive members of society. Or schools within the public sector are very clear that the education they offer is designed to train workers for the economy. Neither of those systems—a rational citizenry-based approach and system for training employees—has much to do with curiosity.

As we chatted, I became interested in von Stumm's own experience as a learner. My social curiosity got the better of me, and I wondered why this clearly successful researcher in her field was so interested in other qualities that led to learning besides the good ol' books and brains approaches.

Von Stumm was the winner of the Excellence in Research Award from the Mensa Education and Research Foundation, and she received The International Society for the Study of Individual Differences Early Career Award. When I asked how she came to research intelligence and cognition from the perspective she did, she told me that she had found that researchers who studied intelligence fell into two categories: those who felt they were very intelligent and were, in a way, furthering that agenda by publicly reinforcing that claim through research and those who were interested in the very idea of smartness.

While she didn't cop to which category she fell into, I was pretty sure von Stumm had dismissed with ego a long time ago and was simply pursuing curiosity out of, well, *curiosity*. And clearly reaping the unsought, but surely appreciated, rewards. I didn't ask her where she felt she fell on the spectrum of I-type or D-type, but I have a hunch she experiences curiosity for its own sake and that the ambiguity of knowledge seeking is what motivates her.

AND YOUR LITTLE DOG, TOO!

I've always lived comfortably in the realm of ambiguity. I don't claim to have an understanding of any of the "big" questions: what's at the end of the universe, do humans have a purpose, or how many deductions I'm supposed to claim on my taxes. But I know that ambiguity—the state of not really knowing, or having multiple meanings—is a fundamental part of learning and may be both a precursor to, and result of, curiosity.

Socrates was no stranger to either ambiguity or curiosity. In *The Apology*, Plato's famous account of Socrates defending himself in 399 BCE on charges that he was corrupting the youth of the city, Socrates embraces ambiguity as the true starting point in the quest for knowledge. "It is only too likely that neither of us has any knowledge to boast of; but he thinks he knows something which he does not know, whereas I am conscious of my ignorance. At any rate it seems that I am wiser than he is to this small extent, that I do not think that I know what I do not know." Socrates, at least, knew that not knowing stuff was an important step in knowledge and that curiosity is a fundamental attribute of the learner.

I'm not Socrates, nor am I Einstein, but he too lived comfortably in the realm of the ambiguous. In the biography written by Walter Isaacson, *Einstein*, the author writes of the frizzy-haired genius: "He retained the ability to hold two thoughts in his mind simultaneously, to be puzzled when they conflicted, and to marvel when he could smell an underlying unity."

Ambiguity is closely connected to curiosity. It's in an ambiguous state—not knowing vital information or entertaining a multiplicity of possibilities—where curiosity often takes root. There's a rich tradition of ambiguity in literature and art. Perhaps the most helpful example is from Michel de Montaigne.

Montaigne, 16th-century essayist and a curious person if ever there was one, started his *Essais* with the statement "What do I know?" This experience of ambiguity, and trying to either solve it or make sense of it, can be the birthplace of curiosity.

In a collection of essays titled *Ambiguity in the Western Mind*, John D. Caputo, a Villanova professor, writes, "What could be clearer than that our lives are ambiguous—deeply, provocatively, dangerously, beautifully ambiguous? I am not complaining, for ambiguity is a gift that gives life its interest, its mystery, its passion."

When I was a kid, I watched the famous film version of Frank Baum's masterpiece, *The Wizard of Oz*. Watching Dorothy's adventures in Oz was a mixed bag. While much of the film seemed unbearably hokey even then, there were parts that were deeply scary as well. The flying monkeys in particular I found unnerving, the same with the Wicked Witch's sheer malevolence. I've seen the movie many times since then. Every time I'm struck by *The Wizard of Oz*'s denouement, which I found to be one of the most wholly unsatisfying endings in the history of cinema, and also one of the best.

As Dorothy, the Tin Man, the Scarecrow, and the Cowardly Lion enter the city of Oz to beg the Wizard for passage home—a heart, a brain, and courage, respectively—the quad is in for a shock. Dorothy's little sooty terrier, Toto, pulls aside a curtain to reveal the "great and mighty Oz" as nothing more than a carnival showman, pulling levers on a smoke machine and making a racket. He's a huckster, not a wizard.

The tension in *The Wizard of Oz* exists in two spheres. One is the adventure of Dorothy, going head to head with the Wicked Witch as she tries to return to Kansas. But another large part of the draw of the film is the ambiguity of the Wizard: who is he? Satan or saint, savior or saboteur? Throughout the movie, my curiosity was intense. I wanted desperately to know what the Wizard looked like, what his powers were. Was he evil or good? My brain was stuffed with imaginings. I was hungry to know who, in fact, the great and mighty Oz really was. I wanted the mystery solved.

And then I didn't. Once I found out who Oz really was—a carny barker whose balloon took him off course and landed him in Oz, where he'd been duping the green citizens ever since with cheap tricks—I was crestfallen. As a kid with a wild imagination, the reality of Oz couldn't compete with the Oz I had fabricated in my head.

This is the lure of ambiguity and the reason for its sweetness. To study the mystery and magic of God is to create a world of inquiry and epic adventures; to know God is boring.

IGNORANCE IS BLISS

All of the Big Questions in life have an innate ambiguity. Is there life after death? What's at the end of the universe? Do our lives have purpose? What exactly was the Awesome Blossom they served at Chili's restaurant? All of these questions are slippery slopes, slicked with ambiguity. Ambiguity denotes multiple meanings or lack of understanding, and it can feed and nurture us. It can compel us to action and inquiry. It's fuel for our heads. Some find ambiguity confusing, even a bit scary.

Ambiguity can be the precursor of curiosity. Not knowing information can lead us onward, either through the pages of a book, the stacks of a library, or deeper into our own imaginative landscape. But as von Stumm noted, school may not offer the kind of space needed to allow for the fruits of ambiguity to thrive.

According to traditional education—and the way we present information as chunks of data to be memorized or consumed—ambiguity is seen as a fleeting, brief episode to be cured as soon as possible. In fact, patently not knowing the answer or how to find it is seen as the antithesis of schooling and learning. Curiosity can often take root in such moments when we're left to our own devices and must deal with the ambiguity.

Our brains invent scenarios, get speculative, and investigate options when we're left in the realm of ambiguity in ways that don't always occur in traditional academic settings. In fact, one of the things teachers often try to do is present lessons in "bite-size" chunks so that students never have to wrestle with big questions that have murky answers. But within that murkiness (ambiguity) we can use curiosity to develop potential answers or solutions.

Within the classroom experience, this is easier said than done. Creating experiences mired in ambiguity can feel like a waste of time. But the connection is vital to the learning process, and schools that embrace alternatives to traditional "drill and kill" methods such as inquiry method pedagogy, place-based education, and experiential learning are making great strides in imbuing learning with the richness of ambiguity.

While schools may not necessarily provide this particular experience all that often, many of us do experience this sense of being unsure, being left in the shadows. Some of us actually live there, in a state of multiple options, realities, and murky boundaries. Theoretical physicists, deep sea explorers, artists, priests, philosophers, and kids—one thing they all share is the lack of certainty—there are no absolutes. This paucity of surety can be a lure and an invigorating gambit for some, torture for others. Depends on circumstances and stakes.

Which is why, even as a kid, I was sort of bummed at the end of *Wizard of Oz*. My heightened ambiguity had been of a pleasurable kind, and the truth of the Wizard's identity was a bit of a disappointment. Curiosity researcher George Loewenstein has noted that this is often the case; when we finally satisfy our curiosity, it's often not all that great. The not-knowingness was what was palpably exciting. Reality is a letdown compared with imagination.

When I was in graduate school, I was lucky enough to have Wyatt Mason as a writing mentor. Mason—translator, book critic, essayist, and all-around good egg—offered our little group of aspiring writers an interesting piece of advice one day during a workshop. He suggested we think about ending essays with what he called "aperture." An aperture is the opening in the lens of a camera that lets in light, and adjusting it determines how much exposure to light a photograph has.

Basically, Mason told us, trying to answer questions in creative nonfiction was a rather skewed enterprise; better to go after bigger fish in deeper waters, even if that means coming home empty-handed. As a writer of nonfiction, I found this to be both energizing and exciting as well as a liberation and relief.

One of the concerns I'd always had was that I didn't really know anything. I wasn't an expert or scholar in any particular discipline, had never done anything all that noteworthy, so what was I doing writing nonfiction? I'd never sashayed through the crowded markets of Kathmandu, never piloted an outrigger canoe through turquoise South Pacific waters. I'd never studied anything, really, never researched some topic until a certain level of expertise manifested itself. I was somewhat at a loss of what to write about.

What Mason pointed at with his description of aperture was, I think, ambiguity. Not that we shouldn't quest for truth and answers in our writing (we should), but accepting ambiguity as a reality was a means to open up our writing and thinking to other worlds and possibilities. The point was not to answer questions; the point was to ask more interesting ones.

So even though ambiguity and her twin, ignorance, had ruled much of my fate as a learner, I learned to embrace that state. I came to see it differently.

The problem with all this, however, is that it directly contradicts much of what psychologists and scientists have determined about ambiguity. Research into the psychological underpinnings of ambiguity has categorized a "deprivation" of information—or what our old buddy Loewenstein termed a "knowledge gap"—as a source of discomfort. Rather than ambiguity being a heady state, it's a condition that gives rise to uncertainty and dislike. We don't like not knowing what's in the box. Or do we?

NOT ALL WHO WONDER ARE LOST

Wonder is almost the default state for children—so much is pleasantly unexplained, wondrous, and full of marvel.

Wonder is in short supply in schools. Finn's teacher, like lots of great kindergarten teachers, no doubt, teaches students to at least be aware of what they're curious about. But how much of how our schools function—within the constraints imposed by either local or federal curriculum mandates such as Common Core—is a way to optimize wonder?

Schools are equipped to teach to the curriculum, which means they are not staffed or provided with resources to respond to the wonder a child may have, for example, about Scandinavian folklore. Let's say a student gets fascinated by the invisible creatures that inhabited pre-Christian Sweden and Norway (little invisible *nisse* and *vittra*, and lumpen *trolls* and terrifying, cow-tailed *huldra*) and is filled with wonder at the stories of these mysterious, supernatural creatures. How deep will their wonder take them? How well are schools designed to truly support their wonder?

Not well at all, I'm afraid. Schools are built around common knowledge and standardized skills, not unique passions and idiosyncratic learning. How could a teacher handle a class of thirty students interested in NASCAR, pro wrestling, the Everglades, Rapunzel, robotics, and astronomy?

The problem with answering this question is that we're locked into the preconceived notion of established curriculum. We think of a classroom where the pursuit of knowledge based on individual wonder is in *competition* with other disciplines and expectations. And, of course, true to form, this would be difficult; when students are forced against their will to learn standardized information to boost test scores, there is a race to the top that leaves wonder, curiosity, and independent thinking in the dust.

But what if we just ditched the bubble tests, threw out federally mandated curricula? This gives even me, a guerrilla educator at heart, a wee bit of the frothing shimmy shams. I mean, wouldn't schools be chaotic? Wouldn't they be forums of the apocalypse, children rending and tearing the very school down to its foundation? How would anyone learn anything?

The problem with this set of fears is that it removes any agency, at all, from the children themselves. As we've seen, kids are naturally primed for knowledge seeking. Curiosity, in its most basic Loewenstein incarnation, is a fundamental drive to close knowledge gaps and reduce uncertainty. It seems by the evidence that it's central to our experience as humans. If not hardwired, then it's at least close to essential as a means of navigating the world with any degree of success.

However, kids left to their own devices—given time outside, access to mentors who are intelligent and thoughtful and able to guide and support their interests—*will* learn. Of course, one of the arguments that could readily be used is that left to their own devices, kids would literally be left to the devices—they'd be playing Mario Kart until their eyeballs exploded. Just like parents would be negligent to allow their children to pick any food they wanted, anytime they wanted it, there would need to be a setting that was conducive to learning, one without an excess of technology that actually impedes creativity.

One of the most persistent obstacles to wonder is distraction. The most fertile ground for wonder (and curiosity, really) is unobstructed stretches of time without interference from the attention-grabbing influence of pixels. My son, for instance, ratchets up his most rapid-fire question sessions when we're in the car, driving somewhere. We don't use an iPad or portable DVD player in the car. My wife and I are firm believers that the unrelieved, unrelenting boredom of a brutal six-hour drive is an experience that all kids need to have.

During these drives, I can almost hear Finn's brain pinging about, from subject to subject. "How big was Titanoboa? Why does Batman wear a cape? Could army ants eat me?" The questions come fast and furious, and in my less glorious moments, I'll respond with a gruff: "I don't know Finn, Daddy's driving."

Later of course, I castigate myself for being so stupid. He was in the thrall of wonder, or experiencing the precursor of curiosity, and I was worried about getting to wherever we were going. Had he been staring with the classic opiated, slack-jawed kid-watching-a-movie expression at the screen, all that wonder would've been replaced by passivity.

All this leads to the question: what is learning, exactly? We all think we know, but capturing some sense of how learning works—it's time frame, persistence, transformative power and importance—is no easy task. But one thing seems clear. Learning and curiosity go hand in hand. And the moments when I stop learning what I'm supposed to and zone out often seem the most fertile fields for imagination.

THIRTEEN

Stop Daydreaming and Get Creative

The Obama administration has an entire section of its Whitehouse.gov website dedicated to innovation. In fact, Obama has a group of policies and plans called the "Strategy for American Innovation." The goal of these strategies is to ensure American competitiveness in the global economy. On January 25, 2011, Obama offered up his administration's vision of how America could succeed in this mission:

> The first step in winning the future is encouraging American innovation. None of us can predict with certainty what the next big industry will be or where the new jobs will come from. Thirty years ago, we couldn't know that something called the Internet would lead to an economic revolution. What we can do—what America does better than anyone else—is spark the creativity and imagination of our people.

The plan calls for increased attention paid to education, particularly in science, technology, engineering, and math (STEM). In the executive summary of the report, it states that the overriding goal of federal policy in regard to education is to ensure that K–12 schools are "graduating every student from high school ready for college and a career."

The way our government intends to achieve this goal is through funding ed tech. They've even created an entire department known as the Advanced Research Projects Agency—Education. This agency will "support research on breakthrough technologies to enhance learning." There's another link here between the public and private sector.

Part of the plan for innovation includes a group called Change the Equation, which is a coalition of entities—businesses, primarily. Change the Equation's board of trustees is sprinkled with CEOs from some of the largest companies in the world: Xerox, Intel, Accenture, DuPont, and Time Warner.

Some of this stuff is really progressive. For instance, it explicitly states that part of the strategy is to get more girls involved in STEM careers, where they have traditionally been woefully underrepresented. But there's no doubt that the relationship between corporate profits and the way education works in our country is beyond casual—it's practically matrimonial.

But the question lingers: how do you help people learn to be innovative? The plan doesn't offer up ideas for how to create the next Steve Jobs or iWoz, for example. What the strategy calls for is teaching toward creating a "world-class workforce." To do this, the plan calls for "injecting performance-based competition into the Head Start Program," which serves children from lower income families. So little Jimmy better bone up on his Lego skills. Things are about to get real.

CREATIVITY GETS SENT TO DETENTION

How do we teach creativity, or to put it more bluntly, *can* we teach creativity? Arguably, innovation is just the commodified version of creativity. Creativity usually refers to creating something original, and innovation is usually more about changing something already in existence and making it different or better. But they're close cousins at least.

Reading through literature that addresses these qualities, most articles on innovation are tied to the business world, whereas descriptions of creativity span multiple disciplines and appear in conversations about art, music, sports, and a multitude of other endeavors. In addition, innovation seems tied to production in the business or industrial sense. Former editor of the *Harvard Business Review*, Theodore Levitt, defined innovation as "action-producing," whereas creativity was "idea-creating."

In a literature review of research on how we can learn to be more creative, Daniel Fasko Jr., a professor at Bowling Green State University, came to some interesting conclusions about the connection between how schools are run and the creative impulse. Titled "Education and Creativity" and published in the *Creativity Research Journal* in 2001, the piece does a good job of looking at a whole bunch of research that addresses whether, in fact, school makes students creative.

The paper delivers some surprises. Students who are out-of-the-box thinkers are actually at odds with how school is taught. Creativity isn't supported; it's endured or even actively punished. Students who are creative and innovative are that way because they want to discover and explore. They have an intrinsic curiosity and seek to find solutions and answers. But the way school is structured—grades, homework, assignments, and assessment—is often an obstacle to those students. That sort of performance-based motivation is external. It's forced upon the student.

In addition, students who found themselves on the creative side of the scale had the courage of their convictions, were strongly motivated to accomplish *their own goals*, and were willing to wrestle with concepts such as doubt and uncertainty—our old friend ambiguity again—more than more traditionally conscientious students. Fasko's description sounds very much like an epistemically curious person.

Sounds great, but the problem Fasko discovered is that personality description is exactly the kind of student that teachers find frustrating. Some researchers even went so far as to suggest that school doesn't nurture creativity. It may not be a safe place for fostering curiosity and new ideas.

Heterodoxy and self-determination were seen as negative traits. Students embodying these qualities mess with the schedule, go off on tangents, don't follow instructions, and ignore the lesson plans. They ask too many questions, aren't interested in the content, refuse to sit still for seven hours a day. They are stubborn, obstinate, and willful. Troublemakers. They are impetuous curiosity seekers.

Biographer Walter Isaacson called Einstein the "patron saint of distracted kids everywhere" for this exact reason. Isaacson writes of the founder of the theory of relativity, "his slow development was combined with a cheeky rebelliousness toward authority." Einstein was creative, sure, but he was at odds with the structure of school. School comes in boxes, and people like Einstein think outside of them. Einstein would go on to say later in life, in various ways, that his rambunctious curiosity was what drove him to become the innovative, creative thinker he was. As he wrote in a letter to a friend in later life, "People like you and me never grow old. We never cease to stand like curious children before the great mystery into which we were born."

History is chock-full of examples of devious little boogers becoming brilliant, creative geniuses. In *Darwin: The Life of a Tortured Evolutionist*, authors Adrian Desmond and James Moore wrote about the early life of the man who structured modern biological thought: "Charles was boisterous and mischievous, and one of his earliest memories was of trying to break the windows in a room where he had been locked for punishment."

It's not just old, dead white men either. George Washington Carver's genius for innovation redefined agriculture in many respects, and Neil DeGrasse Tyson's infectious enthusiasm for cosmology and deeply curious mind have inspired legions of fans. In the East African myth of Marwe, the heroine ditches working in the bean fields for a swim, discovers a door to the underworld, and goes on an adventure that leads to riches and a happy life. One of the consistent heros in Native American folklore is coyote trickster, whose defining characteristic is a sneaky, spry, troublemaker's intellect.

Ultimately, the research undermines all of what school and programs like Obama's Strategy for American Innovation are trying to accomplish. Fasko writes, "Creative people are intrinsically motivated to complete a task. Thus, educators must be aware that, if they implement an extrinsic reward structure with these students, this will undermine their intrinsic motivation."

This isn't true just for school. The workplace undermines creativity, a trait that is curiosity in action.

Curiosity, as we have seen, thrives on ambiguity. It is a sporadic and intense state, and doesn't fit well into time lines, goals, or rigid expectations. It's playful. The problem is that, while most employers *claim* to want out-of-the-box thinkers and creative people, with creativity comes uncertainty, and businesses, in general, don't like uncertainty.

In a study called "The Bias Against Creativity: Why People Desire But Reject Creative Ideas" published in *Psychological Science* in 2012, the authors found that while many employers claim to want to hire and keep creative people, the difficulty faced by creative employees presenting new ideas strongly suggested otherwise. In fact, the researchers found that while we have a culture bent on innovation and celebrating the independently minded, wildly creative individual, in practice we're a bit more boring. We like predictability and practicality. "Our findings imply a deep irony," the authors wrote.

It's an irony shared by educators, apparently. The fact is, curiosity is probably the least admirable trait a student or employee can have—it runs counter to the dominant paradigm of work/study = paycheck/reward.

To spark the creativity and imagination of Americans, it's going to take something different than traditional schooling.

THE HAPPY WORK-BOT

Many individuals express the same lament about their jobs. They feel stifled creatively. We often mistakenly think of creativity only in terms of artists and musicians, but creativity plays a role in everyone's life. New solutions to old problems, novel ways of doing things, a better workflow system, different office configurations—creativity can manifest itself in many ways.

How are creativity and curiosity linked? Curiosity, as we've seen, is a series of traits and behaviors that result from either intrinsic motivation or extrinsic motivation. It's a precursor, certainly, to creativity. While creativity is dynamic and action-oriented, curiosity is directional, in that it gets us moving—intellectually, or even physically—toward answers.

To be creative one must first be curious. Being in an environment that fosters curiosity is vital to the creative process. As we've seen, time, lack of structure, boredom, intellectual freedom, autonomy—all these can and often are ingredients to curiosity. None of them fit very well with traditional workplace mentality, where once you punch the clock, you're on company time; better get hustling. Even boredom gets disrupted, as boredom often is described as a lack of anticipation, and anyone unhappy in their job rabidly anticipates the end of the workday with a kind of fervent desire.

The other thing about curiosity is that it can be satisfying. If we are experiencing that brand of curiosity that is intrinsically motivated, and aren't trying to reduce fear due to uncertainty or trying to close a perceived knowledge gap due to external pressure, curiosity can feel good. Being given free rein to explore our curiosity is a positive.

Researchers Teresa Amabile, director of research at the Harvard Business School, and Steven J. Kramer would agree. In an article they co-wrote for the *Harvard Business Review* in 2007 called "Inner Work Life: Understanding the Subtext of Business Performance," the ability to think creatively ranked at the top in terms of what made employees happy and more effective.

Over ten years, Amabile and Kramer studied the inner emotional lives of employees at big companies. What they found was that the opportunity to think creatively not only improved their positive feelings about work, but dramatically improved the work itself. The conditions that nurtured that creativity in the workplace sound very similar to the circumstances that give rise to curiosity.

According to the studies, people "were more creative when they interpreted the goings-on in their organizations in a positive light—that is, when they saw their organizations and leaders as collaborative, cooperative, open to new ideas, able to evaluate and develop new ideas fairly, clearly focused on an innovative vision, and willing to reward creative work."

It seems fairly obvious that we *like* to work, as a species. The Golden Gate Bridge, the Great Wall of China, strip malls—sure, there are plenty of external motivations such as transportation needs, defense, the desire to make money selling fast food and hair dye, but our industriousness seems a bit over the top. Clearly, we find some internal reward in working. If that is so, is it possible to imagine working without the boss standing over your desk, demanding "deliverables" and "outcomes"?

President Obama chose education as one of his very early core issues, and he has done a great deal toward easing student loan debt, educating women, and supporting students who are immigrants. But his desire to lead in innovation lacks the understanding of how curiosity works—how to be innovative, we must be creative, and how creativity takes root in the soil of curiosity. Take away the time, autonomy, and freedom to be a curious person, and we're left with work-bots, toiling away like WALL-E wishing for some greater purpose.

DR. DAYDREAM'S SCHOOL OF CREATIVITY AND INNOVATION

If we can agree that creativity is the wellspring of innovation, then we have to ask ourselves how we can maximize both our schools and businesses to nurture a creative, dynamic environment. Particularly within the business world, this is tough to achieve. The very things that appear to be a drain on company resources may in fact be the very concepts needed to spur innovative iteration.

If you've ever been in a managerial position, then you will recognize this scenario: Your employees are sitting around, idly chatting, staring out the window. One of them is making a paper clip chain necklace. Another is concentrating deeply on fashioning a rubber band ball the size of her head. You get this particular pang down low and on your side, not coincidentally, near your wallet. Your brow furrows, and you start to grumble. What the hell are you paying these people for? This isn't Club Med, you say to yourself. You may go so far as to lay into the lazy sods. *Let's pick up the pace, people!*

That may be true, but they may also be bored or, more importantly, daydreaming. And this could be a very good thing—for them and for you, their cranky boss.

The father of research into daydreaming is Jerome Singer. A researcher at Yale, Singer spent the greater part of the latter half of the 20th century battling the myth that when we're daydreaming, we're indulging in neurotic or psychotic fantasy. His idea, borne out by decades of research, is that daydreaming is actually a positive, constructive attribute and symptomatic of a healthy inner life.

Singer's work has been bolstered by fascinating research by others, notably Scott Barry Kaufman and John Antrobus. The field of daydream research has never seemed as vital as it does now, as classic dropout types such as Mark Zuckerberg, Steve Jobs, and Bill Gates go about changing the very way we think about the world. It seems that whatever daydreaming is, it has some connection with creativity and innovation—the question is simply to figure out what it is and how to harness it. But what, exactly, is daydreaming?

You know it when you see it, either in your own kids, your students, your employees, or yourself. In a meeting, at work, in the classroom—it can strike anywhere. The jaw slackens, maybe the mouth hangs open a bit. The body slumps. The eyes get glassy. You can just tell they *aren't listening.*

Usually, we take it as a sign of lack of attention—which it most definitely is. In fact, daydreaming is not always a positive. It can focus on negative thoughts, guilt or paranoia, or sometimes the daydreamer just can't pay attention at all, period. But for most of us, it's not that we're not paying attention or listening. It's that we're not focused on the external environment, but rather inward, to our own mind's voice. To the internal dialogue we all run nonstop in our heads. Like boredom, knowledge gaps, or interesting external stimuli, daydreaming can be a precursor to curiosity. It can spur curious questions.

What Singer discovered was that there was a benefit to spacing out. He called it "positive constructive daydreaming." In this state, we plan for the future, explore how to solve problems, and come up with original ideas. Only by unfettering the mind from the here and now can we access this liquid thinking state, where fantasy and reality get all mixed up and can, under some conditions, result in a potent brew of innovative, original thinking.

TREVOR AND BETTY

Maya Angelou once wrote, "Each of us needs to withdraw from the cares which will not withdraw from us. We need hours of aimless wandering or spates of time sitting on park benches, observing the mysterious world of ants and the canopy of trees."

I count myself an adherent of Angelou's plan, yet I doubt most institutions—whether academic, professional, or otherwise—would agree. Time is money, as they say, and the dividends for exactly Angelou's kind of reverie are difficult to assess, harder still to quantify.

Think of a high school student. We'll call him Trevor. Trevor gets straight A's and he scores perfectly on the SAT. He gets into MIT, graduates summa cum laude, and aces the GRE. This is the guy you want at your company. There's no doubt he's smart. Anyone would be proud of this guy if he were their kid.

Trevor has demonstrated an important kind of intelligence, but certainly not the only one. His scores on standardized tests, for example, demonstrate that Trevor can benefit from traditional instruction. He incorporates and retains intellectual systems well, such as trigonometry. The tests and his success in school also demonstrate that he is goal-oriented. He is able to assess the expectations of a given system, and prepare information and deliver it according to those expectations; not a bad skill to have.

Finally, he is apt at analytical, or abstract thinking. *Tungsten* is to *lightbulbs* as *freeways* are to *California* is a comparison that requires just that sort of analogic thinking. The fact is, Trevor does well on those tests and would score high on a traditional IQ test. They're all based around these three skills: traditional learning, goal orientation, and reasoning. Trevor is highly intellectually curious. Trevor is a fine boy, and we should all be proud of him.

But what of his younger sister Betty?

Betty earns poor grades and blows off the standardized tests. She just can't seem to focus in class and spends all her time creating worlds for tabletop gaming or messing about with those computer parts or writing in her journal. Maybe all she wants to do is ski and hike or just hang out at the local swimming pool, watching the water glint in the sun. What a ne'er-do-well!

But Betty may have some skills too, some really interesting things going on in her head. Unless we've got Jerome Singer there to run her through a questionnaire, we just don't know. The thing Betty always says about the SATs, the GREs, the American history tests is that they just don't *matter*. They're *stupid*, she says.

What Betty means is that standardized tests and most metrics we use to assess student performance are decontextualized. They are taken out of the narrative of personal experience. They don't matter to Betty. Nor, really, should they. They matter to Trevor because he's a smart, conscientious boy. Betty doesn't care about what the Educational Testing Service thinks of her academic prowess.

The tests don't allow for Betty to reach into the rich, powerful, internal world that she inhabits. She's got this wild imagination, and her daydreams are like a Peter Jackson movie, robust and complicated and beautiful, baroque in their imagery and associations. But that will do her no good parsing the bubble tests put before her. The tests, the schools, and her eventual workplace will more likely than not require standardized responses.

A student from South Korea would answer the question the same way as one from Croatia—personal mythology and the scope of internal narrative don't matter. An original response that draws on this information that is vital for maintaining Betty's inner world's exacting cartography is not only not wanted; it's wrong. Betty won't score well, though she may well be as smart as Trevor.

The fact is Betty has never done particularly well in school. Her teachers notice that occasionally, maybe even frequently, she interrupts her reading to stare out the window. There she is, when she should be working, staring at the chickadees flitting past the window! It's likely that whereas Trevor is *intellectually* curious, Betty is *epistemically* curious. She seeks knowledge as passionately as her brother, but only that which matters to her, has personal meaning.

This is where things get dicey. It could be that Betty is just a rather unfocused reader. But what if her attention drifts in a positive way, within the construct of Jerome Singer's theories of daydreaming? Her mind may be wandering in order to coerce mental goals that are rewarding *for her*, on a personal level.

Researchers like Mary Helen Immordino-Yang of the University of Southern California have built on Singer's research to give proper due to the moments of reflection peppered throughout Betty's life. So what if she takes forever to read a page of Plato's *Republic*? Her wandering brain may have offered a key clue, finally, to some puzzle that has eluded her thus far; an essential insight into something of importance in her life may have interrupted, and there may even be tangible results from her newly acquired insight.

Or maybe she's considering some really important event, like letting her friends know about some cool new social media platform she's been coding the past couple of weeks. That decision, made while she should be reading, could be the fundamental step toward the achievement of personal goals. Or—and for me, this seems the most likely—maybe there was some little snippet of information that triggered a memory. She read a line, or perhaps it was as simple as a single word, and a whole new configuration of personal experience and meaning presented itself. Worth taking a break from the assigned text, if you ask me.

Here's the other thing about Betty—she's a really nice girl. Super empathetic. She really *gets* you; when you tell her about your feelings, she seems to understand them on a level none of your other friends do. If you can just look past the questionable fashion choices, you can tell that she's super sympathetic. Not like her older brother, Trevor, who's a bit type A and rather selfishly focused on achievement. Not Betty. She's got all the time in the world for you.

Here, again, we see signs of curiosity. It may well be that Trevor achieves more quantifiable results according to society, but Betty's interpersonal curiosity encourages relationships in her life that are fulfilling, lasting, and important.

Sadly, most of us would probably hire Trevor before Betty. Culturally, we like to see clear-cut feats of expertise and excellence, and reward them accordingly. Whether it's a face-melting guitar solo, a brilliant crosscourt backhand, or an articulate closing argument in court, we give accolades to commonly recognizable demonstrations of excellence.

However, Betty has skills that are just as powerful, but somewhat cloistered. She can feel your pain. It's almost like she's walked a mile in your shoes. She understands you so well, and that may be because of her daydreamy way of projecting herself into future scenarios, other people's lives.

The thing about Betty is that she just seems so "deep," and that's because she is. Rather than taking time and energy to satisfy the outward demands of her environment, Betty has fostered a rich and rewarding inner life, and has no compunction about retreating there when life offers the chance of escape. The do-gooders of the classroom, the ones always on their smartphones scrolling through Instagram, haven't given themselves the time to develop the same sense of individualized meaning that Betty has. She has a deeply important personal narrative playing out in her head—everyone else is competing for societal rewards.

One last note about Betty—she's going to achieve things. Part of daydreaming, according to Singer and the rest of the daydreaming crew, is "autobiographical planning." Betty and those like her are preparing themselves for future scenarios. They're laying out the plans for their later life, and usually have a better chance of achieving those goals. Betty is gonna get shit done—eventually.

HE'S SO DAYDREAMY!

Obama is right; the only way for our schools, businesses, and position within the global economy to prosper and grow is for us to lead in innovation. He's also correct in stating that creativity is the place where all this starts. I'm sure lots of countries around the world have smart people who work hard, but it's the creative thinkers—the ones who create new products, new ways of solving problems, new versions of old ideas—who move things forward, who create compelling economic narratives.

The missing part of Obama's plan is how to achieve this creativity. To foster creativity, time must be given to daydreams, curiosity, and the unmediated influence of unstructured playtime—preferably outdoors.

This is all about the future. What is our goal as a country, yes, but also, what's our goal for our children? For ourselves? I once got to meet Brian David Johnson, chief "futurist" at Intel, arguably one of the most dominant tech companies of the past couple decades. His job, I think, is to look at what people will want from their machines and, by extension, in their lives, 5, 10, 15 years down the road. You can YouTube him having a chat with hip-hop producer and rapper will.i.am. Clearly, Johnson is willing to think outside of the box.

When we were chatting, Johnson mentioned his "mentor" and conversations they'd had, ideas they'd cooked up together, and things he'd learned. He later stated that his mentor was a child. He actively seeks out children to help him focus on the future.

What I realized later is that to be creative, and lock into that swirling mix of innovation and dreams and fearless imagination, Johnson realized that he needed to access minds unencumbered by social expectation, conscientiousness, and the very stultifying adult world of metrics and standardization. He relies on the wisdom of daydreamy kids to help pilot the direction of a tech giant with some $90 billion in assets.

Curiosity weaves itself through all of this. It is integral to the creative process. The trajectory can run various ways: We get curious about an idea, then daydream about it, then actualize it. Or, perhaps, we are daydreaming about the future, and get curious about some aspect of our future hopes for ourselves, and seek to inform ourselves about it.

However it works, it seems clear that daydreaming—the positive kind—is very similar to Litman's I-type curiosity. Curiosity with a feeling of interest is like daydreaming—more focused on something, sure, but definitely connected. To achieve Obama's goals seems to say that to spur ourselves and our children to greater levels of creativity and innovation, we've got to allow our brains to wander. Go find a window, slacken that jaw, and watch the squirrels pilfer the bird feeder for a while. You may just get smarter.

The irony in all this is that daydreaming and its accompanying creativity aren't things you can enter into QuickBooks. It's hard to put a price tag on and quantify daydreaming or curiosity. But in the long term, a cost-benefit analysis may support giving students, and ourselves, time to dream—and dream big.

WE DON'T NEED NO EDUCATION

The difficulties in designing a creativity-boosting, curiosity-fostering education comes from the difficulty in connecting authentic learning experiences in school with an educational system that is burdened with preparing students for the workplace. Much of Obama's rhetoric, and that of proponents of charter schools like Secretary of Education Arne Duncan, proposes methods for ensuring that American children grow up to become American workers.

The sticking point comes because many of us believe education is about expanding our students' sense of the world, themselves, and their community, not about preparing them to function as workers per se, though we want that too. However, children who grow up to be adults will need the skills to be competitive in the job market. They'll need basic literacy and numeracy, and to know how to tackle problems.

For most of us, a job where we make ends meet is a godsend. It means we can provide a stable life for our family, keep food on the table, and provide the kind of environment where our own children will have access to higher standards of living. It begs the question: are schools supposed to be designed to produce dreamy Leonardo da Vincis, sketching preposterous flying machines, or are they incubators for workers, constructed to instill work skills, professionalism, and commodified aptitudes?

FOURTEEN

Tapping into Flow

I GOT FLOW LIKE GHOSTBUSTERS GOT SLIME

Within our syllabi, we prescribe certain days to hand in writing for our students. This is essential. Deadlines help everyone. But this also represents an untruth. Writing for some is inexorable—they do it every day, without fail, and make it an unassailable priority. However, for most of us, it comes in fits and starts. We binge, and then disappear from the page. Our students, on the other hand, are expected to churn it out on the daily. Most of what they churn out is absolute spew. Unfortunately, as any writer will tell you, that condition is endemic in the craft.

The same is true for reading.

Some of us binge read. What's going on here? Why with reading, as with writing, are there whole swaths of time that feel productive and engaged and others that lie fallow? When we're talking about writing, we often use the phrase "get into the flow," and while that shorthand is a bit too cliché to be helpful, if we take a moment and really think about it, then we can find a pretty large truth within that expression. Is there a way to enable our schools to get students reading like maniacs, to rev the rpms of their curiosity about learning? Can we get students into the "flow" of learning through curiosity?

The flow. What it is? The quote that titles this section is from John Green's young adult novel, *Looking for Alaska*, and it is—not coincidentally—from a hip-hop song, one of the disciplines that benefits from flow. The first thing we need to appreciate is that it's pervasive. It's not just reading/writing that needs it, but most expressive forms of art. Performers rely on it, not just improvisational jazz but hip-hop MCs, improv comedians—the list goes on. But one of the best examples, and to me the most conducive to thinking about writing, comes in the familiar form of Michael Jordan.

In the 1998 NBA playoffs Michael Jordan was thirty-five years old—no spring chicken in any sport, particularly basketball. Jordan's team, the Chicago Bulls, won the championship, with Jordan averaging over thirty-two points per game during the series.

In commentary after commentary, and in postgame interviews, the word "flow" was mentioned, both in regard to Jordan's performance and by most successful athletes. You hear it from jocks all the time. Hitting streaks in baseball, number of wins during singles season in tennis, or the entire career of Wayne Gretzky are all the result of tapping into the mysterious power of "the flow."

With reading, as with Jordan's six championship rings, there's a whole lot that happens before. Training. Practice. Work. And the boring, mind-numbing exhaustion of repetition. Many adolescents gobble up books. They have that ability to just dive in deep—whether it's *Harry Potter* or *Twilight*, among others—and read for hours. And reread, again and again. That's the practice—the training. As we get older and slower, it becomes harder and harder to tap into that Zen state of flow, but with enough years of training behind us, it's possible. And every once in awhile, we find a book, or a couple of them, and we're "reading and running," in the best Salingerian sense. All of a sudden, we got flow.

One of the things that curiosity allows us to do is enter the flow state. Flow, the ability to become positively absorbed in a task and shut out interfering stimuli, is crucial to pleasure. Our curiosity guru Kashdan has explored this as well and has noted how achieving this level of "absorption" analogous to flow makes us feel good.

Flow is not something you can teach, really. It comes from repetition, from consistent ritual and personal investment. It's intrinsic and epistemic. It comes from within.

Flow is a funny state. In a nutshell, it's when we become super focused and really proficient at a given task—think Prince's guitar solos, Jordan's dominance, Walt Whitman's poetry, Serena Williams crushing opponents late in the game with a blistering backhand. Clearly, when someone is in a state of flow, some cosmic V8 engine is humming along at a speedy, well-tuned clip, while the rest of us putt-putt and bounce along on the rusted springs of our own neural jalopies.

Neuroscientists have discovered that flow floods the brain with happy chemicals like our good friends dopamine, norepinephrine, serotonin, and anandamide. When the dudes in white coats measure our brain waves during states of flow, they find that our brain waves transition from beta waves—our normal, waking, thinking brain patterns—and begin to oscillate between alpha and theta waves. Alpha waves are the sort of brain state we experience during daydreams. Theta waves are associated with REM sleep, or that weird time when we are almost asleep and our thoughts cascade and jumble and mix—dreams swirled with memories, bustling past conscious thought like crowded commuters all running which way to catch the next train to Sleepyville.

In February 2005, author Steven Kotler wrote an interesting overview of flow states and their relation to creativity in *Psychology Today*. In the article, Kotler tackles the role of creativity in the workplace and argues that creativity has become one of the most sought-after skills in the modern workplace.

But in our hunt for the great white whale of curiosity, Kotler offers some interesting clues to how flow may be connected with curiosity. He writes that during flow the brain shuts down certain high-level executive functions. "The dorsolateral prefrontal cortex—the part of the brain charged with self-monitoring and impulse control—goes quiet."

As we've seen earlier, impulsivity, and giving into it under certain circumstances, can have positive effects on learning. It seems that in a flow state, according to the research quoted by Kotler, we liberate our impulsivity and in doing so increase our creativity, productivity, and performance by as much as 500 percent.

The connection between curiosity and flow states seems a bit tenuous, but there seems to be some overlap in terms of neurochemical conditions common to both. The commonalities seem to be a sort of weird, unfocused focus. Athletes describe how time gets warped when they're in the flow state and how they can see the stitches on a 90 mph fastball.

How can we teach flow? Seems like a rather impossible task. Getting to a flow state requires years of practice at any given task. The rule of thumb you hear coaches talk about is that it takes 10,000 hours to become proficient at something. We don't really have that kind of time, do we?

What seems crucial is to provide ourselves and our kids with the time, autonomy, and freedom to explore our curiosity enough to find that experience that resonates so deeply for us that we find our flow.

NO RESEARCH, JUST SEARCHING

One of the routes to rediscovering curiosity, particularly in high schools and colleges, may be through the students themselves.

Take research, for example. Whenever I've taught a research writing course, students look forward to researching about as much as a root canal during a novocaine drought. But there are a couple of research librarians out there who are changing that.

I called Anne-Marie Deitering and Hannah Rempel from Oregon State University. Deitering and Rempel have approached traditional undergraduate research studies through the lens of curiosity and had striking results. Their approach, in essence, favors students moving away from their traditional approach of choosing research topics that are safe (read here: boring) and excavating their own interests by getting in touch with curiosity. They've had remarkable results: by jettisoning the usual safe topics in favor of subjects clouded in ambiguity, students take ownership of their research, but more than that, they get *excited* by it.

Deitering and Rempel have fun in working with students to produce research ideas by bringing in egg cartons repurposed by their own children and encouraging the undergrads to see objects with the same sense of possibility as a young child. In addition, they mention the importance of getting out of the classroom—moving around, exploring the building or campus and finding out what possible ideas exist in the world around them.

Another important facet of their work is that the workshops they run, both for students and for other librarians and teachers, aren't graded. They believe this has made it "easier," and when I asked them what they meant, they explained that when the pressure of grades and performance is at stake, students strongly and automatically revert to safe topics, refusing to tackle other research ideas about stuff they *don't* know about—arguably the whole point of research to begin with.

They were quick to point out that while their experiences were in part anecdotal (though they've also contributed a healthy bit of peer-reviewed research on the subject), it was clear to them that by releasing the strictures of traditional academic assessment, students sought not to satisfy the arbitrary guidelines of the assignment or the expectations of the teacher. They explored their own epistemic curiosity.

Essays, as we traditionally think of them, are the great scholarly vehicle for carrying curiosity. They are assigned throughout high school and college with a madcap, maniacal persistence, as though the last wasn't good enough. Maybe that's the nature of essays—they are not satiating, the way a large, fully researched treatise is. You read Stephen Jay Gould's *The Structure of Evolutionary Theory*, then lean back from the table, gut groaning as you pat your belly contentedly.

Essays, on the other hand, are like a maddening taste of the possible. A winding journey through a street choked with street vendors selling food. Individually they can't fill you up, but the flavor is so transcendent you return to the street, again and again, looking for that flavor. Was it at the dim sum stall? The dumplings? The elote? What was that place that sold them? You can't remember the feeling, so you keep looking. You can't quite put your finger on it.

I'm sure the scientists out there are issuing a collective snort of derision. I don't blame them, but would argue that the very wellspring of science is un-annotated curiosity. The most exacting disciplines are born from an undefined, curious urge to seek further, know more. The curious among us, when the science teacher vivisects the lab rat, lean in to get a closer look.

UNFILLING THE BUBBLES

Figuring out what works—what *really* works—in education is tough. Kids are different, neighborhoods are different, and teachers are different. But identifying obstacles to learning (killers of curiosity) is a bit easier. After all, if there is one thing that seems glaringly apparent, it's that we love to try to create a panacea for complex problems. And we fail.

As we reviewed earlier, education in the West got off on the wrong foot. Traditionally in the West, schools have favored the reinforcement of hierarchy, whether in terms of people or ideas—and relegated the learner to acolyte and subordinate. Enter the industrial age, when schools are modeled on factories, reducing the development of thinking, feeling people to a process whereby information is delivered in chunks to same-age groups, churning out little citizens from the same mold.

In our current educational landscape, we've wholly embraced standardized testing as the means by which we'll teach the children of America. And it's not working. To give a detailed analysis of why is beyond the scope of this book, and others have already blazed that path.

In *The Big Test: The Secret History of the American Meritocracy*, author Nicholas Lemann provides us with a disturbing history of why we torture children by making them sit in a room filling in bubbles on tests like the National Assessment of Educational Progress or the New England Common Assessment Program (ironically, NECAP is usually pronounced "kneecap," which in verb form is a reference used by various groups like the Mafia and the IRA to describe the punishment of breaking someone's kneecaps).

The history of standardized testing strongly suggests that it is, first and foremost, a capitalist venture. Corporations such as the Educational Testing Service provide testing services, and in doing so categorize and catalog information on the tests in such a way as to provide significant results across a wide array of students. It's also rooted in replicating a class system where the haves test better than the have-nots, simply by virtue of the type of questions and the manner in which the test is given.

The main problem is that the tests are really assessing conscientiousness and the ability to take tests. It's also been soundly proved that if you're white and come from a middle- or upper-class background, you'll probably perform better. Statistically speaking, it could be argued that standardized tests are another example of systemic racism. For a black kid in north Philly, it's statistically likely that she's not had the same educationally supportive environment that a kid from Menlo Park has. Not to mention recent immigrants, for whom negotiating street signs in English is enough of a challenge.

Add to this the specter of economic disparity and broken families, where you have kids coming to school hungry, and we have a radically unfair system that measures social capital of the young vis-à-vis the dominant groups in society. So the tests are given, and the kids get relegated to the bottom of the achievement pile, their schools get a hefty slap on the wrist from the federal government, and thoughtful teachers who are using class time to connect and care for their students are fired for not hitting performance targets.

Many of the kids in these scenarios are poor, black, brown. Inherent in all this is the soft bigotry of low expectations. Low-income areas are expected to do poorly on these tests. It's hard to overcome the paradigm of commonly held beliefs, no matter how blatantly untrue they may be.

And yet we keep adopting these macro solutions to individual problems. No Child Left Behind was one of the most spectacular failures we've seen in a while, and Common Core looks like it may be running a close second. As I write this book, states like Indiana and South Carolina have rejected Common Core; New York teachers passed a vote of "no confidence" in the standard.

This isn't to say that schools—and, in the case of Common Core, some schools in traditionally underperforming urban areas—haven't improved through these programs. They have. But the improvements have been made according to tests that don't really measure all facets of learning. They sure as hell don't measure curiosity. Any curiosity seeker worth her salt would take one look at the soul-crushingly boring questions on a standardized test and chuck it in the wastebasket on the way out the door.

The tests measure a student's ability to remember data, not to ask complex questions. Standardized tests demand that the test takers remove, at all costs, ambiguity and exploration from their lives. There is no place for wonder or awe. And certainly no time for contemplation. The teachers are scared witless that if they don't crack the whip and up those scores they'll lose their jobs, so they hurry students from "content area literacy" lessons to "number word problems" with nary a thought to any nuance or creativity.

I don't blame them. In fact, I was one of them. But it's not hard to see that standardized tests and educational reforms such as No Child Left Behind crush curiosity. While some curiosity could, theoretically, exist in these circumstances, it wouldn't be robust. Loewenstein originally postulated that curiosity was a way to solve uncertainty, which is true. But that's simply a sliver of how curiosity works, as we've seen.

Epistemic, perceptual, sensory, and intellectual curiosity is chucked to the wayside in favor of answers, answers, answers. In a world where we need to be asking tough questions about our role as global citizens, how we'll face climate change, growing income gaps and markets out of control, the rise of extremism, and the shocking human-caused erosion of biodiversity due to development around the globe, we're training the next generation to be passive collectors of information.

Rather than fostering curiosity and nurturing a sense of exploratory behavior, we're creating a fear-based model of educational consumption. Pay for this information with your time and effort, and you'll be rewarded with social and material gain.

In July 2014, Rachel Aviv wrote an article for *The New Yorker* magazine titled "Wrong Answer." The story was about the experience of Parks Middle School in Atlanta. Parks was populated predominantly by students of color and had struggled to meet state standards year after year.

Georgia uses the Criterion-Referenced Competency Test scores to determine whether schools statewide meet federal targets, namely those dictated by No Child Left Behind. The story is a simple one. The pressure to raise test scores was so intense—teachers and administrators felt their jobs were on the line—that a massive cheating ring emerged. Teachers would go in after the kids took the tests and correct answers just enough to ensure that the school as a whole would perform well. As the article points out, this is no isolated incident: Toledo, El Paso, Baltimore, Houston, Philadelphia, and Cincinnati have also had huge cheating scandals as a result of high pressure standardized testing.

The result of the Atlanta cheating scandal, which affected not just Parks Middle School but many schools in the region, was that 178 educators were listed in the report on the incident. Many were subsequently fired. Teachers who had let homeless students sleep on their couches and done laundry for them were fired for trying to keep their school afloat by cheating on an arbitrarily constructed and unrealistic test.

One of the most interesting points of the article is a quote made by John Ewing, who was the executive director of the American Mathematical Society: "The end goal of education isn't to get students to answer the right number of questions. The goal is to have curious and creative students who can function in life."

GET RID OF THE TRIVIAL AND ENTER THE CONVIVIAL

Ivan Illich, poster boy for the disgruntled, anti-institutional hippie, wrote two books that bear on our conversation of curiosity. *Deschooling Society* and *Tools for Conviviality* both concern themselves, in broad strokes, with how institutions such as schools take away personal agency. They replace communal consensus with authoritarian rule. Hierarchies replace more autonomous collectives, and we're left marching to the beat of the corporate drum.

Much of Illich's life and work centered around the Centro Intercultural de Documentación in Cuernavaca, Mexico. He founded the school in 1965 ostensibly to train Catholic missionaries (Illich began life as a Catholic priest), but it soon became a sort of free university for liberal and radical thinkers of the day.

Of all the counterculture ideas Illich produced, one of the most enduring is that standardized, educational institutions stymie authentic learning. Illich saw education as a "service industry" and disagreed with the emphasis on improving hardware and software to improve education, expanding the responsibility of teachers into more and more of students' lives in an attempt to have a greater impact on learning, and the homogeneous approach to content and delivery represented by modern educational institutions. Illich preferred to talk about learning from the perspective of a "web," wherein all parts of life, professional, domestic, public, and private, are learning experiences.

In his later book, *Tools for Conviviality*, Illich postulates that there is a "war on subsistence" that is fostered by dependence on corporate- or state-controlled institutions such as schools, governments, and medicine. It's hard not to hear echoes of a "war on subsistence" in current research by the likes of Peter Gray, who argues for a more autonomous form of learning.

While the homeschooling and unschooling movements in the United States have embraced the idea that independent learning is a valuable, important alternative to compulsory public education, it still seems risky, even to me. What happens when you remove the directedness of governmentally scripted (and underwritten) educational institutions? As the French writer Anatole France once said, "The whole art of teaching is only the art of awakening the natural curiosity of young minds."

MIND THE GAPS

It may very well be that teaching curiosity isn't everyone's priority. It's certainly not the priority of public education as it exists currently. But what are the stakes when we talk about curiosity as a means to improving the lives of our children and ourselves? This isn't some nebulous fantasy. Plenty of schools and organizations have embraced the means by which curiosity is fostered.

Vivien went to a Waldorf school, and her teachers created nature tables with artifacts from the woods representing the seasons. She worked with clay, beeswax, and woolen felt. They told stories of gnomes and fairies. They practiced eurythmy, a dance-like movement program that reinforced ideas about rhythm and structure, timing and focus. They baked bread and sang songs, and much of their kindergarten days were spent outside. It was a place of curiosity and wonder.

We were lucky to send her, thanks to scholarships and financial aid, but that type of education is available to only a select few. This kind of education costs money. What of the students who can't afford a Waldorf or Montessori program, or those who may not rate curiosity-fostering environments as a priority?

My son has attended public schools where he's had caring, smart teachers. They're constrained by the expectations of standards. Their own creativity languishes. I wonder what they would do with their students if given free rein. Where would their curiosity take them?

Any attempt to reform education by injecting curiosity into the curriculum would fail. Reform never seems to take hold the way we'd like—it flops. Despite the best efforts of a lot of people over the past several decades, we've made limited progress toward equity, better learning, and improving our schools.

The reason is that education in America is a fundamentally flawed system based in a society suffering from massive economic and social inequality. Public education is a bureaucratic nightmare, a budgetary glutton with splintered political agendas undermining the efforts of teachers and students at every turn. We hold closely to it because it's all we know, save those brave souls who opt for homeschooling or unschooling, or have the economic privilege to send their children to non-traditional private schools.

Charter schools have tried to rewrite the rules, but they haven't been the revolution everyone (including yours truly, who worked at an urban charter school in Los Angeles) was hoping for. It's scary to think about what would happen if we dumped it all. We've put so much into building education. It's vital to our national infrastructure, economic competitiveness, political stability, and global participation. And yet, it is a deeply flawed system, a brittle crutch propping us up.

Is this the best we can do—what we want schools to be? Often, the conversation about learning veers into these areas dealing with issues that seem to be of a different ilk entirely from the piecemeal, daily, quotidian nature of learning like economics, politics, and public policy. And thus it's always been; while many individual teachers profess a love of igniting the spark of curiosity, they have to work within a system that denigrates teachers' personal agency, that places quantitative results before qualitative analysis, and that favors competition over collaboration—competencies instead of curiosity.

The criticism that often follows this line of thinking is that it comes from a position of privilege: duly noted. I work in higher education, and while I'm not wealthy, my children have a huge number of advantages because I'm a white, middle-class, American male. They, however, are both biracial and will grow up in a world where the specter of inequality is everywhere: from the church shooting in Charleston, South Carolina, to anti-Islamic protests in Germany.

Granted, it is a position of entitlement to even consider these questions of curiosity. A low-income family may not have the same concerns, and more immediate needs may take precedence. That's because the system we're locked into, where success in a school system that favors the dominant social class unfairly, may be one of the only ways to gain leverage in terms of earning potential and future careers.

Marginalized populations like ethnic minorities, low-income populations, and immigrants may be in a position that demands they focus on the clear-cut, transactional dividends of education rather than lofty philosophical goals like inspiring curiosity. This is despite the fact that the educational deck is stacked against them, and the very system they hope to capitalize on is rigged, and not in their favor. According to the National Center for Education Statistics, 85 percent of white students graduate from high school, whereas 68 percent of black students do. We live in a society that has strong ties to a racist past. Schools are a part of that historical continuum.

David Berliner is professor emeritus at Arizona State University. In an essay from *Teachers College Record*, a publication of Columbia University, Berliner trounces reform movements as failures in the face of an economic background that has a massive gap between the haves and have-nots. "The achievement gaps between blacks and whites, Hispanics and Anglos, the poor and the rich, are hard to erase because the gaps have only a little to do with what goes on in schools, and a lot to do with social and cultural factors that affect student performance," Berliner writes.

He goes on to deconstruct the failure of school reform movements over the past several decades, citing the fact that the United States has "the largest income gap between its wealthy and its poor citizens," of all the wealthy nations of the world. It is this massive discrepancy that underpins our society, and thus our schools' ability to equally educate young people. The reform movements can't fix this systemic, deeply embedded national inequity and are therefore ineffectual. Reforms are useless, according to Berliner. "These efforts have failed. They need to be abandoned." Good-paying jobs for those in poverty, Berliner argues, would be an effective reform.

In a way, this is a very radical and inspiring notion. If reform is doomed to failure, then we can rethink schools entirely—rewrite the way we introduce our children to curiosity, knowledge, compassion, each other, and the world. Curiosity is just the elemental, explosive ingredient needed on this tabula rasa wherein we could launch a whole new way to learn, both for our children and *ourselves.*

THE SCHOOL OF CURIOSITY

What if how we've learned traditionally was erased? What if we had a blank slate? What would we do—how would we learn, and what would we want for our children?

What I want for my children—and I have to believe this is what all parents want on some level—is for them to be fulfilled. To lead active, engaged, conscious lives. To be compassionate, and empathetic. To follow their reckless dreams fearlessly.

Only curiosity opens the door to this exciting, new world.

Curiosity will never be a part of any reform because it refuses to be tamed; it will remain forever wild. It is the expression of our truest selves, our most fervent desires. To know, and know more, to seek, to explore — this is the insistent push of curiosity, and any attempt to corral it ends in killing it.

Curiosity is subversive at its core. It leads not just to authentic learning—curiosity liberates us. It gives us the freedom to script and narrate our self-mythologies ourselves and not to kowtow to social demands or picayune obligations. By fully embracing curiosity, we blow up the confines of institutional demands and discover the manifestations of our true selves.

Being wildly curious sets us free, at last, from a society that compels us to obey.

Afterword

To Build a Fire

It was too cold, but we went sledding anyway. Finn and I wound our way through the patches of field and forest that surround our little suburban neighborhood to get to the sledding hill, a short but steep little pitch near some local baseball fields.

The wind whipped gritty, late-winter snow in our faces. After only a half-dozen runs, we decided to bag it and head home. Our cheeks were bright red, and the tips of our noses stung from the cold as we slogged along our favorite "shortcut," though it was anything but. The path was a snow- and tree-choked ravine that bisects the woods near our condo development.

Finn was tired and cold, and in the tradition of six-year-olds everywhere, would flop down in the snow periodically to complain. "I just want to lay here," he'd whine.

To inspire movement, I started telling Finn about the short story "To Build a Fire," by Jack London. It's a fantastic little cautionary tale about a man and his dog hiking through the Alaskan wilderness in freezing temperatures.

The man falls through some ice, gets wet, and begins to freeze. When it's 70 below, it doesn't take long for that situation to become fatal. He desperately builds a fire to thaw out, but unthinkingly gets it roaring under some snow-laden pine boughs. The snow, softened by the upward-wafting heat of the fire, slides off the branches and comes cascading down and extinguishes the fire.

Things get worse from there, but I'll let you go out and read the story on your own.

The point is that Finn was so intensely *curious* about the Jack London story. He fired question after question at me. His need to know led to a discussion of how hypothermia affects blood flow: recall the scene from *The Empire Strikes Back* when Han Solo slices open a Tauntaun like a piece of pita bread and stuffs Luke Skywalker into the body cavity to keep him from freezing to death on the ice planet Hoth or how Mount Everest climber Beck Weathers froze off his nose.

Finn couldn't get enough. I couldn't seem to answer his questions with the right information. He just kept wanting more, as though there was some secret I was keeping from him. He was so hungry—enraptured and full of wonder, really—and his curiosity seemed to keep us warm all the way home.

We made our way through the woods to the little patch of forest behind our condo.

I love this little patch of woods. It is Finn's playground. Since he was about three years old, we've spent winters while the ground is frozen and the undergrowth is hibernating, making it easier to walk about by hacking trails. The trails now snake around the woods, seeming to converge at bristly, old white pines, their spreading boughs shading out undergrowth and creating clearings.

I wonder at the way Finn and I have designed the trails, if it can be called design. He walks one way, with no real destination. I try to clear out eye-poking branches and make the passage possible, and before you know it, a trail.

"Trailblazing" seems a bit extreme for what we do. We wander, and because of that, our trails are tight, twisted, silly things created by whim, necessity, and a desire to go there, over here, this way. We are living out our lives in these woods, as father and son, but also as individuals carving out our wants in the underbrush.

We let our curiosity determine our course. When we're gone, it'll grow back. The woods are hungry for growth, and our trails will be sunshine and space for many a competing branch. The trails are us, our project. Destiny is too loaded a word. But they are a picture, a topography of who we are. Maybe of who we want to be.

One day, we watched two pileated woodpeckers hammer a dead silver birch, excavating the bugs and larvae. Finn watched with heightened attentiveness. He watched with wonder.

We've seen foxes and deer, and smelled skunks. One day, we saw moose tracks, and our tracking abilities were confirmed by a neighbor who said that a moose was sighted near the playground nearby that same day. But it's not the forest primeval. It's borderland, neither true forest nor developed park.

Nearby are fields and forests maintained by the city that are lovely, large hemlock stands, a university-owned ropes course, paved bike trails, basketball and tennis courts, mowed fields perfect for kite flying, the ball fields near the sledding hill. But I like the stumpy, dense, growth-choked stand behind our house.

These will be Finn's woods as he grows up. As spring turns to summer this year and next, he'll play out there with his friends. He calls one raised piece of ground "Smaug's Mountain," where he pretends Smaug, Tolkien's dragon, lives. He loves the reeds—*Phragmites australis*—an invasive species that has cleaned out almost all the indigenous cattails.

I break off whippet branches of maple saplings for him, and he hacks away at the brittle, dry, 12-foot-high grassy stalks. Whenever we walk the dog out there, he asks me an exhaustive stream of questions about whatever topic is front and center: *Where did the ice slide go that we played on last year?* Under the snow. *Is that woodpecker a boy?* I don't know. It might be a girl or a boy. *Why so much snow?* Lots of snow fell this year. *Why is it sparkly?* Because snow is little crystals, frozen like little chunks of ice. And so on.

I've dreamed and discarded many plans for the woods: Finn's own ropes course, a tree house, maybe a mountain bike trail he can use when he's older. But I probably won't do any of those things. Instead, I'll probably just keep hatching our little trails. Some go in loops. Some peter out in bracken. Some I've given up on. Others I've just started.

Acknowledgments

I imagine there are some writers who tidily compartmentalize their lives, keeping the creative act of writing separate from friends and family, thus ensuring that their writing exists in a pure sphere of unsullied intellectualism. But what fun would that be? For me, my creative life is inextricably wrapped up in family, friends, work, and the mad tangle of everyday life. From this cacophony come ideas about learning and reading; parenting and the outdoors. Thus, there are quite a few folks to thank for their role in this book, and in my life in general.

Profound thanks is due to my editor, Sarah Jubar, who has been a constant source of support and whip-smart advice from the get-go. There's also the competent and kind crew at Rowman & Littlefield who have helped this project along; Christine Fahey, Meredith Nelson, and Ethan Feinstein—thanks to all of you. In addition, special gratitude is due to Mary-Ellen Phelps Deily at *Education Week* for publishing the original article that prompted this book.

Everyone I interviewed took time away from busy lives to patiently answer the questions of some random guy who kept pestering them about curiosity; Jordan Litman, Sophie von Stumm, Rolf Potts, Lynn Fairbanks, Donald Lyman, Roy Baumeister, Natasha Tokowicz, Jeana Frost, Ethan Bromberg-Martin, Audrey Watters, Armando Carmona, Charan Ranganath, Marie Deitering, and Hannah Rempel were generous with their time and expertise. They have my thanks.

A decent portion of this book is based on experiences I've had in the outdoors as a wilderness educator. If there is a single individual to thank for that, it's Tahoe Rowland, one of the instructors I had when I took an Outward Bound course as a longhaired, confused eighteen-year-old. Tahoe would hilariously bark like a dog at random moments; yelled "whooo-hoo!" every time he carved a turn on skis; snuck up into the mountains at night and delivered an entire chocolate cake to me during my first wilderness solo because it coincided with my birthday, and ignited in me a love of the outdoors and the freedom to be found there. Tahoe died in a mountaineering accident years ago—I never got to thank him in person for his inspiration, so I'll do so here. Thanks, Tahoe.

During my years teaching students both in the classroom and in the woods, I've come to know and love hundreds of individual kids, who have mystified me, had me tearing my hair out in paroxysms of frustration, and filled my life with laughter, tears, and stories galore. To all of them; thank you for all the unhelpfully-timed bowel movements on the trail; for eating my terrible camp cooking (I'll never live down the mortar-like consistency of the famous "cheddar risotto"); your heedless rush to experience anything and everything the world has to offer; and for including me in your wild, unfettered adventures.

A few years ago I attended Bennington College's MFA program, and since that time I've drawn daily on the wisdom and encouragement of my mentors. Thank you to Dinah Lenney for her infectious enthusiasm and for encouraging me to write about animals and the woodsy ramblings of my youth; Wyatt Mason for keeping me on track and focused and getting me to constantly pare away the text to get to the point; Susan Cheever for believing in—encouraging, even—my crazy obsession with Melville; and Sven Birkerts, who got me thinking about reading and writing in a way that has changed the way I see the world.

There is a scattered group of individuals from whom I get all kinds of support, advice, and ideas: all the Bennington MFA alumni out there, in particular Dan Webster. In addition; Tim Brookes, Eliza Garrison, April Ruedaflores, Kari Kurto, Ina Neugebauer, and Danielle Zimmerman. Thank you all.

Champlain College has provided me with a culture and community that celebrates innovation, creativity, and ideas that go against the grain. In particular, the Core Division is filled with thoughtful, welcoming people whose ideas and conviviality have helped me feel like a part of some larger endeavor of learning. Special gratitude is due to Linda Goodrum, who tirelessly supports folks like me behind the scenes making our lives easier; and Betsy Beaulieu, for believing in me and giving me the time, space, and trust I needed to get this book written. You guys rock.

Smoke jumpers are elite firefighters who descend from helicopters into the flaming wilderness to fight forest fires in the remote backcountry. Katheryn Wright, Cyndi Brandenburg, Mike Kelly, Jeff Rettew, and Kristin Novotny leapt into the flaming chaos of the early drafts of this book, dug trenches, brought the flames under control, and saved lives— they have my thanks.

There's a whole crew of folks who make up the supportive clan I depend on—in various ways they are the village that surrounds me with the hum of loving support, and fortify me with the strength of love and friendship that make it possible for me to sneak away every once and awhile and scribble. Ferene Paris-Meyer and her kids; the Simons; Jamie Kelly and the boys; Mark, Thomas, and Jonathan Generazio; Troy Headrick and Marianne DiMascio; Steph Rettew and her little ones; Sarah and Aaron Flinn and their family; Nick Negrete, Sarah Childs, Jenn and Deanna Garrett-Ostermiller; Liz and John Siddle and their progeny. Josh Meyer and Rashad Shabazz—thanks for all those conversations about flow, Prince's guitar solos, and basketball—some of that stuff ended up in these pages.

Special thanks and love to Amanda Levinson, Sal, and Leo, who have filled many a day with their antics and rare breed of loud, whirling love—we may not share DNA, but you are as much a part of my family as anyone and I am so grateful to all of you.

I want to take a moment to especially thank Adam Rosenblatt, who has been a constant source of advice, inspiration, and friendship while writing this book. I roughed out entire chapters in conversation with Adam as we tramped along the winding trails of the 'Dacks, foraged for Cheerios to feed our hungry kids, and drank Vermont microbrews waist-deep in Lake Champlain. He reviewed every single word of the draft, and his enthusiasm for the book made me believe in myself. His friendship makes me a better writer and thinker and a happier person. Thanks, dude.

A few years ago I wrote a blog called "Wild Tracts." I was worried about putting my writing out there, but got encouragement from one of my oldest friends, Matthew Power. "You've got some good ideas in there," he said. It meant the world to me to hear that. Matt was a journalist of incredible skill and courage; he was a writer that made me want to read and a friend that made me want to write. It was a shock and tragedy when Matt died while on assignment in Uganda in 2014. I was never able to tell him how much his kind words meant to me, how they made me think that maybe I could pull off this whole writing thing. Showing him this book would've made me so proud. Matt, wherever you are, you are much loved and missed, my friend.

A good deal of my life as a kid and adult has been spent outdoors; discovering curiosity and initially forging many of the observations that ended up in this book, and the person who first got me out exploring the mountains was my father, Mike Shonstrom. His Scandinavian stoicism in the face of inclement weather; his obsessive drive to be skiing, biking, and moving through the world, and the way he valued outdoor experiences instilled in me a love of nature and an inability to hold a desk job for very long. Dad, thanks. Love you. My step-mother Amy has been a constant enthusiast and kind supporter—she deserves my love and gratitude not just for that but for having the temerity to put up with my father. You are a brave and wonderful person, Amy. My thanks to all my family members flung far and wide, my sister Kirsten Hollander, and especially my cousin Kristine Schmidt, with whom I had many conversations about creativity and innovation that inspired sections of this book while shopping for Thanksgiving victuals.

Like Tatooine, my entire world orbits around two suns; Vivien and Finn. Being a parent has been a wild ride—their constant curiosity has inspired me time and again, and there is not a day that passes that I don't feel an immense, soul-softening gratitude that I get to share the world with two such incredible human beings. I didn't realize that being a parent would be such an all-consuming task—but I let it consume me every day and am so filled with gratitude because of it. Even when you two drive me bonkers, I love you so much.

Almost thirteen years ago I got down on one knee in the parking lot of the Los Angeles Zoo and asked the woman of my dreams to marry me. Thankfully, she said yes, and since that time the world has sped up; our kids have grown like weeds and eaten us out of house and home; our family has moved across a continent; changed jobs about three dozen times; made new friends, had new adventures, and lived a chaotic and messy life that has me so filled with love for her that now my life just wouldn't make sense without her in it. Cindy makes me happier than I ever imagined it possible to be. She is my first reader and best editor. Her tough honesty, fierce belief in truth, and compassion have made me a better person. I have no idea what possessed her to say yes to that scruffy guy at the zoo all those years ago, but man, am I glad she did.

Bibliography

"About NSTA." NSTA Overview. Accessed March 26, 2015. http://www.nsta.org/about/overview.aspx.

Amabile, Teresa, and Steven Kramer. "Inner Work Life: Understanding the Subtext of Business Performance - HBR." Harvard Business Review. May 01, 2007. Accessed January 09, 2015. https://hbr.org/2007/05/inner-work-life-understanding-the-subtext-of-business-performance/ar/1.

Aviv, Rachel. "Wrong Answer." July 21, 2014. http://www.newyorker.com/magazine/2014/07/21/wrong-answer.

Baumeister, Roy F. "Conquer Yourself, Conquer the World." *Scientific American* 312, no. 4 (April 2015).

Berliner, David C. "Effects of Inequality and Poverty vs. Teachers and Schooling on America's Youth." TCRecord: Article. 2013. Accessed June 16, 2015. http://www.tcrecord.org/Content.asp?ContentID=16889.

Berlyne, D. E. *Conflict, Arousal, and Curiosity*. New York: McGraw-Hill, 1960.

Berman, Marc G., John Jonides, and Stephen Kaplan. "The Cognitive Benefits of Interacting with Nature." *Psychological Science* 19, no. 12 (2008): 1207-1212. doi:10.1111/j.1467-9280.2008.02225.x.

Berridge, Kent C., and Terry E. Robinson. "What Is the Role of Dopamine in Reward: Hedonic Impact, Reward Learning, or Incentive Salience?" *Brain Research Reviews* 28, no. 3 (1998): 309-69. doi:10.1016/S0165-0173(98)00019-8.

Bidwell, Allie. "More States Seek to Repeal Common Core." US News. January 31, 2014. Accessed June 29, 2015. http://www.usnews.com/news/articles/2014/01/31/more-states-seek-to-repeal-common-core.

Birkerts, Sven. "The Decline of the West & Other Animadversions." AGNI Online. Accessed March 16, 2015. http://www.bu.edu/agni/essays/online/2004/birkerts-nytbr.html.

Birkerts, Sven. *The Gutenberg Elegies: The Fate of Reading in an Electronic Age*. Boston: Faber and Faber, 1994.

Blyth, Catherine. *The Art of Conversation: A Guided Tour of a Neglected Pleasure*. New York: Gotham Books, 2009.

"Board of Directors." Change the Equation. April 17, 2014. http://changetheequation.org/board-directors.

Bromberg-Martin, Ethan S., Masayuki Matsumoto, and Okihide Hikosaka. "Dopamine in Motivational Control: Rewarding, Aversive, and Alerting." *Neuron* 68, no. 5 (2010): 815-34. doi:10.1016/j.neuron.2010.11.022.

Bunzeck, Nico, and Emrah Düzel. "Absolute Coding of Stimulus Novelty in the Human Substantia Nigra/VTA." *Neuron* 51, no. 3 (August 3, 2006): 369-79. doi:10.1016/j.neuron.2006.06.021.

Caci, Hervé, Vianney Mattei, Franck J. Baylé, Liliane Nadalet, Christelle Dossios, Philippe Robert, and Patrice Boyer. "Impulsivity But Not Venturesomeness Is Related to Morningness." *Psychiatry Research* 134, no. 3 (2005): 259-65. doi:10.1016/j.psychres.2004.02.019.

Caci, Hervé, Liliane Nadalet, Franck J. Baylé, Philippe Robert, and Patrice Boyer. "Cross-Cultural Study of the Impulsiveness-Venturesomeness-Empathy Questionnaire (IVE-7)." *Comprehensive Psychiatry* 44, no. 5 (2003): 381-87. doi:10.1016/S0010-440X(03)00105-6.

Carey, Benedict. "Living on Impulse." *The New York Times*. April 03, 2006. Accessed November 03, 2014. http://www.nytimes.com/2006/04/04/health/psychology/04impulse.html.

Carr, Nicholas G. *The Glass Cage: Automation and Us*. New York: W.W Norton, 2014.

Carr, Nicholas G. *The Shallows: What the Internet Is Doing to Our Brains*. New York: W.W. Norton, 2010.

Clay, Rebecca. "Green Is Good for You." American Psychological Association. April 2001. http://www.apa.org/monitor/apr01/greengood.aspx.

"The Condition of Education." National Center for Education Statistics. http://nces.ed.gov/programs/coe/indicator_coi.asp.

"Curiosity Doesn't Kill the Student." Association for Psychological Science RSS. October 26, 2011. http://www.psychologicalscience.org/index.php/news/releases/curiosity-doesnt-kill-the-student.html.

Degani, Tamar, Anat Prior, and Natasha Tokowicz. "Bidirectional Transfer: The Effect of Sharing a Translation." *Journal of Cognitive Psychology* 23, no. 1 (2011): 18-28. doi:10.1080/20445911.2011.445986.

De Paulo, Craig J. N., Patrick A. Messina, and Marc Stier. *Ambiguity in the Western Mind*. New York: Peter Lang, 2005.

Dillon, Sam. "U.S. Is Urged to Raise Teachers' Status." *The New York Times*. March 15, 2011. http://www.nytimes.com/2011/03/16/education/16teachers.html?_r=0.

Dobbs, David. "Restless Genes." National Geographic Magazine. January 2013. http://ngm.nationalgeographic.com/2013/01/125-restless-genes/dobbs-text.

"The Duckworth Lab." The Duckworth Lab. Accessed June 29, 2015. https://sites.sas.upenn.edu/duckworth.

"El Capitan's Dawn Wall: Coverage of the Ascent at Yosemite." *The New York Times*. January 14, 2015. http://www.nytimes.com/2015/01/15/sports/el-capitans-dawn-wall-climbers-near-top-yosemite.html?_r=0.

Fairbanks, Lynn A., Matthew J. Jorgensen, Adriana Huff, Karin Blau, Yung-Yu Hung, and J. John Mann. "Adolescent Impulsivity Predicts Adult Dominance Attainment in Male Vervet Monkeys." *American Journal of Primatology* 64, no. 1 (2004): 1-17. doi:10.1002/ajp.20057.

Fasko, Daniel. "Education and Creativity." *Creativity Research Journal* 13, no. 3-4 (2001): 317-27. doi:10.1207/S15326934CRJ1334_09.

Fowler, Harry. *Curiosity and Exploratory Behavior*. New York: Macmillan, 1965.

Fuller, Robert G. *Wonder*. Chapel Hill: University of North Carolina Press, 2006.

Gade, Daniel W. *Curiosity, Inquiry, and the Geographical Imagination*. New York: Peter Lang, 2011.

Goldsmith, Belinda. "Is Surfing the Internet Altering Your Brain?" Reuters. October 27, 2008. http://www.reuters.com/article/2008/10/27/us-technology-ibrain-tech-net-idUSTRE49Q2YW20081027.

Goswami, Usha. "Neuroscience and Education: From Research to Practice?" Nature.com. April 12, 2006. Accessed November 03, 2014. http://www.nature.com/reviews/neuro.

Guterl, Sophie. "Is Teaching to a Student's 'Learning Style' a Bogus Idea?" *Scientific American*. September 20, 2013. http://scientificamerican.com/article/is-teaching-to-a-students-learning-style-a-bogus-idea?

Harari, Yuval N. *Sapiens: A Brief History of Humankind*. New York: HarperCollins, 2015.

"HMS." Curiosity Seekers. Accessed March 25, 2015. http://hms.harvard.edu/news/harvard-medicine/curiosity-seekers.

Homer, and Barry B. Powell. *The Odyssey*. New York: Oxford University Press, 2014.

"How to Apply: Summer Pre-College." Accessed March 25, 2015. http://www.brown.edu/academics/pre-college/pc-apply.php.

Illich, Ivan. *Tools for Conviviality*. United Kingdom: Marion Boyars, 1973.

Immordino-Yang, M. H., J. A. Christodoulou, and V. Singh. "Rest Is Not Idleness: Implications of the Brain's Default Mode for Human Development and Education."

Perspectives on Psychological Science 7, no. 4 (2012): 352-64. doi:10.1177/1745691612447308.

"Intellectual Curiosity." *Psychology Today*. Accessed November 03, 2014. http://www.psychologytoday.com/blog/ethics-everyone/201404/intellectual-curiosity.

Jepma, Marieke, Rinus G. Verdonschot, Henk Van Steenbergen, Serge A. R. B. Rombouts, and Sander Nieuwenhuis. "Neural Mechanisms Underlying the Induction and Relief of Perceptual Curiosity." *Frontiers in Behavioral Neuroscience* 6 (2012). doi:10.3389/fnbeh.2012.00005.

Kaiser, Tiffany. "DailyTech - Study: GPS Units Cause Memory and Spatial Problems." November 16, 2010. http://www.dailytech.com/Study+GPS+Units+Cause+Memory+and+Spatial+Problems/article20169.htm.

Kang, Min Jeong, Ming Hsu, Ian M. Krajbich, George Loewenstein, Samuel M. McClure, Joseph Tao-Yi Wang, and Colin F. Camerer. "The Wick in the Candle of Learning: Epistemic Curiosity Activates Reward Circuitry and Enhances Memory." *Psychological Science* 20, no. 8 (2009): 963-73. doi:10.1111/j.1467-9280.2009.02402.x.

Kashdan, Todd. *Curious? Discover the Missing Ingredient to a Fulfilling Life*. New York: William Morrow, 2009.

Kashdan, Todd B., C. Nathan Dewall, Richard S. Pond, Paul J. Silvia, Nathaniel M. Lambert, Frank D. Fincham, Antonina A. Savostyanova, and Peggy S. Keller. "Curiosity Protects Against Interpersonal Aggression: Cross-Sectional, Daily Process, and Behavioral Evidence." *Journal of Personality*, 2012, N/A. doi:10.1111/j.1467-6494.2012.00783.x.

Kashdan, Todd B., and John E. Roberts. "Trait and State Curiosity in the Genesis of Intimacy: Differentiation from Related Constructs." *Journal of Social and Clinical Psychology* 23, no. 6 (2004): 792-816. doi:10.1521/jscp.23.6.792.54800.

Kashdan, Todd B., Paul Rose, and Frank D. Fincham. "Curiosity and Exploration: Facilitating Positive Subjective Experiences and Personal Growth Opportunities." *Journal of Personality Assessment* 82, no. 3 (2004): 291-305. doi:10.1207/s15327752jpa8203_05.

Kaufman, Scott B. "Dreams of Glory." *Psychology Today*. March 11, 2014. https://www.psychologytoday.com/articles/201402/dreams-glory.

Kaufman, Scott B. "The Real Neuroscience of Creativity | Beautiful Minds, Scientific American Blog Network." *Scientific American Global RSS*. August 19, 2013. http://blogs.scientificamerican.com/beautiful-minds/2013/08/19/the-real-neuroscience-of-creativity/.

Keller, Heidi, and Hans-Georg Voss. *Curiosity and Exploration: Theories and Results*. New York: Academic Press, 1983.

Keltner, Dacher, and Jonathan Haidt. "Approaching Awe, a Moral, Spiritual, and Aesthetic Emotion." *Cognition & Emotion* 17, no. 2 (2003): 297-314. doi:10.1080/02699930302297.

Kenny, Neil. *Curiosity in Early Modern Europe: Word Histories*. Wiesbaden: Harrassowitz, 1998.

Kincaid, Jamaica. *A Small Place*. New York: Farrar, Straus & Giroux, 1988.

Konnikova, Maria. "What's Lost as Handwriting Fades." *The New York Times*. June 02, 2014. Accessed June 29, 2015. http://www.nytimes.com/2014/06/03/science/whats-lost-as-handwriting-fades.html?_r=0.

Krupicka, Anton. "RTW Ruminations: Jan 19–25." Anton Krupicka. January 22, 2015. http://www.antonkrupicka.com/blog/rtw-ruminations-jan-19-25/.

Krznaric, Roman. *Empathy: Why It Matters, and How to Get It*. New York: Penguin Group, 2014.

"Learning to Learn." Why Waldorf Works. Accessed March 18, 2015. http://www.whywaldorfworks.org/01_WhyWaldorf/learning.asp.

Litman, Jordan. "Curiosity and the Pleasures of Learning: Wanting and Liking New Information." *Cognition & Emotion* 19, no. 6 (2005): 793-814. doi:10.1080/02699930541000101.

Litman, Jordan A., Robert P. Collins, and Charles D. Spielberger. "The Nature and Measurement of Sensory Curiosity." *Personality and Individual Differences* 39, no. 6 (2005): 1123-133. doi:10.1016/j.paid.2005.05.001.

Louv, Richard. *The Nature Principle: Human Restoration and the End of Nature-Deficit Disorder*. Chapel Hill, NC: Algonquin Books of Chapel Hill, 2011.

McCredie, Scott. *Balance: In Search of the Lost Sense*. New York: Little, Brown, 2007.

McMillan, Rebecca L., Scott Barry Kaufman, and Jerome L. Singer. "Ode to Positive Constructive Daydreaming." Frontiers in Psychology. September 23, 2013. http://www.ncbi.nlm.nih.gov/pmc/articles/PMC3779797/.

McNally, Gavan P., and R. Frederick Westbrook. "Predicting Danger: The Nature, Consequences, and Neural Mechanisms of Predictive Fear Learning." Learning and Memory. http://learnmem.cshlp.org/content/13/3/245.full.

Melville, Herman, Howard C. Horsford, and Lynn Horth. *Journals*. Evanston: Northwestern University Press, 1989.

Mineka, Susan, and Arne Öhman. "Phobias and Preparedness: The Selective, Automatic, and Encapsulated Nature of Fear." *Biological Psychiatry* 52, no. 10 (2002): 927-37. doi:10.1016/s0006-3223(02)01669-4.

Moeller, F. G. "Psychiatric Aspects of Impulsivity." *American Journal of Psychiatry* 158, no. 11 (2001): 1783-793. doi:10.1176/appi.ajp.158.11.1783.

Mueller, J. S., S. Melwani, and J. A. Goncalo. "The Bias Against Creativity: Why People Desire But Reject Creative Ideas." *Psychological Science* 23, no. 1 (2012): 13-17. doi:10.1177/0956797611421018.

Munsey, Christopher. "Frisky, But More Risky." American Psychological Association. July/August 2006. http://www.apa.org/monitor/julaug06/frisky.aspx.

Neem, Johann N. "Experience Matters: Why Competency-Based Education Will Not Replace Seat Time." Association of American Colleges & Universities. October 03, 2013. https://www.aacu.org/liberaleducation/2013/fall/neem.

Norton, Michael I., Jeana H. Frost, and Dan Ariely. "Less Is More: The Lure of Ambiguity, or Why Familiarity Breeds Contempt." *Journal of Personality and Social Psychology* 92, no. 1 (2007): 97-105. doi:10.1037/0022-3514.92.1.97.

"Open Digital Pedagogy = Critical Pedagogy." Hybrid Pedagogy. January 06, 2015. Accessed June 29, 2015. http://www.hybridpedagogy.com/journal/open-digital-pedagogy-critical-pedagogy/.

Peterson, Christopher, and Martin E. P. Seligman. *Character Strengths and Virtues: A Handbook and Classification*. Washington, DC: American Psychological Association, 2004.

Pinker, Susan. *The Village Effect: How Face-to-face Contact Can Make Us Healthier, Happier, and Smarter*. New York: Spiegal and Grau, 2014.

President Barack Obama, January 25, 2011. "Innovation." The White House. February 2011. http://www.whitehouse.gov/issues/economy/innovation.

"Program History." Learning to Learn Office. Accessed March 18, 2015. http://www.bc.edu/offices/ltl.

Reilly, Mary. *Play as Exploratory Learning: Studies of Curiosity Behavior*. Beverly Hills, CA: Sage Publications, 1974.

"Rest Is Not Idleness: Reflection Is Critical for Development and Well-Being." Association for Psychological Science RSS. July 2, 2012. http://www.psychologicalscience.org/index.php/news/releases/rest-is-not-idleness-reflection-is-critical-for-development-and-well-being.html.

Rogerson, Christine, and Elsje Scott. "The Fear Factor: How It Affects Students Learning to Program in a Tertiary Environment." *Journal of Information Technology Education* 9 (2010).

Rudd, Melanie, Kathleen Vohs, and Jennifer Aaker. "Awe Expands People's Perception of Time, Alters Decision Making, and Enhances Well-Being." *Psychological Science*, August 10, 2012.

Russell, George K., ed. *Children & Nature: Making Connections*. Great Barrington, MA: Myrin Institute, 2014.

Sachs, Naomi A. "TLN Blog: Exploring the Connection between Nature and Health." Therapeutic Landscapes Network. January 2011. http://www.healinglandscapes. org/blog/2011/01/its-in-the-dirt-bacteria-in-soil-makes-us-happier-smarter/.

Salamone, John D., and Mercè Correa. "The Mysterious Motivational Functions of Mesolimbic Dopamine." *Neuron* 76, no. 3 (November 8, 2012): 470-85. doi:10.1016/ j.neuron.2012.10.021.

Schneider, Mercedes. "Those 24 Common Core 2009 Work Group Members." Deutsch29. April 23, 2014. https://deutsch29.wordpress.com/2014/04/23/those-24-common-core-2009-work-group-members/.

Schultz, W. "A Neural Substrate of Prediction and Reward." *Science* 275, no. 5306 (March 14, 1997): 1593-599. doi:10.1126/science.275.5306.1593.

Sharma, Zubin. "A Culture of Curiosity." *The Huffington Post.* April 4, 2014. http:// www.huffingtonpost.com/zubin-sharma/a-culture-of-curiosity_b_5190214.html.

Shiota, Michelle N., Dacher Keltner, and Amanda Mossman. "The Nature of Awe: Elicitors, Appraisals, and Effects on Self-Concept." *Cognition & Emotion* 21, no. 5 (2007): 944-63. doi:10.1080/02699930600923668.

Slingerland, Edward, and Mihaly Csikszentmihalyi. "The Way of Spontaneity." On Point with Tom Ashbrook RSS. April 2, 2014. http://onpoint.wbur.org/2015/01/15/ the-way-of-spontaneity-dao-tao.

Strafella, Antonio P., Tomas Paus, Jennifer Barrett, and Alain Dagher. "Repetitive Transcranial Magnetic Stimulation of the Human Prefrontal Cortex Induces Dopamine Release in the Caudate Nucleus." *The Journal of Neuroscience,* 2001.

Strauss, Valerie. "Why Almost All School Reform Efforts Have Failed." *Washington Post.* October 17, 2012. Accessed June 16, 2015. http://www.washingtonpost.com/ blogs/answer-sheet/wp/2012/10/17/why-almost-all-school-reform-efforts-have-failed/.

Tamir, D. I., and J. P. Mitchell. "Disclosing Information about the Self Is Intrinsically Rewarding." *Proceedings of the National Academy of Sciences* 109, no. 21 (2012): 8038-043. doi:10.1073/pnas.1202129109.

Thompson, Clive. *Smarter than You Think: How Technology Is Changing Our Minds for the Better.* New York: Penguin Press, 2013.

Tokowicz, Natasha, Erica B. Michael, and Judith F. Kroll. "The Roles of Study-Abroad Experience and Working-Memory Capacity in the Types of Errors Made during Translation." *Bilingualism: Language and Cognition* 7, no. 3 (2004): 255-72. doi:10.1017/S1366728904001634.

"Trinity College Curriculum." Accessed March 25, 2015. http://www.trincoll.edu/ Academics/Pages/Curriculum.aspx.

Tsai, Chin-Chung, Hsin Ning Jessie Ho, Jyh-Chong Liang, and Hung-Ming Lin. "Scientific Epistemic Beliefs, Conceptions of Learning Science and Self-Efficacy of Learning Science among High School Students." *Learning and Instruction,* 2011. doi:10.1016/j.learninstruc.2011.05.002.

Urgo, Joseph R. *In the Age of Distraction.* Jackson: University Press of Mississippi, 2000.

"Use Spatial Memory to Reduce Risk of Dementia." Douglas Mental Health University Institute. December 14, 2010. http://www.douglas.qc.ca/news/1072/file_en/press-release-bohbot-spatial.pdf.

Whiteside, Stephen P., and Donald R. Lynam. "The Five Factor Model and Impulsivity: Using a Structural Model of Personality to Understand Impulsivity." *Personality and Individual Differences* 30, no. 4 (2001): 669-89. doi:10.1016/S0191-8869(00)00064-7.

"Will.i.am and Intel Futurist Brian David Johnson Brainstorm." YouTube. Accessed March 12, 2015. https://www.youtube.com/watch?v=kbkpveP6J5c.

Zuckerman, Marvin. *Behavioral Expressions and Biosocial Bases of Sensation Seeking.* Cambridge: Cambridge University Press, 1994.

Zull, James E. *The Art of Changing the Brain: Enriching Teaching by Exploring the Biology of Learning.* Sterling, VA: Stylus, 2002.

About the Author

Erik Shonstrom is a professor of rhetoric and interdisciplinary studies at Champlain College and a graduate of the Bennington Writing Seminars. He has been a teacher for twenty years, working in both traditional and outdoor education, and for the past four years has run Nomad Youth Adventures, an experiential wilderness program. Erik grew up in Vermont, where he lives with his family. Find out more at www.erikshonstrom.com.